acts of art
in Greenwich Village

acts of art
in Greenwich Village

Edited by Howard Singerman with Re'al Christian and Katie Hood Morgan

HUNTER COLLEGE
ART GALLERIES

HIRMER

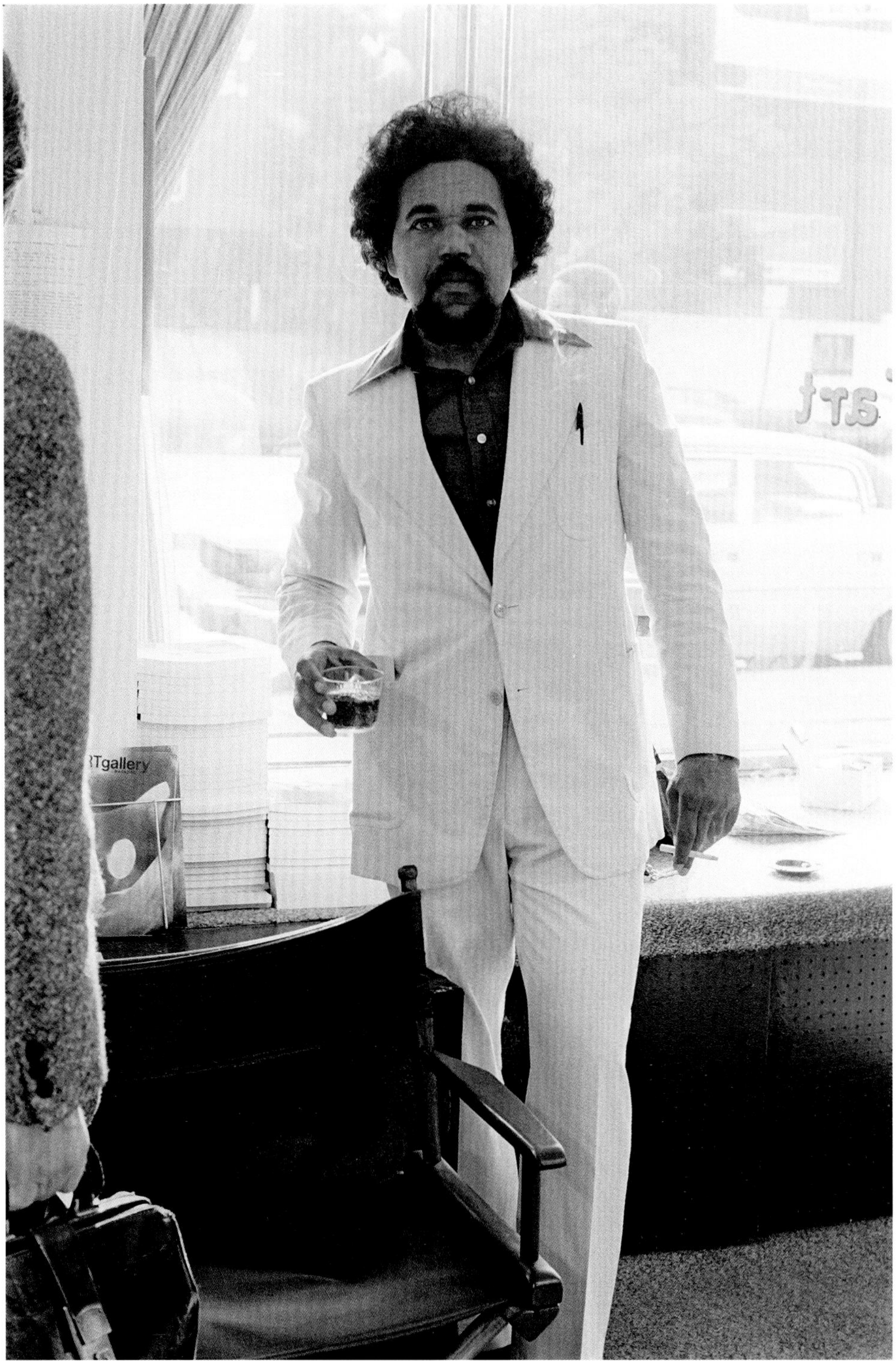

Chester Higgins, *Portrait of Nigel Jackson*, 1974

CONTENTS

FOREWORD

This publication, *Acts of Art in Greenwich Village*, is the result of a two-semester-long seminar taught by Dr. Howard Singerman, Phyllis and Joseph Caroff Professor of Art History in Hunter College's Department of Art and Art History. It accompanies the exhibition of the same name presented in Hunter's Bertha and Karl Leubsdorf Gallery from November 7, 2024, to March 22, 2025. Thirteen students enrolled in the university's nationally recognized graduate Art History and Studio Arts programs—many of whom are also earning an Advanced Certificate in Curatorial Studies—worked with Dr. Singerman on the research that brought to light the institutional histories and artistic practices chronicled in this book, narratives that substantially enrich and expand the history of Black art in 1960s and '70s New York. Both this publication and the exhibition mark the first curatorial practice seminar and exhibition realized with the generous support of Leonard A. Lauder, who has endowed a fund to support Hunter's unique program of organizing research-based exhibitions by students and faculty.

The Leonard A. Lauder Exhibition and Catalogue Fund gift lends vital support to a long-standing practice in Hunter's Department of Art and Art History and it is an enormous pleasure to acknowledge *Acts of Art in Greenwich Village* as the first of many publications and exhibitions supported by this gift. Thanks to this gift, Dr. Singerman and the students were able to execute crucial primary research, interviewing artists and their descendants, visiting private collections, seeking out gallery directors, and scouring archives—public and private—in their efforts to present new research on the activities of the Acts of Art Gallery and the many artists with whom it intersected. Additional support for this book was provided by the Wolf Kahn Foundation and the Emily Mason and Alice Trumbull Mason Foundation. We extend our gratitude for their commitment to Hunter. Lastly, we acknowledge Hunter College President Nancy Cantor, and Professor and Ruth Stanton Chair of Art and Art History, Sara Greenberger Rafferty, for their support of the work of the Hunter College Galleries.

Harper Montgomery
Associate Professor and Susan and David Bershad Director of the Hunter College Art Galleries

Nigel Jackson's Acts of Art

HOWARD SINGERMAN

Acts of Art in Greenwich Village presents the six-year history of the gallery Acts of Art, founded by artists Nigel Jackson and Patricia Grey in 1969 to showcase the work of Black artists in downtown Manhattan. There has been scant art historical research into the gallery or its community of artists. If Acts of Art is known at all, it is as the site of the Black Emergency Cultural Coalition's *Rebuttal to the Whitney Museum Exhibition: Black Artists in Rebuttal* in 1971—their response to the Whitney's *Contemporary Black Artists in America*. That same year, the Greenwich Village gallery also hosted the first exhibition of Where We At, the Black women artists collective founded by Kay Brown, Dindga McCannon, and Faith Ringgold. (For more on both exhibitions, see essays by Brianna Golub and Mary Lisette Morris and Nicolas Poblete in this volume.) These two shows have been referenced in recent texts and exhibitions as they intersect with other stories—of the Whitney, of Black women artists—or as part of broader surveys and fuller narratives of Black art and artists in the 1960s and 1970s.[1] This book and the exhibition it accompanies center Acts of Art, charting its particular history not only as it intersects with and sometimes draws out other histories—of the Black Emergency Cultural Coalition (BECC), the Weusi collective, Where We At, and of other earlier exhibitions and formations—but also as its own project and curatorial vision.[2] Acts of Art closed in November 1975, and for the next three decades, Nigel Jackson, the gallery's co-founder who passed away in 2005, had no contact with the art world he had been part of or the artists he showed. He left behind no papers we have been able to uncover, no mailing lists or sales records or inventory. Thus the history we present—some fifty years on—has been built from the reminiscences of artists and family members, fleeting mentions, newspaper calendar listings, and ephemera.

The artist Benny Andrews was closely associated with the gallery for its first few years. The earliest appearance of Acts of Art in the archival record is in Andrews's journal, in an entry dated September 9, 1969: "I attended a meeting of Black artists at the Acts of Art Gallery, 31 Bedford Street, New York, Nigel L. Jackson owner. I advised Mr. Jackson that I could not come in his gallery but I would donate a painting toward the success of his gallery."[3] A founder of the BECC, Andrews was a meticulous journal keeper and archivist, and his diary entries between 1969 and 1972, along with letters and ephemera that now rest with his papers at the Rose Library at Emory University, offer entryways into the history of Acts of Art. While Andrews didn't join the gallery at that September meeting, he did loan works to its opening exhibition. There is a listing in his journal on October 1, 1969, noting the opening of what he referred to as Acts of Art's "Black Art Show," and his loan of three paintings to it: *Washerwoman* (1963); *Immigrants, Southern Style* (1966); and *Lady in a Parade* (1969).[4] An ad for the show appeared in *The Village Voice* on October 2, announcing the gallery's "first ethnic showing, featuring Black Art in America." A flyer of the same design is in Andrews's papers at Emory University.

There is no other record of that first show or of the artists included beyond Andrews, though there is a brief accounting of it in a draft grant application likely crafted sometime in the late summer of 1970, which is also now among Andrews's papers. "The show included 150 pieces by fifteen different Black artists, and attracted about two hundred people to the opening."[5] The gallery disappears from Andrews's journal for nearly seven months following the October 1969 exhibition, but it does surface in a couple of notices that winter in the Harlem-based *New York Amsterdam News*, the city's largest circulation newspaper for the Black community. Both mentions note the continuation of an untitled exhibition of eight artists—the gallery's second public exhibition—on view from February to March 1970. The March note appears as a caption to a photograph of Jackson and Grey with two works from the exhibition. Grey stands next to Jackson's painting, *The Seekers* (1970); Jackson next to a painting, perhaps by Grey, that owes much to Robert Gwathmey.[6] In addition to the Acts of Art co-founders, the exhibition included work by Andrews, J. Hill Ainsworth, Gil Edwards, Moses Groves, John Johnson, and Enid Richardson Moore. With the exception of Andrews, few if any of the artists were recognizable names. Andrews, Edwards, and Richardson Moore would show with Acts of Art again in one-person and group shows over the life of the gallery. The group included both Black and white artists, but unlike the few other galleries in New York at the time that showed Black artists, at Acts of Art it was the minority who were white: co-founder Patricia Grey and Ainsworth, a Canadian-born artist who taught at SUNY Plattsburgh. As Jackson would say in a 1972 interview, "myself being Black meant that most of the people that I knew were Black and most of the artists that I knew were Black."[7] A brochure for the gallery published sometime during its year on Bedford Street doesn't note a focus on Black artists or mention race at all. Andrews's painting *Washerwoman* is at the center of the salon-hung wall pictured on its cover panel.[8]

While the inaugural exhibition—billed as the gallery's "first ethnic exhibition"—showcased the work of Black artists, the gallery's fully-formed mission is not announced until 1970 in a profile in the local weekly, *The Villager*, published in late August. It is a commitment whose formalization one can trace again through Andrews's papers and journals. There is no origin story for the gallery or its goals, but a version appears in the summer 1970 grant application in Andrews's papers. Acts of Art, the draft reads, was founded in the belief that art was:

> One way of bringing people together, whatever their racial background may be… With each showing we hope to involve one ethnic group with others, and in doing so, create a social interest in the development and achievements of one group with another.…The art presented by Acts of Art will always keep foremost in mind, cultural and ethnic contributions. We believe in Acts of Art.[9]

We don't know whether the grant was ever filed or—if it was—what relationship this text has to the final version, but we know from an entry in Andrews's journal dated August 26, 1970, and from the *Villager* profile published on August 27, that the "ethnic and cultural contributions" the gallery planned to focus on were those of Black artists. On August 26, Jackson and Andrews met with the artist and critic Brian O'Doherty in his capacity as an officer of the National Endowment for the Arts to discuss how the NEA could support the gallery's mission of "aiding unknown Black artists." The phrase "unknown Black artists" appears twice in Andrews's journal entry for August 26, with "unknown" inserted with a caret each time.[10]

In the August 27 article, Jackson verbally edited Andrews's "unknown" out, telling reporter Nancy Burton that he and Grey "agree on the fact that there has to be a market for Black artists." Burton identifies Grey as a "white artist whose idea it was to open the gallery in the first place," but it is Jackson's voice that dominates the piece. He speaks to questions of audience and the gallery's location in Greenwich Village directly: the purpose of Acts of Art is "to promote Black artists and provide a showplace for Black art outside the ghetto."[11] Burton's text continues, "Jackson describes the difficulties—and roadblocks—to opening a showcase outside ghetto areas where original works are typically shown in church halls and community centers." He explains, "If it's an all-Black thing, it doesn't belong outside the ghetto, people would say, if it's to go outside the ghetto, then it must be integrated." That geographical calculation and its ramifications were central for Jackson and the goals of the gallery. While Acts of Art's first membership brochure was silent on both race and geography, a similar leaflet published in 1971 and using the same cover image of Jackson's sister, Fay Leeper, in front of Andrews's *Washerwoman* in the space on Bedford Street, returned to the language of the *Villager* and made their conjunction clear. "If you're not a Black artist, you cannot fully realize the great need for an art gallery specializing in fine art by Black artists, located outside the ghetto areas.... For the Black artist to emerge at all, a gallery outside the ghetto must accept his work."[12] Jackson's argument for the gallery's presence in Greenwich Village was that if a Black audience embraced the artists, the work, and the gallery, a white audience would follow—as white audiences had for Black music, Black dance, and Black language. "The Black man must support his own institutions," he told the *Villager*'s reporter. "Then you have to turn the Black experience into money, and to do that you have to make it fashionable. For fear of missing something, the whites will support it."[13] Jackson took white appropriation of Black culture as given and historical; he understood the value of Black visibility strategically. The case for Greenwich Village was not one for integration and the invisibility it had resulted in for a generation of Black artists, but a way of insisting on the presence of a Black movement, at once political and aesthetic. In answer to the questions "What about the location of Acts of Art—Greenwich Village? Why not Harlem?" Jackson answers in part, "Greenwich Village is the place to present Black artists because every movement in American art started here. It's better for an educational setting."[14]

The Villager offered a quick overview of the gallery's September group show and named at least some its artists—Andrews, Grey, Richardson Moore, and James Denmark—and noted both a two-week summer exhibition of the Jamaican painter Lester Gunter, which had recently closed, and Andrews's forthcoming exhibition scheduled for November. Andrews was decidedly not the unknown Black artist he had emphasized in his August 1970 journal entry, and his decision to show at Acts of Art and Jackson's reliance on him was strategic on both sides. While Andrews had resisted a solo exhibition when he first met with Jackson in 1969, he acceded to one in April 1970, writing "I tentatively agreed because I personally feel that it would be a principled gesture toward helping Nigel get a foothold as a commercial Black art dealer."[15] The exhibition opened on October 31, 1970.

Gallery Hours:

Monday Closed
Tues thru Fri 12-9PM
Saturday 2-9PM
Sunday 2-7PM

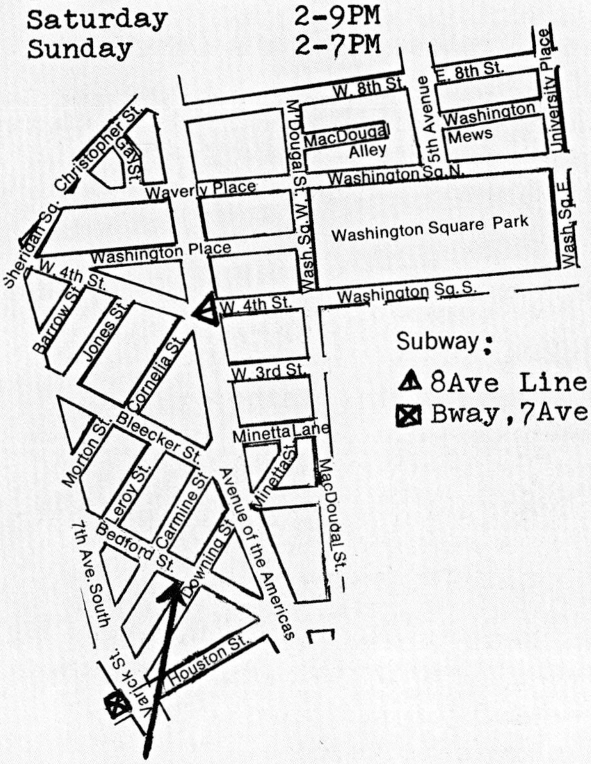

Subway:
▲ 8Ave Line
⊠ Bway, 7Ave

acts of art
gallery

corner of 31 bedford & downing sts., nyc, 10014 (212)989-8335
in greenwich village

acts of art
gallery

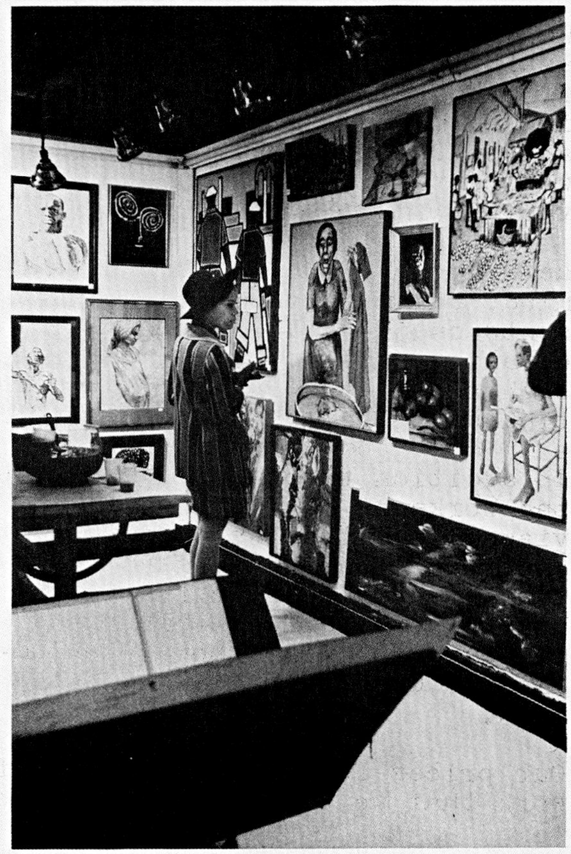

31 bedford street, in greenwich village, new york city, 10014

Acts of Art gallery brochure, c. 1970

A review in *Artforum*—the gallery's only appearance in the art world's magazine of record—took the exhibition that way: it understood that Andrews had chosen to show with the gallery to help it gain a foothold and an audience. "A note on the Acts of Art Gallery: it's a Black-run, Black-owned commercial gallery to which Andrews is contributing his reputation in this show to help it gather prestige and get further off the ground."[16] Andrews had an exhibition record in New York that went back to 1962 and included multiple one-person exhibitions at the integrated Forum Gallery along with various prizes and awards. But he had been particularly visible—and visible in a particular way—since the winter of 1969, beginning with his role as a leader of the Black Emergency Cultural Coalition and its public demonstrations at the Metropolitan Museum of Art in January of that year. (See the essay by Ansley Browning in this book.) The demonstrations were followed in the summer of 1970 by Andrews's debate in print with Hilton Kramer in *The New York Times* over the latter's review of Edmund Gaither's exhibition *Afro-American Artists: New York and Boston.* Andrews's contribution to Gaither's show at the Museum of Fine Arts, Boston—a painting of a seated boxer entitled *Champion* (1967)—had been reproduced in *The New York Times* alongside Kramer's second salvo, under the headline "'Black Art' and Expedient Politics."[17] Acts of Art featured *Champion II* (1970)—a drawing based on that painting—on its October mailer.

Afro-American Artists: New York and Boston was one of a number of larger group exhibitions of Black artists organized in the late 1960s and early 1970s. In February 1969, with the intense publicity and backlash to the Metropolitan Museum of Art's exhibition *Harlem on My Mind* still fresh, Grace Glueck of *The New York Times* noted a "rash of 'Black' exhibitions."[18] The historian and curator Carroll Greene, Jr., who had curated one of the first of these new forays, *Evolution of the Afro-American Artist, 1800–1950* at the City College of New York with Romare Bearden in 1967, wrote in *Art Gallery Magazine* in April 1970 of the necessity of such exhibitions and of the irritation of both Black artists and white audiences. His essay opens: "'Every time I turn around nowadays there is a Black art show,' comments a gallery owner. 'What's all this fuss and flurry about Black artists all of a sudden?'" Greene answers his unnamed, presumably white gallery owner this way: "The recent spate of group exhibitions, aside from creating mere awareness that these artists exist, serves other purposes." Together, they stand for a brace of questions posed to mainstream galleries and museums: "Are there any Black American artists on your roster and if not, why not?" And how can those "who have been traditionally ignored or excluded…now be given a fair chance of representation on the same basis as that accorded non-Black artists?"[19] Edmund Gaither's introductory essay for *Afro-American Artists New York and Boston* also begins with a nod to the recent "so-called 'Black shows'" and works to situate them and his contribution historically and strategically. Tracing a history of exhibitions and formations across the twentieth century, Gaither cites, among others, the Harmon Foundation exhibitions of the 1920s and the Atlanta University Art Annuals organized by Hale Woodruff beginning in 1941. Still, the new "'Black shows' of the sixties" were different. They were often hosted by "major museums and universities"—by white institutions—and often organized in the face of "pressure of militant Black arts organizations and the heightened demand for relevancy," and increasingly by "Black organizers." "In the sixties, after Birmingham, Harlem, Watts and the others, cultural institutions re-discovered the Black man and his world, and the groundwork for Black studies programs and new 'Black shows' was laid."[20] Gaither's linking of the new exhibitions to the emergent Black studies programs on campuses nationwide suggests a new generation of artists coming to consciousness in the decade.

Exhibitions like *Afro-American Artists* and the other "all-Black" exhibitions mounted in the wake of *Harlem on my Mind* and the broader Black Arts Movement introduced a younger generation of Black artists to at least parts of the art world and, at times, to one another. In "The War Years: 1969–1972," an unpublished manuscript in his archives, Andrews describes meeting Reginald Gammon for the first time at the opening of *New Voices: Fifteen New York Artists* in March 1968, and recalls the subsequent new conversations he would have with Melvin Edwards, Tom Lloyd, and Jack Whitten, who were also among the *New Voices*.[21] The exhibition was sponsored by the American Greetings Corporation and installed at their gallery in Pan Am Building, but it was organized by the staff of the nascent Studio Museum in Harlem, which was then some six months away from opening. In part, the exhibition served as a way to publicize the museum and its mission. Two members of the exhibition's selection committee were officers of the Studio Museum and affiliated with the Museum of Modern Art's Junior Council; the other two were on the staff of the public relations firm Ruder and Finn. All four were white. The artists, all younger, most without gallery affiliation (as the *The New York Times* would point out in its review[22]), were assembled in part by two young artists from the Studio Museum's founding board: Betty Blayton-Taylor and Mahler Ryder, both of whom were included in the exhibition. *New Voices: 15 New York Artists* was a savvy exhibition, Andrews wrote in "The War Years": "It wasn't just that 15 Black artists were being shown someplace together…it was how Ruder and Finn went about putting the show together.…With the exception of known Black artists like Jake Lawrence, Charles White, Charles Alston, Hale Woodruff, Norman Lewis, Ernest Crichlow, Richard Hunt, Ray Saunders, and Romare Bearden and Richard Mayhew, there weren't any more as far as the art world was concerned."[23] Ruder and Finn "had to find some." All of the artists on Andrews's list—artists that a white art world turned to as representatives and gatekeepers—had "one basic weakness…their work had been seen so damn much until it wasn't anything special to show as a 'new happening on the Black scene.' Ironically up till now that had been most of their strength." Most of the artists on Andrews's list were born before 1920 and had first worked together in the Harlem Arts Workshop in the 1930s; thirteen of the fifteen artists of *New Voices* were born in 1930 or after.[24] Ruder and Finn would double the size of *New Voices* in October 1968, adding members of the older, more familiar generation of artists, and make clear its racial mission. Renamed *Thirty Contemporary Black Artists*, the exhibition traveled from the Minneapolis Art Institute to four further venues before returning to New York and the IBM Gallery of Arts and Sciences in May and June 1969. It then traveled one more time, heading out again in July as *Contemporary Black Artists* with a shifted and further expanded roster that included James Denmark and Lloyd Toone to the Rhode Island School of Design Museum and five subsequent locations.

Jackson would draw Acts of Art's roster of artists from this generation. In addition to Andrews and Denmark, Reginald Gammon, Ben Jones, and Lloyd Toone were also among the artists in Gaither's *New York-Boston* exhibition and one version or another of the Ruder and Finn show. Still other key artists on Acts of Art's roster (along with many of those previously mentioned) had been included in the *Counterpoints 23* exhibition at Lever House in 1969. Organized by the collector and gallerist Bertina Hunter, again with Betty Blayton-Taylor of the Studio Museum, *Counterpoints* included Andrews (who was included in nearly everything), Arthur Coppedge, Denmark, Gammon, Ann Tanksley, and Frank Wimberley. As *The New York Times* noted of the artists of *New Voices*, few had gallery representation, and of the thirty-three artists included in the expanded version of Ruder and Finn's *Contemporary Black Artists*, over half did not list a single one-person exhibition in New York; the only artists with regular and repeated commercial gallery representation were Bearden, Laurence, Lewis, Richard Mayhew, and Raymond Saunders—all artists from Andrews's list of the old guard. Acts of Art took its place in that void, a place downtown; it was the only venue operating as a regular commercial gallery for the artists that these large exhibitions had introduced. As James Denmark would later recall, "Many other galleries existed at that time, but most of them were [private galleries] in apartments, open on a by-appointment-only basis. Acts of Art was located on the street level and it was open during normal business hours and after business hours."[25] Denmark, like Andrews, was an important nexus for Acts of Art. The artist Lloyd Toone, who had his first of two solo shows at Acts of Art in April 1972, shared a studio with Denmark at 224 Centre Steet in SoHo in 1969–70. Ann Tanksley—who also had two solo exhibitions with the gallery and whose works were included in a number of group shows—recalls meeting the psychologist Audreon Bratton (who dealt primarily Haitian art but also works by Black American artists from his apartment on Washington Square) and the collector and librarian Vivian Hewitt through Denmark. And Denmark introduced her to Jackson and Pat Grey as well. Ademola Olugebefola, one of the founders of the Weusi artists group in Harlem in 1965, remembers seeing Denmark's work and meeting him at the Harlem supper club 22 West, where Olugebefola also showed in the mid 1960s.

If the large Black exhibitions provided one network of artists for Acts of Art, Harlem provided the other. While "Neo-Africanism" was a category in Gaither's *New York-Boston* show, the artists most closely associated with cultural nationalism and the Black Arts Movement, particularly those engaged with institution-building within Black communities—the artists of Weusi in New York and AfriCobra in Chicago—were to the greatest extent left out of larger group exhibitions; they occupied a very different art world and envisioned a significantly different audience. The Weusi Artist Collective was formed in 1965 out of a schism within a larger group of artists who had joined together in 1964 as Twentieth Century Creators to organize the first Harlem Annual Out-Door Art Show on 7th Avenue from 127th Street to 135th Street. As Laura Luo discusses in her essay in this book, Weusi shared its goals with a broader Black Arts Movement emergent in Harlem and other Black communities. Weusi continued the annual Outdoor Art Festivals through 1970 and, in 1967, members Abdullah Aziz, Otto Neals, G. Falcon Beazer, Taiwo DuVall, and Rudy Irwin (Baba Kachenga) opened the gallery Nyumba Ya Sanaa (House of Art). It would become a cooperative run by the full Weusi membership in 1969 and would show artists from beyond the collective including Ted Gunn, Ben Jones, Valerie Maynard, and AfriCobra members Barbara Jones Hogu and Frank Smith; it also staged the second exhibition of the Black women artist collective, Where We At. There were a handful of galleries in Harlem and in Brooklyn's Bedford-Stuyvesant—the "ghetto areas" Nigel Jackson had called out. Weusi Nyumba Ya Sanaa and the Harlem Art Gallery, opened by Twentieth Century Creators co-founder James Sneed, were both aligned with the mission that had initially organized the Twentieth Century Creators artists group in Harlem in 1964: "Black art for Black people." After 1969, the Studio Museum, under the very different leadership of Edward Spriggs, was also an important venue for movement artists and artist groups. Spriggs was close to the community around Acts of Art; his name appears on gallery letterhead as a member of Acts of Art's "honorary board" in

1972 and 1973, and an extended interview with him was featured in Jackson's short-lived publication *Raven Art Rap* (see the essay by Eve Arballo and Erin Chase in this volume). "Nigel was plugged into Harlem politics," Olugebefola would say, and to the Harlem-based artists most closely associated with the Black Arts Movement as it emerged in Harlem.[26]

Both Ademola Olugebefola's exhibition at Acts of Art in November and December 1971 and Dindga McCannon's in January 1972 foregrounded the transit from Harlem downtown. There was, Olugebefola would recount to Camille Billops in 1979, "a downtown group and an uptown group... That was a very serious schism between some of the mainstream artists, who did primarily abstract art, and some of the artists like those in the Weusi group, who did a lot of cultural nationalistic work.... We were set on making things very African.... At that point in history, we felt that art needed to be involved in politics, because that was the need of our people at that time."[27] From the other side of that schism, Senga Nengudi has recounted the geographical-cum-political decision she was called on to make when she moved to New York from Los Angeles in 1971. The painter William T. Williams, then living on Broadway a couple of blocks above Houston, counselled her: "you're going to have to make up your mind whether you want to be down here or if you want to be with the nationalists."[28] McCannon had been showing in Harlem's outdoor art shows since 1964 and alongside Weusi's members since the group's founding. Her January 1972 show at Acts of Art claimed Harlem in its title: *from Harlem to Haiti and a few stops in between.* Olugebefola's exhibition at the end of 1971 drew in part on the research into Dogon and Yoruba cosmologies he had begun with Baba Oseijeman who founded the Yoruba Temple in Harlem. Titled *Reflections: Orion*, the exhibition grew from stories of Africa's extraterrestrial origins, crossing the celestial Orion with Yoruba *orishas* and, in particular, the concept of *Ori* (literally head), referring to the before-life, consciousness, and destiny. The exhibition featured a suite of etchings made at the Robert Blackburn workshop; performers from Ed Bullins's ritual play *To Raise the Dead and Foretell the Future* at Harlem's New Lafayette Theater, where Olugebefola was an artist-in-residence, sang and chanted at the opening. They again mark the kind of intervention into Greenwich Village—and another art world—that the gallery represented.

Part of that intervention was political. Clearly it was in the case of an exhibition like the *Rebuttal to the Whitney Museum Exhibition*, the Black Emergency Cultural Coalition's response to the Whitney's *Contemporary Black Artists in America.* The two shows opened on the same evening in April 1971; the press that paid attention reviewed the two shows together and measured them against one another, from *The East Village Other* and *The Village Voice* to the *New York Daily News* and *The New York Times.* John Canaday of the *Times* deemed Acts of Art's *Rebuttal* as the Blacker of the two exhibitions. The Communist Party USA's newspaper, the *Daily World*, was the only paper to give a serious review to *Where We At: Black Women Artists 1971*, the exhibition that followed the *Rebuttal.* The gallery's political profile also included fundraisers and readings devoted to issues of prison reform and criminal justice. Ann Tanksley recalls that Bruce M. Wright, then a judge in the New York City Criminal Court and one of the state's first Black judges, frequented the gallery; like Ed Spriggs, he was on the gallery's letterhead as a member the honorary advisory board and bought Tanksley's painting *Atlantic City* (1970) from the *Rebuttal.*[29] A vocal advocate for bail reform—"Bail is not a game of money to be won only by the rich"—he was a lightning rod for the police union and city politicians.[30] But, as Tanksley notes, "Nigel and Pat shared these politics. They were about justice, rebuttal, revolution, and the work that they showed could be identified with their philosophy." James

Denmark's recollection of the Acts of Art's community underlines the intersections of art and political activism at the gallery, and Jackson's use of the visibility that each offered. Acts of Art was "the focal point of what was then known as 'the Black art movement' in New York City."

> The community started to support the gallery, in terms of the number of people who visited it and attend its various events. Not all of these events were artistic in nature. Some were kind of political. Each time a non-art event or fundraiser was held at the gallery, it brought in people who got a chance to also see artwork. And, as a result, people got involved with the artwork, they got involved with the artist at that particular point in his development and many works were sold, many contacts were made and the gallery became stronger and stronger.[31]

Speaking to a reporter for *The New York Times* a few months after the *Rebuttal*, Jackson was blunt about the visibility that came with activist politics, offering: "We use politics only to get an audience.... Once we've gotten that, we concentrate on the art."[32] In reality, the two were never quite so separable. The art the gallery showed and where it showed it embodied a political position. Speaking of his own work, "as a speaker softly spewed out the WLIB sound of James Brown or Herbie Hancock," Jackson told Zita Allen, a Black writer for the neighborhood weekly the *Chelsea-Clinton News*, "These are my relatives, acquaintances and friends. These are the people I find both interesting and beautiful." As Allen writes, "The human figure is the most important thing for Nigel now and the reasons he gives for this could loosely fall under the heading of ideology."[33]

By mid 1973, the gallery's core was well established: Denmark, Jackson, Gammon, McCannon, Olugebefola, Richardson Moore, Tanksley, Toone, and Wimberley (all of whom are represented in *Acts of Art in Greenwich Village* at Hunter), along with Lester Gunter, Philippe Smith, and Robert Threadgill who also had one-person exhibitions and were regularly included in group shows. All but one of them were figurative artists, like Jackson, invested in images and imaginaries of Black people. Howard University-trained Wimberley was the only fully abstract artist Jackson showed regularly. In the summer of 1973, Acts of Art hosted a survey exhibition of Loïs Mailou Jones; a longtime member of the Howard faculty, she had been one of Wimberley's teachers. The show was drawn from Jones's retrospective at the Museum of Fine Arts, Boston: she had been the first Black woman to graduate from the museum's art school in 1927, and her Boston survey was also a first. Jones's relationship with Acts of Art was a fruitful one. In 1974, she curated a large group exhibition, *Caribbean and Afro-American Women Artists*, which was the outcome of research funded by Howard (see the essay by Sondra McGill and Chloe Ming in this volume). In 1975, the gallery's final year, Jackson mounted exhibitions by Abdullah Aziz, one of Weusi's founders, and Ben Jones, who had shown early on at Nyumba Ya Sanaa and whose painted plaster casts of arms and faces had been praised in *The New York Times'* otherwise scathing review of *Blacks: USA: 1973*, a very late entry into the spate of Black shows.[34] The gallery also presented one-person exhibitions by two artists of Loïs Jones's generation—elder statespersons within a project of Black art—both of whom were abstract painters. Harlan Jackson had studied with Clyfford Still at the California School of Fine Arts (later the San Francisco Art Institute) and with Hans Hofmann in New York, and showed widely in California in the 1940s and 1950s. His March 1975 exhibition at Acts of Art was among his last. His show was followed by a Hale Woodruff exhibition in April.

***** PRESS RELEASE ***** IMMEDIATE RELEASE ***** PRESS RELEASE ***** PRESS RELEASE*****

GROUP EXHIBITION: " BLACK ARTISTS IN THE NEW YORK SCENE "

ROMARE BEARDEN	JAMES DENMARK	NORMAN LEWIS	GREG. RIDLEY	FRANK WIMBERLEY
CAMILLE BILLOPS	AL HOLLINGSWORTH	TYRONE MITCHELL	FAITH RINGGOLD	PAT DAVIS
VIVIAN BROWNE	MANUEL HUGHES	DINDGA MC CANNON	DON ROBERTSON	FRED FLOYD
ART COPPEDGE	NIGEL JACKSON	OTTO NEALS	ERN.ROBIBSON	RANDOLPH FLOYD
LLOYD TOONE	VIRVINIA SMIT	VINCENT SMITH	HALE WOODRUFF	BUNNIE BRISSETT
GRACE WILLIAMS				

SEPTEMBER 10,---- OCTOBER 1, 1974
ACTS OF ART, 15 CHARLES STREET NEW YORK 10014
GALLERY HOURS: TUES-SAT. 2-8 PM and by appointment
CONTACT: Mr Nigel L. Jackson, Director (212) 989-8335

****** PRESS RELEASE

" BLACK ARTIST IN THE NEW YORK SCENE " TWENTY-SIX INTERNATIONAL and NATIONALLY KNOWN PRODUCERS OF ART. ALL REGULARS ON THE NEW YORK ART SCENE. UNIQUE THOUGH THEIR WORKS MIGHT BE. FOR MANY RECOGNITION HAS NOT COME.

FOR YEARS MANY HAVE SOUGHT MAINSTREAM GALLERY AFFILIATIONS IN THE NEW YORK ART SCENE. ONLY TO BE IGNORED AND PASSED OVER.

THE TIME HAS COME TO DEMAND POSITIVE CHANGES. AND THE INCLUSION INTO THE MAINSTREAM OF AMERICAN ART... BLACK EXPRESSIONS IN THE PLASTIC ARTS... THE ATMOSPHERE DESIRED IS ONE WHERE ABILITY, CREATIVITY AND PROFESSIONALISM IS THE CRITERIA. AND NOT ONE WHERE IT IS CONSTANTLY THE OPPRESSED VERSUS THE OPPRESSOR.

ACTS OF ART OPENED IN 1969 AS AN ALTERNATIVE EFFORT. OFFERING THE BLACK ARTIST EXHIBITION OPPORTUNITES TO AN AUDIENCE MADE UP OF THE GENERAL PUBLIC. AND IS A NON-PROFIT ORGANIZATION. REVIEWS AND ENTHUSIASM ON THE PART OF THE PUBLIC HAS BEEN ENCOURAGING..... BUT A VISIT AS A BLACK ARTIST TO A MAINSTREAM GALLERY, WILL REMIND YOU OF WHO IS BEING OPPRESSED.

THIS EXHIBITION OFFERS A VARIETY IN QUALITY STYLES AND MEDIUMS. AND YOU ARE INVITED TO ATTEND.... AND DO WHATEVER YOU CAN TO ERASE THE UGLY STIGMA ON THE NEW YORK ART SCENE.

Press release, *Black Artists in the New York Scene*, September 10 to October 1, 1974

Woodruff was a legendary educator who taught at Atlanta University from 1930 to 1946 and founded the national exhibition for Black artists there. While he was best known and widely recognized for his *Amistad* murals at Talladega College (1939–40) and his genre scenes of Black life in the rural South, Woodruff's work after his move to New York University was increasingly gestural and abstract. The show at Acts of Art—one of his few solo shows in the city after 1960—presented sixteen works from the decade in oil on canvas, many whose stacked, gridded forms were drawn from the geometric figures on Ashanti gold dust weights. Woodruff's 1975 exhibition was reviewed in *The Villager* with critic Ann-Sargent Wooster focusing on his largescale drawings, "imaginary figures… made up of a rigorous scaffolding of lines which dig the figure out of space and construct it much like building sculpture."[35] Wooster's thoughtful review was something of an exception; by 1973, most shows at Acts of Art went unnoticed by the mainstream art press. Up until that point, *ARTnews* had been the most dutiful. Its staff writers—among them Laurie Anderson and April Kingsley—reviewed eleven exhibitions at Acts of Art, but all of the magazine's reviews date from the spring of 1971 to the end of 1972. Almost all of the press Acts of Art received in the mainstream art magazines and New York City's white newspapers came in those months, in the wake of the *Rebuttal*. After the echo of *Rebuttal*, they disappear.

When Acts of Art mounted *Black Artists in the New York Scene* at the beginning of the 1974–75 season, visibility and a "fair chance of representation" remained driving aims for Jackson as they had been for Carroll Greene and Edmund Gaither in 1970. The exhibition was intended to be a statement, a way of reclaiming some of the spotlight that the *Rebuttal* had shone on the gallery. The exhibition was also a mark of Jackson's frustration and he let his weariness show in the exhibition's press release, built of sentence fragments separated by ellipses and typed out in all caps. The release reads in part: "Twenty-six international and nationally known producers of art. All regulars on the New York Scene. For many recognition has not come. For years many have sought mainstream gallery affiliations…only to be ignored and passed over. The time has come to demand positive changes and the inclusion into the mainstream of American art."

Insisting that these twenty-six artists are at once both well-known and invisible, Jackson maps two parallel versions of "the New York scene"—one white, one Black—occupying the same space, an art world demonstration of sociologist George Lipsitz's insight that "the lived experience of race has a spatial dimension, and the lived experience of space has a racial dimension."[36] As June Kitahara's essay in this volume explains, the exhibition drew together representatives of a number of circles of Black artists in New York. Included were artists who had shown regularly at Acts of Art since its opening along with other artists associated with Weusi and Where We At including Otto Neals and Faith Ringgold. But there was also a cohort of senior artists who had never shown in the gallery, artists who had been members of Spiral and the generation of the Harlem Arts Workshop—some of Andrews's old guard: Romare Bearden, Alvin Hollingsworth, Norman Lewis, and Hale Woodruff, whose solo show would come the following year. And alongside them were artists from SoHo lofts and a younger downtown Black art world: Camille Billops, Vivian Browne, and Tyrone Mitchell.

Black Artists in the New York Scene closed on October 1, 1974. Linda Goode Bryant's gallery, Just Above Midtown (JAM), opened six weeks later at 50 West Fifty-Seventh Street. Billops, Browne, and Lewis were among the artists included in JAM's inaugural exhibition, the title of which suggests both the nexus that *Black Artists in the New York Scene* formed but also the difference and the break that JAM represented: *Synthesis: A combination of parts or elements into a complex whole.*[37] While Acts of Art would continue to operate for another year, Just Above Midtown can be seen as displacing Acts of Art.

Like Acts of Art, Just Above Midtown was a geographic intervention; its name announced it as such. And Bryant described the relationship between her gallery's mission and its geography in language quite close to Jackson's own. "The rationale for JAM," Bryant told Tony Whitfield in a 1994 interview, was "primarily...about allowing African American artists to function on the same platform equal to their white counterparts. To have been in Harlem or Bedford-Stuyvesant would not have afforded that. It was to get the work consideration in the context of the larger art world."[38] But Just Above Midtown was also a critical, generational response to the vision of Acts of Art. The artists of Acts of Art worked in decidedly traditional media: painting, carved and assembled pedestal-bound sculpture, printmaking. While JAM's circle included painters and more conventional sculptors, the artists Bryant championed and for whom she envisioned the space "worked in a non-commercial, non-representational vein," in performance, installation, and video, and the idioms of postminimalism and conceptual art. JAM's origin story also includes Bryant's explicit rejection of the nationalism and the Afrocentrism of the Studio Museum where she worked under Ed Spriggs in 1973 and, by extension, an implicit rejection of the representational politics of Acts of Art.

Bryant and the artists of Just Above Midtown were in a more tense and engaged negotiation with the mainstream art world and its media. Sometimes that conversation was quite direct, as in the gallery's 1976 exhibition *Statements Known and Statements New*. Installing works by David Hammons, Noah Jeminson, Jorge Luis Rodriguez, and Raymond Saunders alongside and in dialogue with works by Jim Dine, Helen Frankenthaler, Jasper Johns, Robert Motherwell, and Robert Rauschenberg, Bryant's exhibition both demanded and troubled readings of difference and identity. The shift from Acts of Art to Just Above Midtown could be thought of as an instance of a broader shift within cultural practices labeled the "linguistic turn." But it is situated, too, within specific debates over race and representation, and a shift from a politics of visibility (with its insistence on identity and singularity) to reading and the shifting ground that practice entails: a theorization of race as relational and situated. Still, looking back from 1994, Bryant was concerned to make clear that:

> JAM was not about appealing to, accommodating, or speaking to a white marketplace. That was not the intent of JAM. The intent of JAM was to expand upon and build a stronger infrastructure within the Black community....We are not producing for ourselves, or for our communities, and that's dangerous. So, if I did it again, I would be more sensitive to stressing that. I am right now trying to conceptualize infrastructures that can shore up the cultural infrastructure within the community. I think we have to.[39]

There is much in Bryant's language that suggests a shared mission with Nigel Jackson's Acts of Art, and sense of shared need.

There were brief mentions of *Black Artists in the New York Scene* in the *Daily World* and in the new weekly *Black American*, and little else except for the *Amsterdam News*, where artist, illustrator, and columnist Mel Tapley praised Jackson and the artists he assembled. "These artists represent a variety of styles but they share one determination—that Black artists be recognized! Acts of Art, which was founded in 1969, has been struggling to help them reach that goal." Tapley exhorted his readers: "It is up to all of us AND our cultural institutions to see that these artists and galleries like Acts of Art, Weusi, Cinque, Genesis II, Storefront Museum, Sunday Gallery, Melca and Aub-Ray are not detoured by lack of funds. The road for Black artists is rocky enough."[40] Given Jackson's ambitions for Acts of Art, it is an odd and perhaps disappointing list. With the exception of Acts of Art and Cinque (the gallery Bearden, Crichlow, and Lewis founded on Lafayette Street in the Public Theater's headquarters), all of the spaces Tapley mentions are inside Black communities—in Bedford-Stuyvesant, Jamaica, and Harlem. They were part of the necessary infrastructure Bryant argued for, but not the political space both Jackson and Bryant wanted to claim.

For the *Amsterdam News*, these were the circuits and connections of the other New York Scene and other possibilities for community. Long a champion for Jackson as "one of the first to envision a showcase outside of Harlem for the work of Black artists," it wasn't until the summer of 1975 that Tapley began to report on the gallery's difficulties. On August 15, he asked whether "economic conditions, slowness of private and public cultural funding agencies or the urgent need for time to do his own painting started to make Nigel Jackson to consider either a new administration or a final act for his Acts of Art Gallery?"[41] Despite his confidence in Jackson's resilience, Tapley was back a week later writing that Jackson's "dream, 'Acts of Art,' is giving him some sleepless nights and tormented days."[42]

Nigel Jackson closed Acts of Art in November 1975 and left soon after for Botswana. He returned to New York some months later but resumed few—if any—ties to the art worlds he had occupied or the artists he had worked with. Benny Andrews had fallen out with Jackson well before the gallery closed, but in a letter written to Reginald Gammon in August 1997, he recounted running into Jackson on the street and recorded his half of the conversation: "I said to him, 'You know Nigel…you really were a pioneer in Black owned galleries and it's too bad you don't get credit for that. Some of us do remember what you did and will never forget that.'"[43]

NOTES

1 Important texts include Susan Cahan, *Mounting Frustration: The Art Museum in the Age of Black Power* (Durham: Duke University Press, 2016); Darby English, *1971: A Year in the Life of Color* (Chicago: University of Chicago Press, 2016); and the exhibition catalogues *We Wanted a Revolution: Black Radical Women 1965–1985*, eds. Catherine Morris and Rujeko Hockley (Brooklyn Museum, 2018); and *Soul of a Nation: Art in the Age of Black Power*, ed. Mark Godfrey (Tate Modern, 2017).

2 I borrow this term from Lisa Meyerowitz's dissertation "Exhibiting Equality: Black-run Museums and Galleries in 1970s New York," University of Chicago, 2001, p. 145. She defines "curatorial vision" as "the program or agenda defined by an institution over time." While the definition is hers, she credits art historian Richard Powell for suggesting the concept of a "curatorial vision" as a way to encapsulate the history and complexity of an art museum or gallery.

3 Journal entry 655, September 9, 1969, Estate of Benny Andrews, Brooklyn, NY.

4 Journal entry 677, October 1, 1969, Estate of Benny Andrews, Brooklyn, NY. In Andrews's inventory, *Lady in a Parade* was referred to as *Lady on Parade.* This painting was destroyed by the artist in 1971 and incorporated into a new work entitled *Down the Road, 1971.* Andrews's inventory also records *Immigrants, Southern Style* as *Immigrants: American Style.*

5 Benny Andrews papers, MSS 845, box 18, folder 2, Stuart A. Rose Manuscript, Archives and Rare Book Library, Emory University, Atlanta.

6 *New York Amsterdam News*, February 12, 1970, p. 16; and March 28, 1970, p. 18.

7 Nigel Jackson, December 1, 1972, Camille Billops and James V. Hatch archives, MSS 927, Series 6: Oral History Interviews, box 4, folder 441, Stuart A. Rose Manuscript, Archives and Rare Book Library, Emory University, Atlanta.

8 Benny Andrews papers, MSS 845, box 56, folder 2, Stuart A. Rose Manuscript, Archives and Rare Book Library, Emory University, Atlanta.

9 Andrews papers, Emory University, MSS 845, box 18, folder 2.

10 Journal entry 928, August 26, 1970, Estate of Benny Andrews, Brooklyn, NY. The entry identifies O'Doherty as director of the National Council on the Arts; he was Program Director for Visual Arts at the National Endowment for the Arts from as early as January 1970 through 1975.

11 Nancy Burton, "Gallery has a People Following," *The Villager*, August 27, 1970, p. 7.

12 Acts of Art membership brochure, c. 1971, Reginald Gammon papers, 1927–2007, bulk 1960–2005, Series 2: Correspondence, box 1, folder 20, Archives of American Art, Smithsonian Institution, Washington, D.C.

13 Burton, "Gallery has a People Following," *Villager*, 7.

14 "The Black Identity is There," *Contact*, January 1972, p. 21.

15 Journal entry 837, April 8, 1970, Estate of Benny Andrews, Brooklyn, NY.

16 Kasha Linville, "Benny Andrews at Acts of Art," *Artforum* 9, no. 5 (January 1971): 82.

17 Hilton Kramer, "'Black Art' and Expedient Politics," *The New York Times*, June 7, 1970, p. 107.

18 Grace Glueck, "Negroes' Art Is What's In Just Now," *New York Times*, February 27, 1969, p. 34.

19 Carroll Greene, Jr., "Perspective: The Black Artist in America," *Art Gallery Magazine* 13, no. 7 (April 1970): 1–2.

20 Edmund Gaither, "Introduction," *Afro-American Artists: New York and Boston*, exhibition catalogue (Boston: Museum of the National Center of Afro-American Artists and the Museum of Fine Arts, Boston, 1970), unpaginated.

21 Benny Andrews, "The War Years: 1968–1972," manuscript dated December 12, 1973, and subtitled "Autobiography, Book #4." The Estate of Benny Andrews, Brooklyn, NY. See also, Campbell Wylly, "New Voices: 15 New York Artists," *Art Gallery Magazine* 11, no. 7 (April 1968): 33–36. The fifteen artists were Emma Amos, Benny Andrews, Betty Blayton-Taylor, Emilio Cruz, Avel DeKnight, Melvin Edwards, Reginald Gammon, Alvin C. Hollingsworth, Tom Lloyd, William Majors, Earl Miller, Mahler Ryder, Raymond Saunders, Jack H. White, and Jack Whitten.

22 Grace Glueck, "Art Notes: A Box is a Box is a Box," *New York Times*, March 10, 1968, p. D23.

23 Andrews, "War Years."

24 Richard Hunt and Raymond Saunders were outliers on Andrews's list of the old guard. They were younger than the Harlem Arts Workshop group and indeed younger than Andrews, and Saunders was one of the fifteen *New Voices*. Both worked abstractly and both had built significant reputations and exhibition records outside New York City before gaining gallery affiliation in New York; Saunders in San Francisco and Hunt in Chicago.

25 In "When That Time Came Rolling Down, panel II," *Artist and Influence* unnumbered (1985): 144.

26 Ademola Olugebefola, interview with the author, December 3, 2020.

27 Ademola Olugebefola, interview by Camille Billops, August 14, 1979, *Artist and Influence* 23 (2004): 116.

28 Oral history interview with Senga Nengudi, July 9–11, 2013. Archives of American Art, Smithsonian Institution.

29 Ann Tanksley, interview with the author, November 19, 2020.

30 "The Law: The Game of Bail," *Time Magazine*, January 15, 1973. <https://content.time.com/time/subscriber/article/0,33009,906772-1,00.html>

31 "When That Time Came Rolling Down, panel II," *Artist and Influence* unnumbered (1985): 144.

32 David L. Shirey, "Gallery in the Village Seeks to Inspire Black Artists," *New York Times*, February 5, 1972, p. 26.

33 Zita Allen, "Nigel Jackson: Figures of a Black Artist," *Chelsea-Clinton News* 36, no. 51, May 18, 1972.

34 Henri Ghent, "Why, in 1973, a 'Black Art' Show?" *New York Times*, October 14, 1973, p. 151.

35 Ann-Sargent Wooster, "At the Galleries: From Old Posters to New Use of Light," *Villager*, April 17, 1975, p. 12.

36 George Lipsitz, "The Racialization of Space and the Spatialization of Race: Theorizing the Hidden Architecture of Landscape," *Landscape Journal* 26, no. 1 (2007): 12.

37 In addition to Billops, Browne, Lewis, and Mitchell, *Synthesis* included Elizabeth Catlett, Dan Conchelar, Alonzo Davis, David Hammons, Suzanne Jackson, Valerie Maynard, Roho, Russ Thompson, and Randy Williams. For a full and valuable history of Just Above Midtown, see the exhibition catalogue *Just Above Midtown: Changing Spaces*, edited by Thomas (T.) Jean Lax and Lilia Rocio Taboada in collaboration with Linda Goode Bryant (New York: Museum of Modern Art and the Studio Museum in Harlem, 2022).

38 Interview of Linda Goode Bryant by Tony Whitfield, May 15, 1994, *Artist and Influence* 13 (1994): 31.

39 Interview of Linda Goode Bryant, 33, 31.

40 Mel Tapley, "About the Arts," *New York Amsterdam News*, September 14, 1974, p. B6.

41 Mel Tapley, "About the Arts," *New York Amsterdam News*, August 13, 1975, p. D8.

42 Mel Tapley, "About the Arts," *New York Amsterdam News*, August 20, 1975, p. D7.

43 Letter from Benny Andrews to Reginald Gammon, August 18, 1997. Reginald Gammon papers, 1927–2007, bulk 1960–2005, Series 2: Correspondence, box 1, folder 22, Archives of American Art, Smithsonian Institution, Washington, D.C.

acts of art
exhibition history

OCT 1969
31 Bedford Street Opening

The first six months were spent rebuilding a dilapidated old store in Greenwich Village into an elegant little shoppe called acts of art galleries. While it is located only three blocks from the main subway entrance to the Village (West 4th Street), it is on a relatively out of the way corner, which tends to lend itself to the atmosphere that impresses people upon their entering and "discovering" the gallery.... The gallery opened in October, 1969. The theme of the opening was "Black Art in America." The show included 150 pieces by fifteen different Black artists, and attracted about two hundred people to the opening of the show.

—Undated grant application, summer 1970

1969

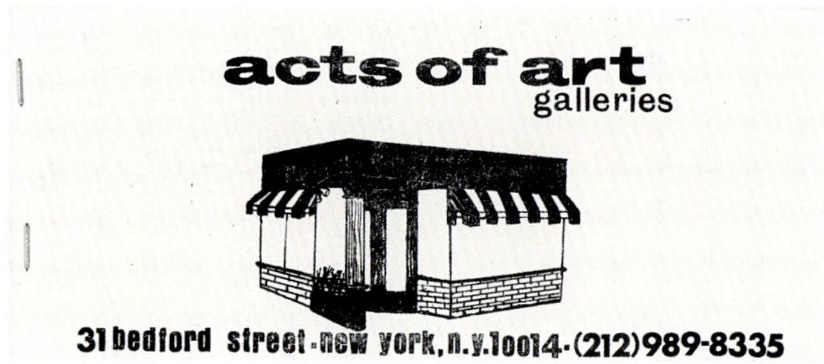

FEB–MAR 1970
Group Show

Jill Ainsworth, Benny Andrews, Gil Edwards, Patricia Grey, Moses Groves, Nigel Jackson, John Johnson, and Enid Richardson

JUL 1970
Lester Gunter

AUG–SEP 1970
Group Show

Benny Andrews, James Denmark, Patricia Grey, Enid Richardson, and others

1970

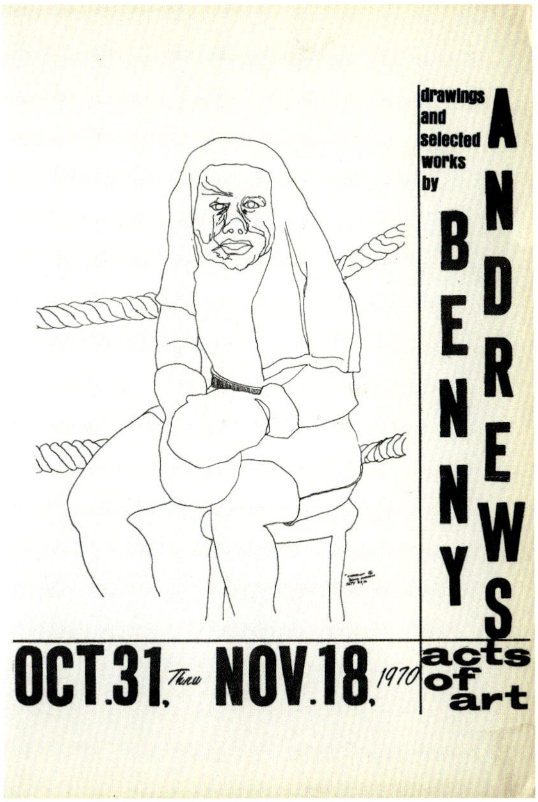

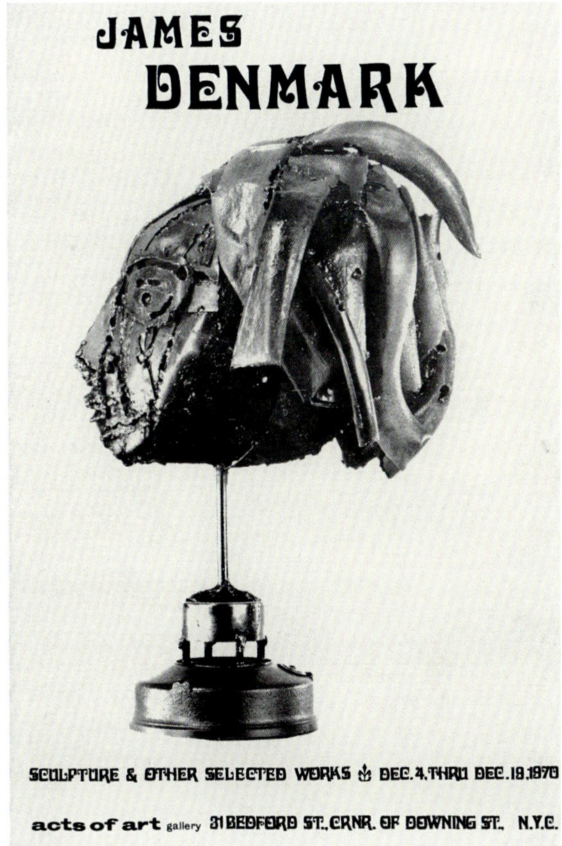

OCT 31–NOV 18, 1970 Benny Andrews: Drawings and Selected Works

The exhibition was a realization of a wish I'd had for a long time, rhetoric aside, and that was to break through to several different groups and make a point of proving that with good art work, a conscientious art dealer…a good exhibition can be put on. It does not matter that we are Black, that the gallery has only 500 square feet of exhibition space, that it is hard to find, etc. What does matter at this stage of art history in general and Black in particular, is "heart and soul." I was especially pleased to see Black people in regular Western dress, mingling with Black people in African dress, students Black & white, artists Black & white, collectors, friend[s], and passersby, all were happy to be there. It was more than my show, it was a place to meet, talk, and relax for a while. The long-term gains should be to establish in the minds of the art world that Black art expertise is coming of age.

—Benny Andrews, journal entry, October 31, 1970

DEC 4–19, 1970 James Denmark: Sculpture and Other Selected Works

This tiny corner gallery, an appealing eye-catcher on a deadish street, is the only one outside Harlem specializing in the work of Black artists.…The best of Mr. Denmark's sculpture…consists of found-wood wall assemblages whose cubistic motifs are unified by a coat of matte black paint. Yes, it does evoke Nevelson—but there's something extra here, a kind of elegant African liveliness that lifts them well above the level of pastiche. A more fully-realized work is "Struggle," a free-standing architectural sculpture whose twisting planes are pieced of found-wood components. It's a powerful statement.

—Grace Glueck, *The New York Times*, December 11, 1970

ART IN BLACK AMERICA

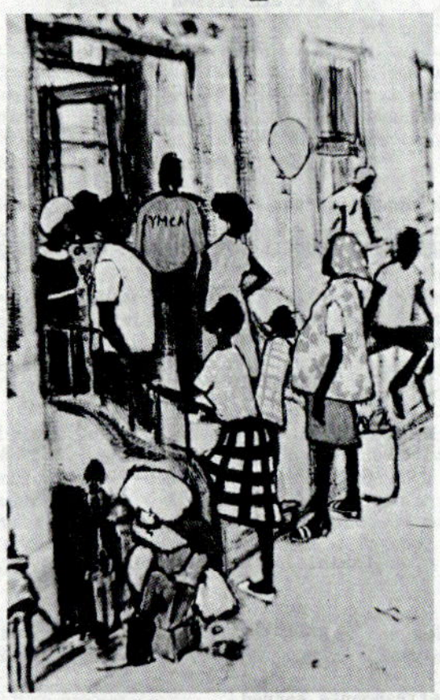

GROUP SHOW

BENNY ANDREWS
VIVIAN BROWN
JAMES DENMARK
LESTER GUNTER
NIGEL JACKSON
DINDGA MC CANNON
ENID RICHARDSO

MARCH 9 THRU 19

You and your guests are cordially
invited to attend the opening preview
art exhibition

ART
IN BLACK AMERICA

MARCH 9
5 - 7 PM

Presented at the National office of the
INTERRACIAL COUNCIL FOR BUSINESS OPPORTUNITY
470 PARK AVENUE SOUTH, NYC, 3rd Fl.
(31st & 32nd St.)

MARCH 10 - 19
5 - 7 PM

For information or appointments -
(212) 889-0880

Exhibition courtesy of
acts of art
galleries, inc.

Refreshments served

COVER...
"Waiting for the Number" by
ENID RICHARDSON
(23" x 30")

ICBO is taking another step forward. In addition to assisting in the development of minority business through educational, advisory and financial aid, ICBO is now rounding out its assistance to also include a cultural contribution. We take great pride in presenting this exhibition of "Art in Black America," in our National office.

The artist, especially the minority artist, needs all of us. He needs us to acknowledge his existance. He needs us to realize that he too is making a contribution. That, because he is of a minority group, he has a point of view, which must be heard. He is expressing himself through his art and is asking us to relate to it.

The art work included in this exhibition is of varied subject matter, style and medium. Included are paintings, drawings, prints and sculpture. All of the art work was created by young black artists whose accomplishments are briefly described in the following pages.

All of the art work on exhibit is for sale. ICBO welcomes you to: Art in Black America.

Darwin W. Bolden
National Executive Director

acts of art has expanded into new and larger quarters. We've moved to 15 Charles Street (at 7th Avenue and Waverly Place), N. Y. C. (in Greenwich Village)

* * * * * * * * * * * * * * * * * * *

You and your friends are invited to attend a

GROUP SHOW
Jan 12 thru Feb 13

BENNY ANDREWS
JAMES DENMARK
LESTER GUNTER
NIGEL JACKSON
ENID RICHARDSON

* * * * * * * * * * * * * * * * * * *

* SPECIAL FEATURE *

Jan 13 to Jan 27
Wednesdays-4 to 7PM
Saturdays -3 to 7PM
and by appointment

PORTRAITS IN OIL BY...

LESTER GUNTER

Visiting artist Lester Gunter will be on hand at acts of art for immediate sittings or portraits from photos. Portrait prices begin at $75. Come meet the visiting artist.

* * * * * * * * * * * * * * * * * * *

GALLERY HOURS: TUES thru SAT 2 - 8PM
FOR APPOINTMENT CALL: (212)989-8335

JAN 12–FEB 13, 1971
Group Show
First Exhibition at 15 Charles Street

Benny Andrews, James Denmark, Lester Gunter, Nigel Jackson, and Enid Richardson

MAR 9–19, 1971
Art in Black America
Exhibition in the offices of the Interracial Council for Business Opportunity

Benny Andrews, Vivian Browne, James Denmark, Lester Gunter, Nigel Jackson, Dindga McCannon, and Enid Richardson

1971

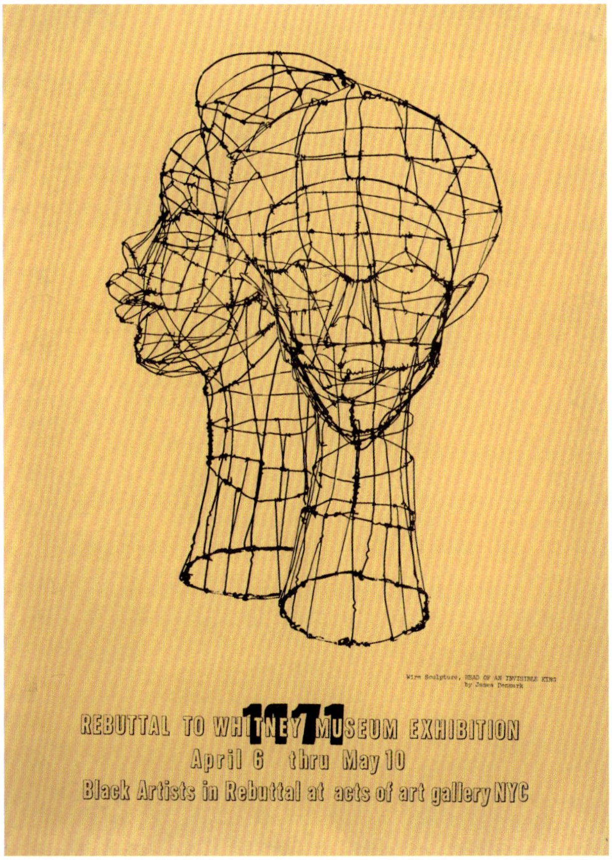

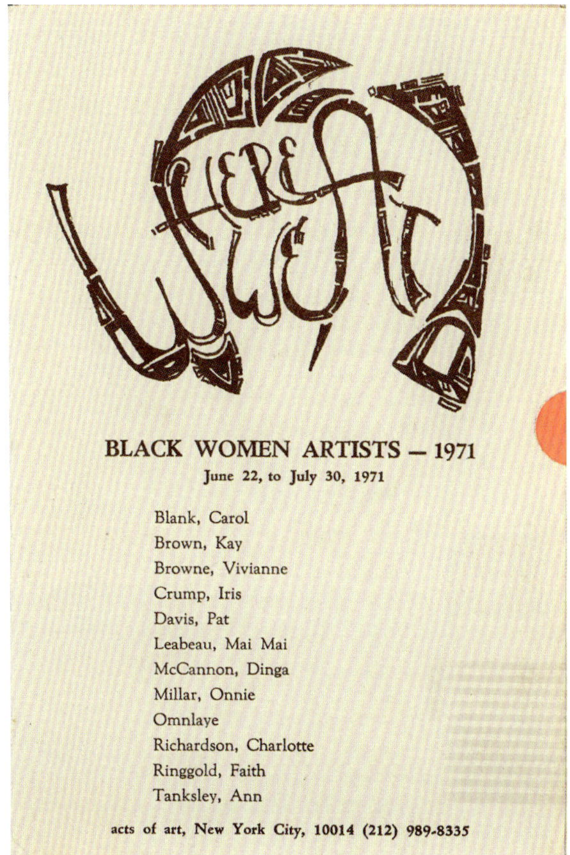

APR 6–MAY 10, 1971
Rebuttal to the Whitney Museum Exhibition

"I'm showing the real stuff and they're showing a watered down standard," said Nigel Jackson of Acts of Art gallery, currently housing the Rebuttal to the Whitney Museum Exhibition. *Both exhibitions previewed April 5th and opened the following day.*

The Whitney, allegedly showing a "national representation of Black artists," has incurred the disfavor of a large segment of this country's community of Black artists. Hence the rebuttal.

Acts of Art, a small Village gallery run and owned by a Black painter who lives in Chelsea, overflowed preview night with painters, actors, their friends and some press. Even some of the artists who were showing at the Whitney were there the night of the preview.

—Z. D. Allen, *Chelsea-Clinton News*, April 15, 1971

JUN 22–JUL 30, 1971
Where We At: Black Women Artists 1971

The theme of the show was: "WHERE WE AT" – BLACK WOMEN ARTISTS 1971. *The title depicted the significant role of the Black woman artist and showed the community that we did exist—in numbers. Heretofore, the viewing public appeared to believe that the Black artists was synonymous with the Black male artist. Many of the artists who had worked for years had not been given opportunities for exhibiting their works. The "WHERE WE AT" BLACK WOMEN ARTISTS is a real "coming together" of creative and talented Black women, unique in its philosophy of mutual support of Black women artists in the creative endeavor. The group is relevant to today's African-American women and is vital to the Black Community. The artists exchange information and resources for the mutual benefit of all and is dedicated to the cultural education and enrichment of the community.*

—Kay Brown, *Feminist Art Journal*, April 1972

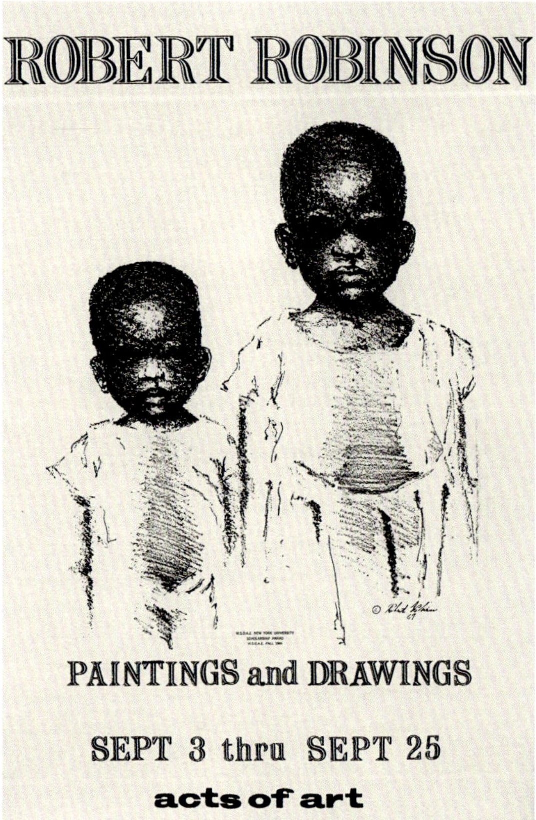

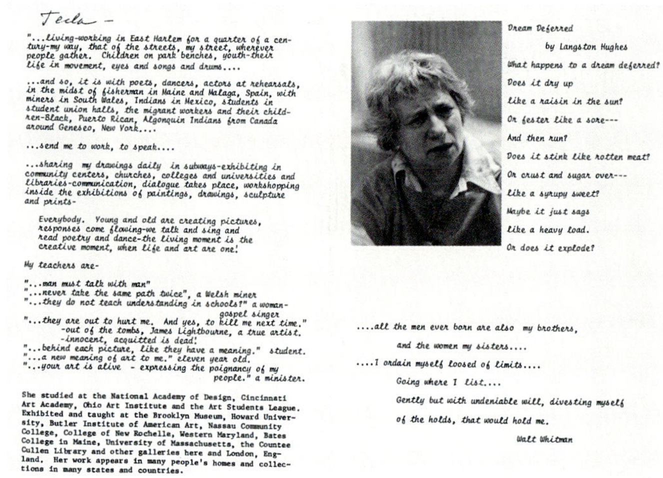

Tecla –

"...living-working in East Harlem for a quarter of a century-my way, that of the streets, my street, wherever people gather. Children on park benches, youth-their life in movement, eyes and songs and drums....

...and so, it is with poets, dancers, actors at rehearsals, in the midst of fisherman in Maine and Malaga, Spain, with miners in South Wales, Indians in Mexico, students in student union halls, the migrant workers and their children-Black, Puerto Rican, Algonquin Indians from Canada around Geneseo, New York....

...send me to work, to speak....

...sharing my drawings daily in subways-exhibiting in community centers, churches, colleges and universities and libraries-communication, dialogue takes place, workshopping inside the exhibitions of paintings, drawings, sculpture and prints-

Everybody. Young and old are creating pictures, responses come flowing-we talk and sing and read poetry and dance-the living moment is the creative moment, when life and art are one!

My teachers are-

"...man must talk with man"
"...never take the same path twice", a Welsh miner
"...they do not teach understanding in schools?" a woman-gospel singer
"...they are out to hurt me. And yes, to kill me next time."
-out of the tombs, James Lightbourne, a true artist.
-innocent, acquitted is dead!
"...behind each picture, like they have a meaning." student.
"...a new meaning of art to me." eleven year old.
"...your art is alive - expressing the poignancy of my people." a minister.

She studied at the National Academy of Design, Cincinnati Art Academy, Ohio Art Institute and the Art Students League. Exhibited and taught at the Brooklyn Museum, Howard University, Butler Institute of American Art, Nassau Community College, College of New Rochelle, Western Maryland, Bates College in Maine, University of Massachusetts, the Countee Cullen Library and other galleries here and London, England. Her work appears in many people's homes and collections in many states and countries.

Dream Deferred

by Langston Hughes

What happens to a dream deferred?
Does it dry up
like a raisin in the sun?
Or fester like a sore---
And then run?
Does it stink like rotten meat?
Or crust and sugar over---
like a syrupy sweet?
Maybe it just sags
like a heavy load.
Or does it explode?

....all the men ever born are also my brothers,
and the women my sisters....
....I ordain myself loosed of limits....
Going where I list....
Gently but with undeniable will, divesting myself
of the holds, that would hold me.

Walt Whitman

SEP 3–25, 1971
Robert Robinson: Paintings and Drawings

SEP 28–OCT 19, 1971
Phillippe Smith: Marble, Bronze, and Wood Sculptures

OCT 22–NOV 13, 1971
Tecla in Retrospect

Tecla Selnicks' show is a retrospective of the past 20 years. She has worked largely in an East Harlem studio, and her portraits are of the people of that vicinity. Subjects and backgrounds are fused together through fast brushing and direct application. This attack extends itself to the portraits of James Lightbourne, a former prisoner and artist in New York's Tombs. His face and the heads he sculpts contain an equal measure of life.

—Bill Beckley, *ARTnews*, November 1971

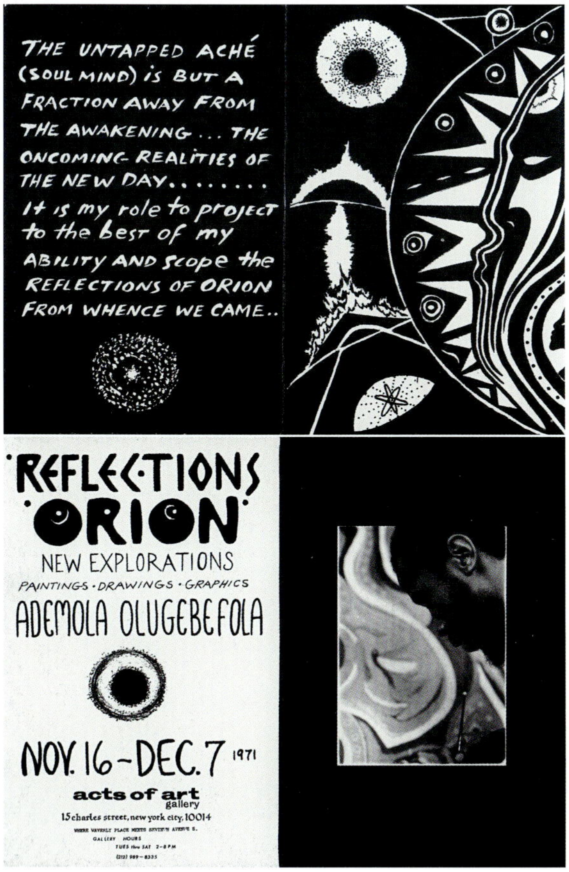

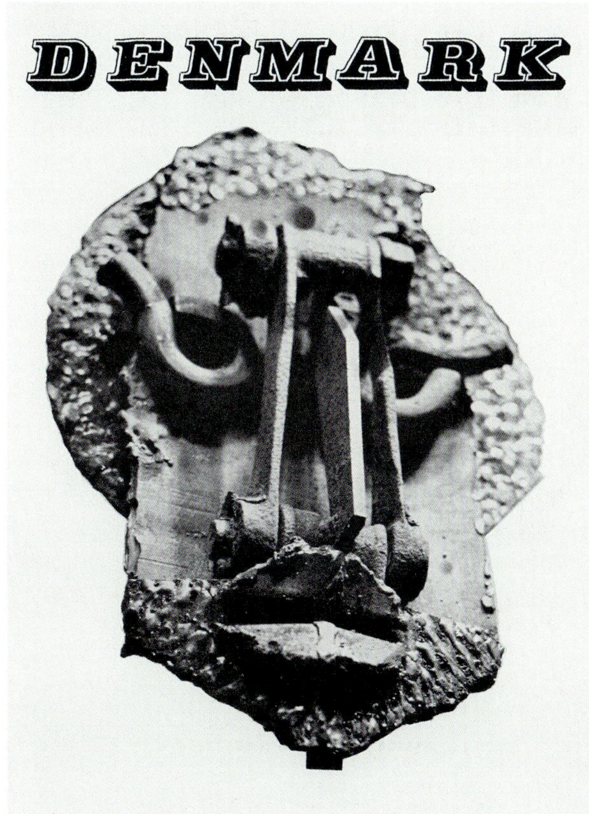

NOV 16–DEC 7, 1971
Ademola Olugebefola: Reflections Orion

Olugebefola's pictorial images are flat, abstracted human and natural forms intertwined with solar and planetary elements. Despite the abstract and ambiguous meanings represented by the works, the communication between artist and viewer seems immediate and highly personal due to the universality of its appeal.... The drama of the exhibition is heightened by a form of jazz chant to "Orion" playing in the background.

—M.L.B, *The Villager*, December 2, 1971

DEC 10, 1971–JAN 7, 1972
James Denmark: Sculpture, Paintings, Drawings

His current show, which will be at the Acts of Art Gallery until January 7, demonstrates anew his versatility and enthusiasm. From his wood or welded steel sculptures to his collages, woodcuts, charcoals and watercolors, Denmark shows he is an accomplished artist and a master craftsman. Take "Spirit of the Dance," which captures the vital upsurge of the Black artist. At first glance, it looks like a simple depiction of the graceful exuberance of a tribal dancer—a smooth swirl from the earth stretching skyward. Then one realizes the movement isn't just skyward—it's heavenward.

—Melvin Tapley, *New York Amsterdam News*, December 18, 1971

1972

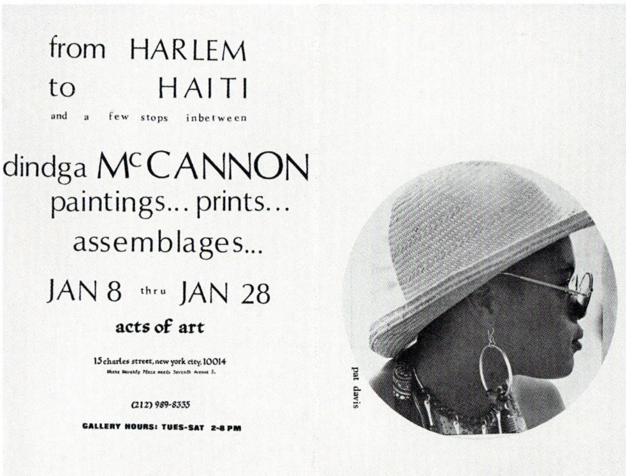

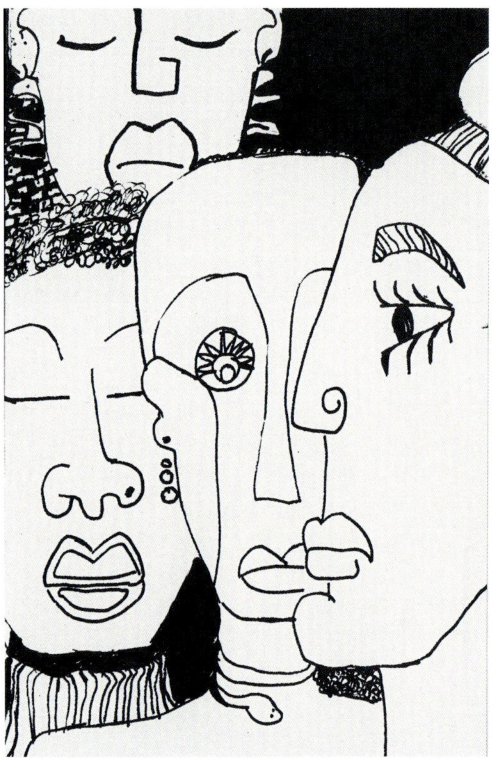

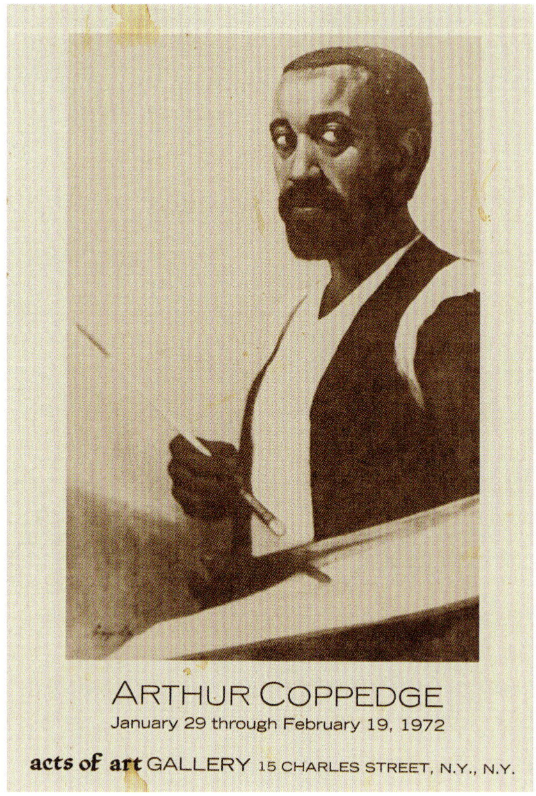

JAN 8–28, 1972
Dindga McCannon: from Harlem to Haiti and a few stops in between

---

JAN 29–FEB 19, 1972
Arthur Coppedge

The current first one-man show of Arthur Coppedge, a young Black from Brooklyn, is one of the best the gallery has offered so far. A figurative artist with a sharp eye for the urban landscape, Mr. Coppedge is a skilled technician whose images of city streets, city people, Black and white, have a feeling and style reminiscent of Edward Hopper and a wry wit suggestive of Daumier.

—David L. Shirey, *The New York Times*, February 5, 1972

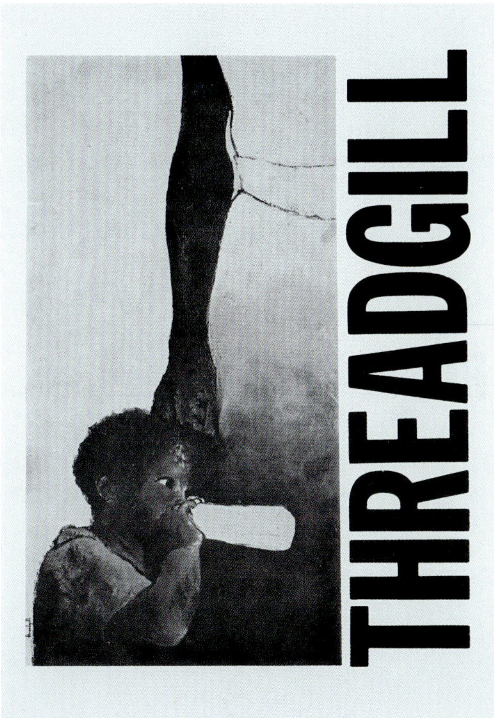

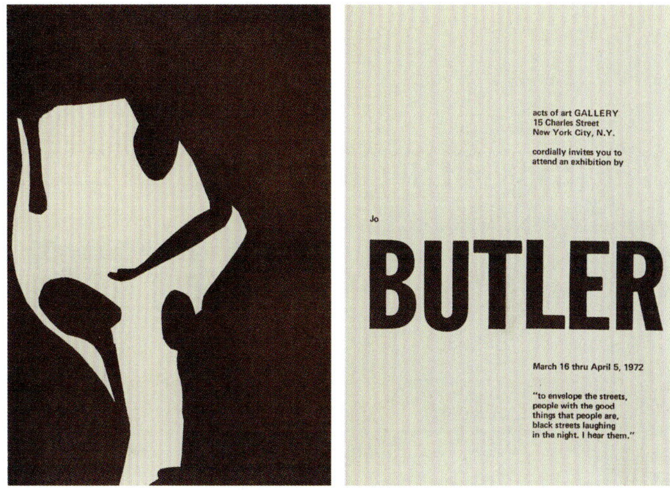

FEB 22–MAR 14, 1972
Robert Threadgill

Threadgill avowedly paints his memories and demands that the viewer identify himself with the figures and situations he paints. To criticize the work is not to deny the appeal of the small child shown tugging at his father's knee; or the reality of the Black experience.

—Jane Gollin, *ARTnews*, April 1972

MAR 16–APR 5, 1972
Jo Butler

Jo Butler's suggestive canvases, with groups of people engaged in unexplained activities, beg for interpretations. Even her small drawings and collages want to be symbolic, though she gives no key for interpreting them. Reinforcing the notion of acceptable alternatives, Butler bolsters background space with strong colors and lets her subjects fend for themselves as left-behind white shapes with features barely indicated.

—Jane Gollin, *ARTnews*, March 1972

1972

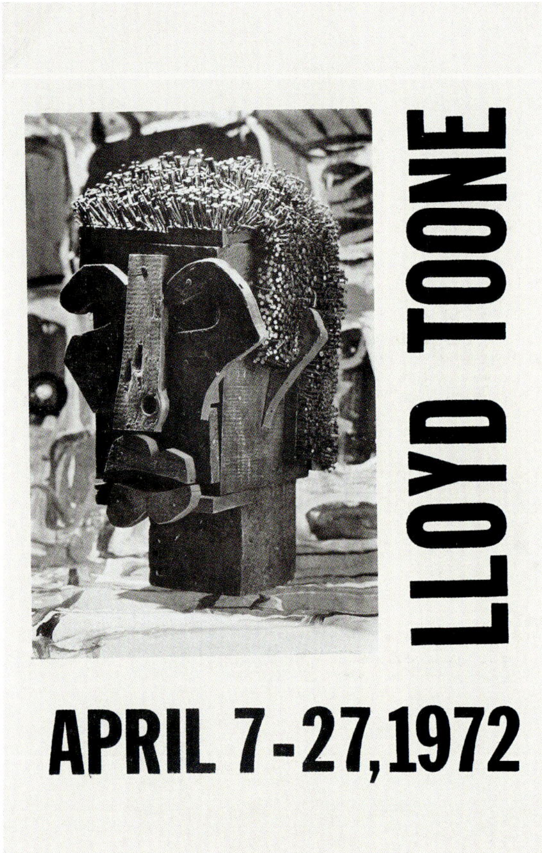

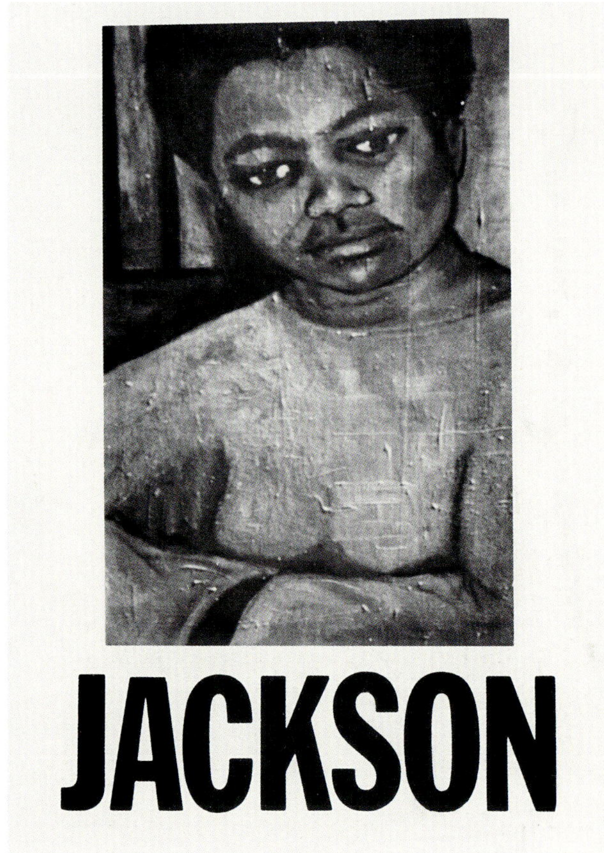

APR 7–27, 1972
Lloyd Toone

Lloyd Toone is a young Black artist bursting with ideas. In plastic and sculptural reliefs, Toone creates patterns of letters or keys and locks. Some of his collages utilize assorted papers and textures; others combine photographs in figure studies. In still another group, he uses collage only as a ground for highly colored crayon-and-acrylic abstractions. Some of these look almost ceramic. In his sculptures, Toone combines leather, wood and nails to create heads and masks. His work is quiet, yet full of energy and admiration for both African and Western sources.

—Jane Gollin, *ARTnews*, April 1972

APR 29–MAY 20, 1972
Nigel Jackson

Nigel Jackson has some very clear ideas about the role of a Black painter in today's world. He feels that it is essential for a Black artist, at least in the beginning, to make crucial connections with his audience in terms of subject matter. As a result, most of Jackson's portraits show strong Black individuals with intense characters. His treatment of them is powerful. Rich color, expressive brushwork, strong vertical and horizontal compositions which lock the figures in the picture plane, work in conjunction with photographic cropping devices to force the sitter's presence up to the forefront of the viewer's attention.

—April Kingsley, *ARTnews*, May 1972

MAY 23–JUN 13, 1972
James Denmark, Ann Tanksley, and Frank Wimberley

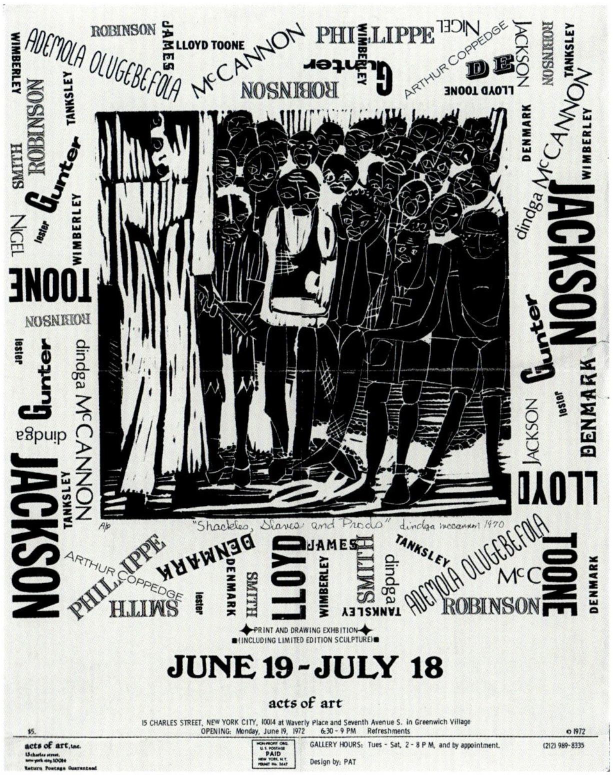

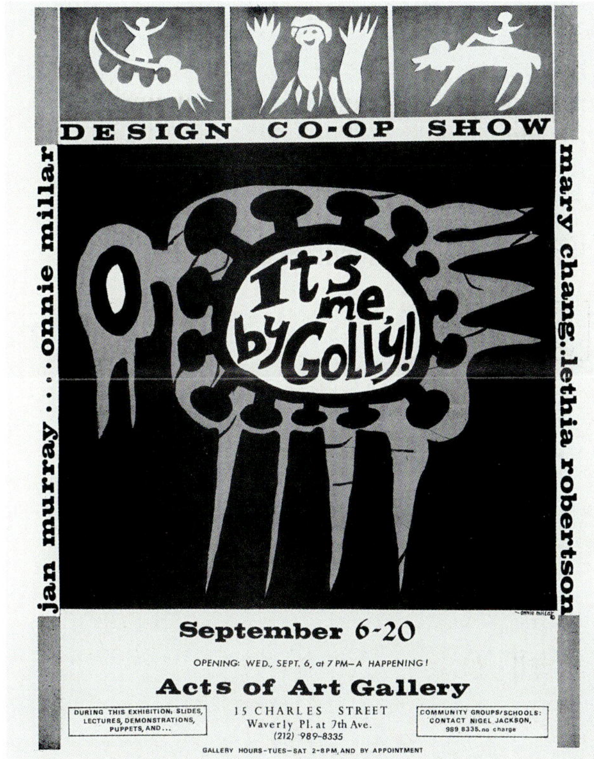

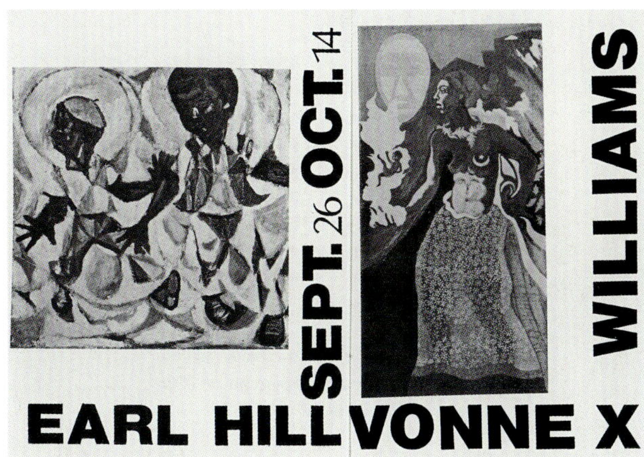

JUN 19–JUL 18, 1972
Group Show

Arthur Coppedge, James Denmark, Lester Gunter, Nigel Jackson, Dindga McCannon, Ademola Olugebefola, Robert Robinson, Philippe Smith, Ann Tanksley, Lloyd Toone, and Frank Wimberley

SEP 6–20, 1972
"It's Me, By Golly": Design Co-op Show

Mary Chang, Onnie Millar, Jan Murray, and Lethia Robertson

SEP 26–OCT 14, 1972
Earl Hill and Yvonne X. Williams

1972

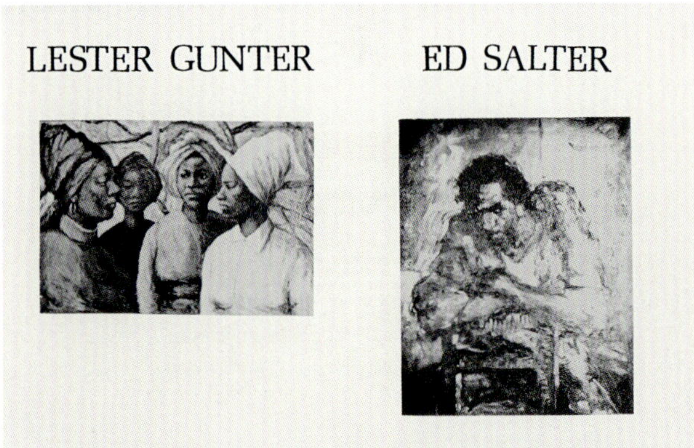

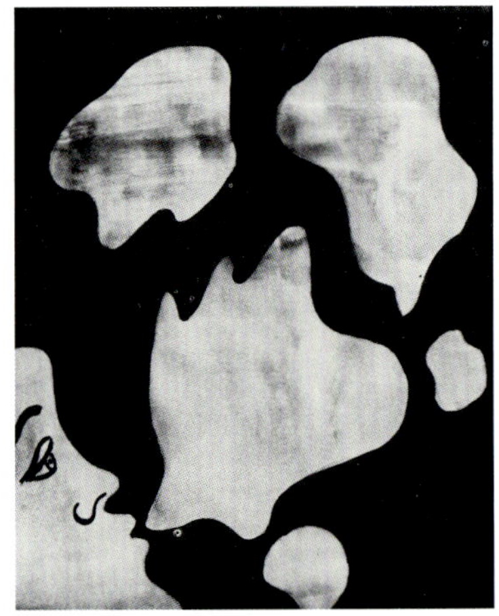

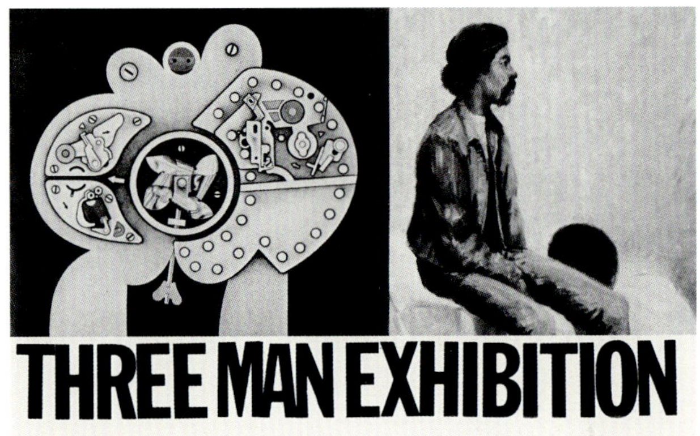

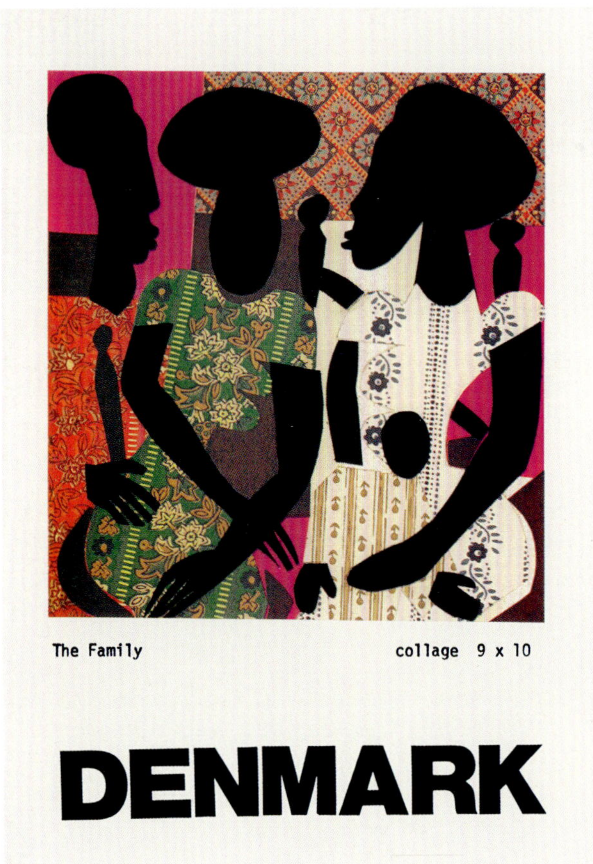

OCT 16–NOV 11, 1972
Lester Gunter and Ed Salter: Paintings and Drawings

NOV 6–DEC 2, 1972
James Denmark: Sculpture, Paintings, Drawings

JAN 4–27, 1973
Three Man Exhibition

Manuel Hughes, Robert Robinson, and Keith Simon

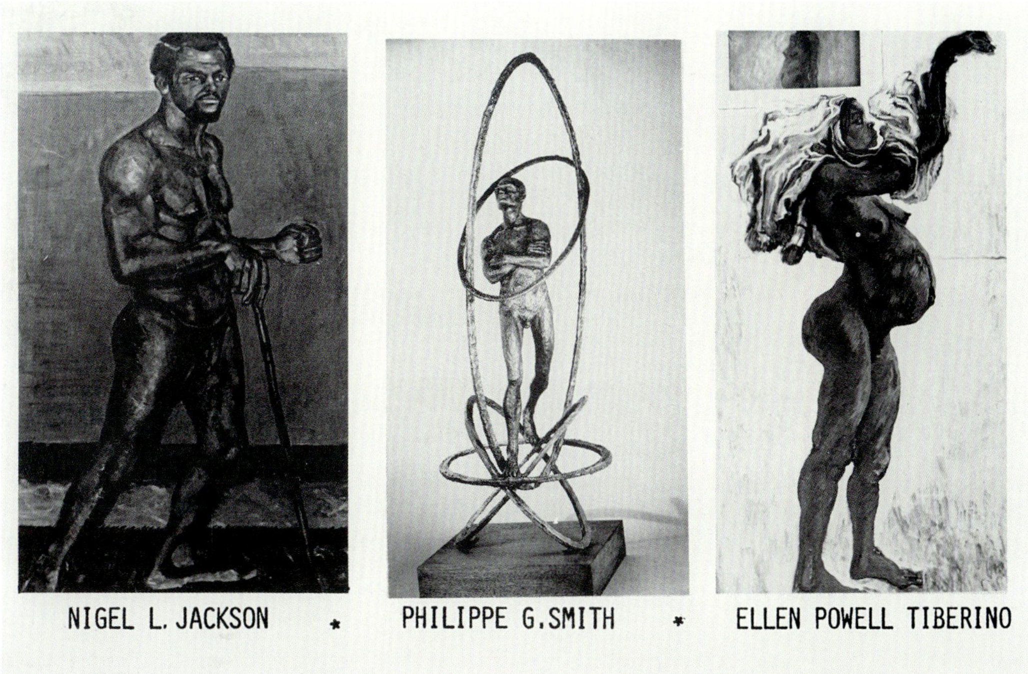

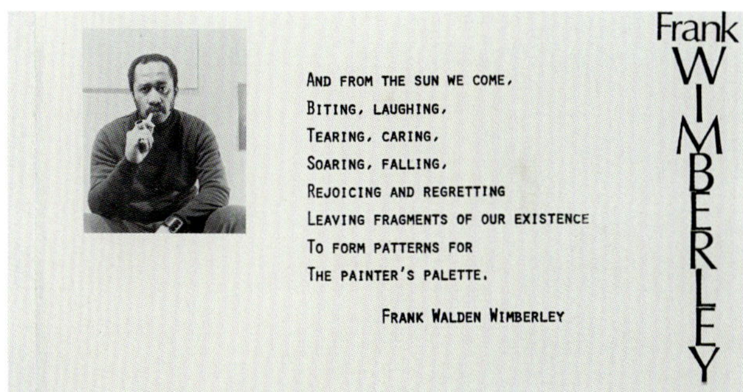

JAN 30–FEB 17, 1973
Frank Walden Wimberley

FEB 20–MAR 13, 1973
Bob Threadgill: Paintings and Drawings

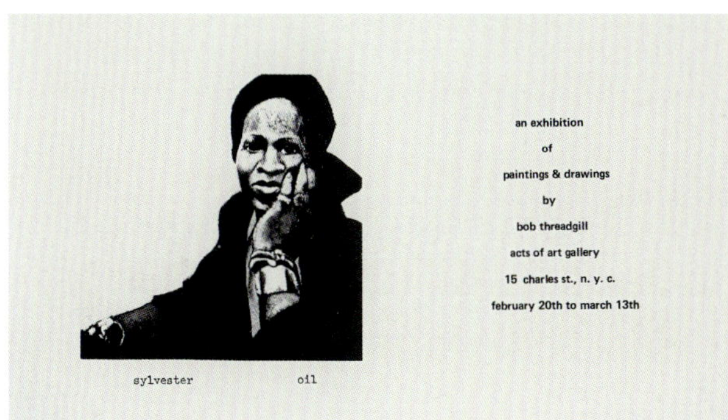

MAR 15–APR 3, 1973
Group Show

Nigel Jackson, Philippe G. Smith, and Ellen Powell Tiberino

1973

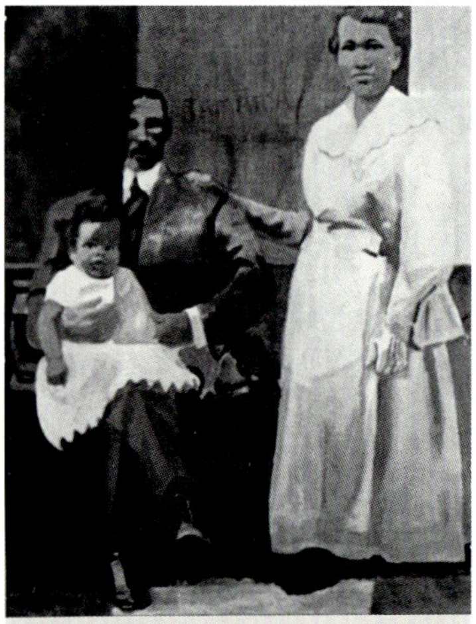

REGINALD GAMMON

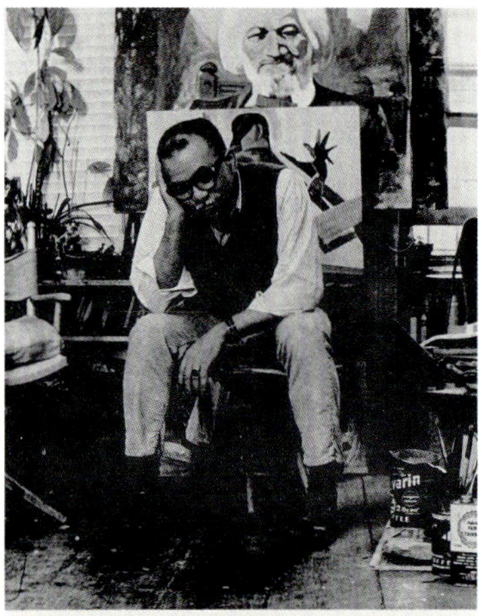

photo by MaryEllen Andrews

REGINALD GAMMON

PAINTINGS DRAWINGS PHOTOGRAPHS

APRIL 5 THRU 24, 1973

ACTS OF ART IS PROUD TO REINTRODUCE THE ARTWORK OF REGINALD GAMMON, TO NEW YORK. A NATIVE OF PHILADELPHIA AND A WELL-KNOWN, VERY FINE ARTIST, HE IS CURRENTLY ASSISTANT PROFESSOR OF ART AND GENERAL STUDIES AT WESTERN MICHIGAN UNIVERSITY, KALAMAZOO, MICHIGAN.

THE EXHIBITION, "THE GAMMON FILE" INCLUDES THE ARTIST'S SECRET LIFE, BITS AND PIECES OF HIS PAST AND HIS PRESENT, SOME PUBLIC, SOME FANTASTIC IN NATURE, SOME HISTORIC AND SOME EVEN A LITTLE HISTRIONIC.

COVER: "FAMILY ALBUM"
(THE ARTIST'S FAMILY)
ACRYLIC ON CANVAS & BURLAP-1972

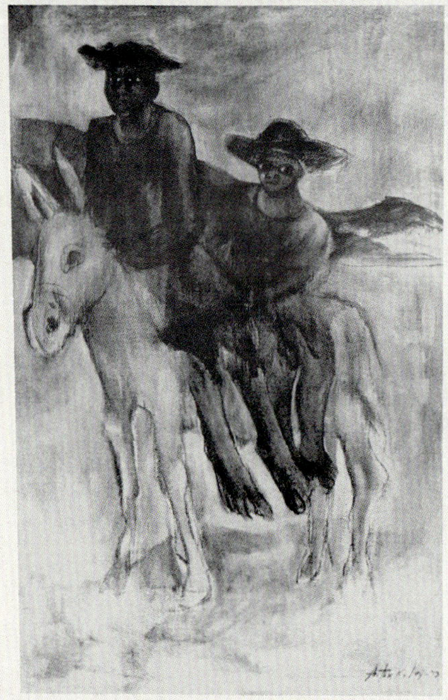

ANN TANKSLEY

APR 5–24, 1973
The Gammon File:
Paintings, Drawings, Photographs

APR 26–MAY 15, 1973
Ann Tanksley:
Paintings, Drawings, Collage

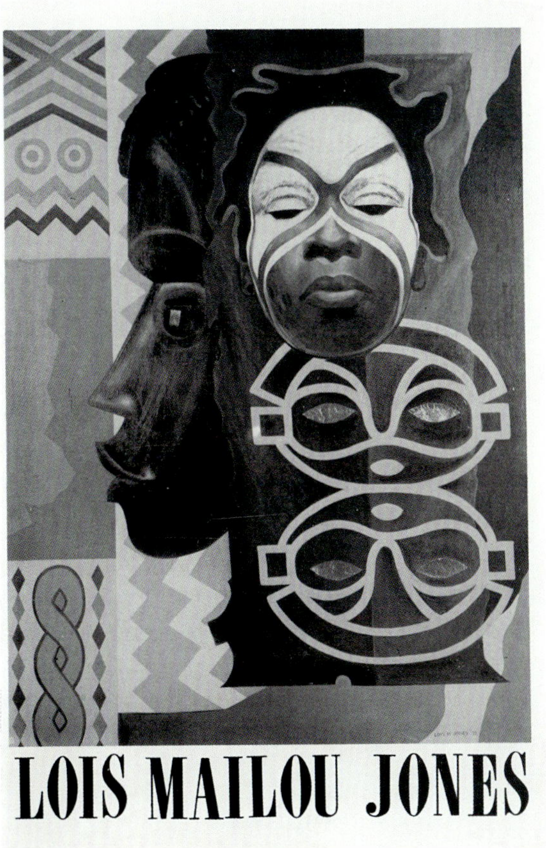

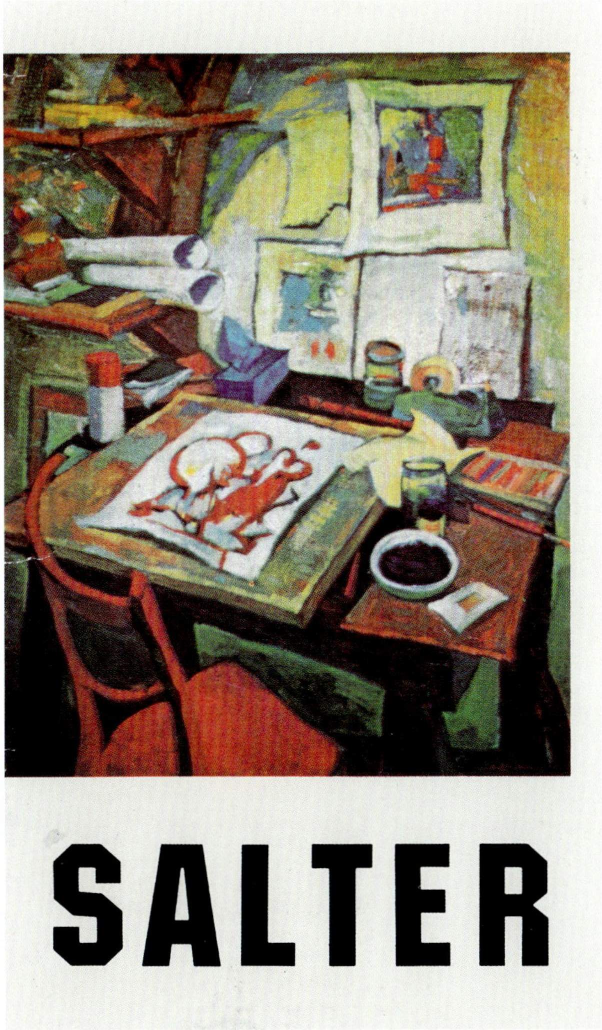

JUN 11–JUL 2, 1973
Loïs Mailou Jones: In Retrospect

JUL 9–28, 1973
Summer of '73

James Denmark, Reginald Gammon, Earl Hill, Nigel Jackson, Ademola Olugebefola, Enid Richardson, Ernestine Robinson, Robert Robinson, Ed Salter, Philippe Smith, Ann Tanksley, Lloyd Toone, and Frank Wimberley

SEP 6–27, 1973
Ed Salter: Paintings and Drawings

1973

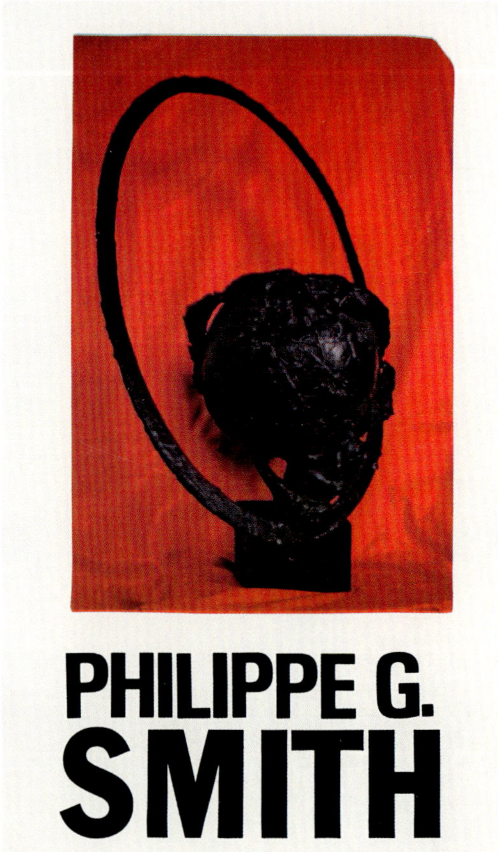

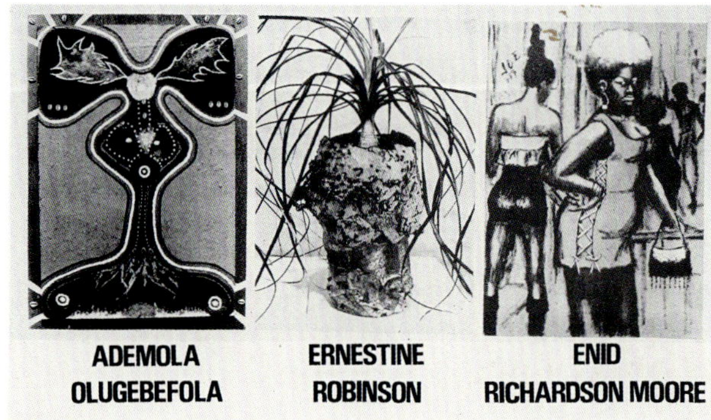

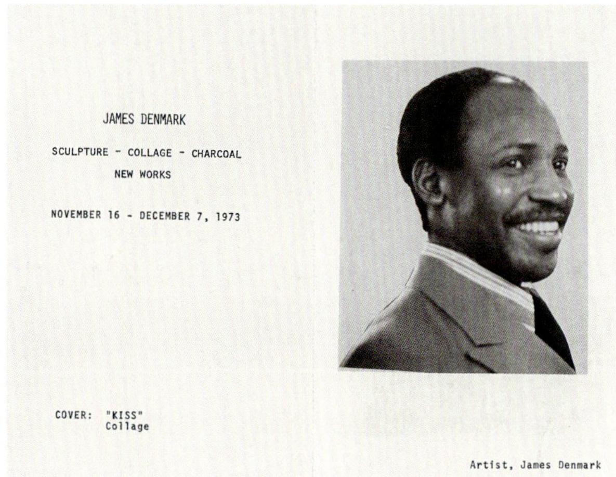

SEP 29–OCT 18, 1973
Group Show

Ademola Olugebefola, Enid Richardson Moore, and Ernestine Robinson

OCT 20–NOV 14, 1973
Philippe G. Smith: Sculpture (New Works)

A Haitian-born sculptor, Mr. Smith is exhibiting a number of modestly scaled pieces, generally in stone, on such themes as birth and womanhood. The artist handles the materials—alabaster and pink Tennessee marble, for example—quite handsomely, bringing out the color and veining. But the forms themselves are generally executed in the sleek, stylized manner associated with nineteen-thirties modern.

—James R. Mellow, *The New York Times*, November 3, 1973

NOV 16–DEC 7, 1973
James Denmark: Sculpture, Collage, Charcoal, New Works

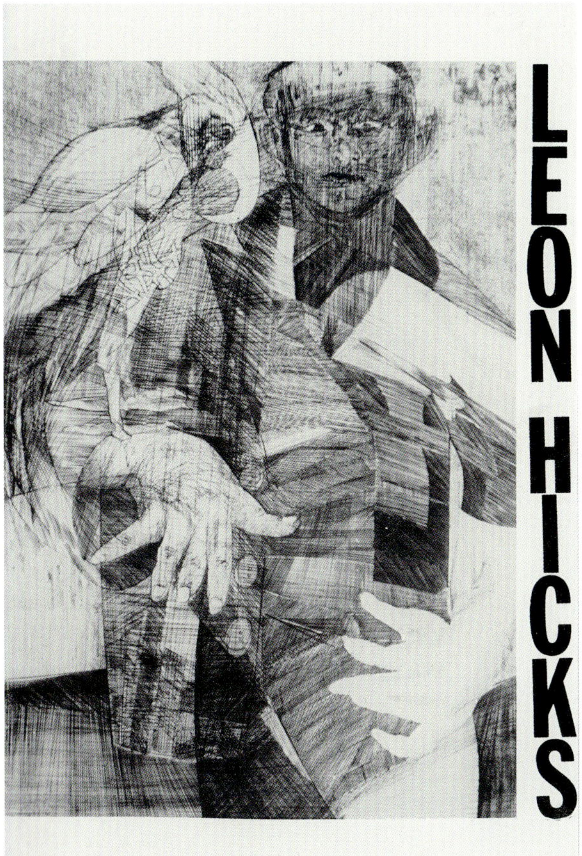

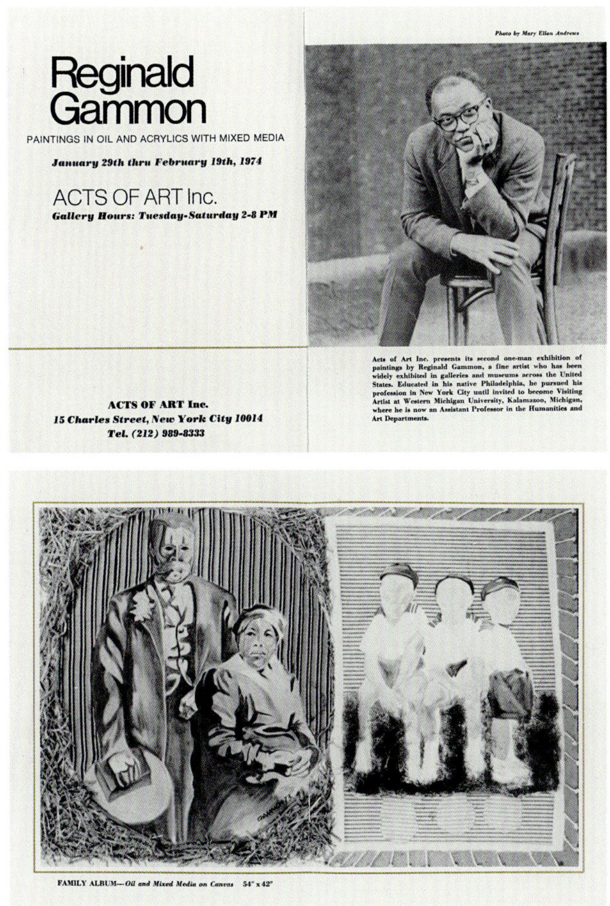

DEC 11, 1973–JAN 2, 1974
Season's Greeting

James Denmark, Leon Hicks, Earl Hill, Nigel Jackson, Enid Richardson, Ernestine Robinson, Robert Robinson, Ed Salter, Ann Tanksley, Lloyd Toone, and Frank Wimberley

JAN 4–24, 1974
Leon Hicks

JAN 29–FEB 19, 1974
Reginald Gammon: Paintings in Oil and Acrylics with Mixed Media

1974

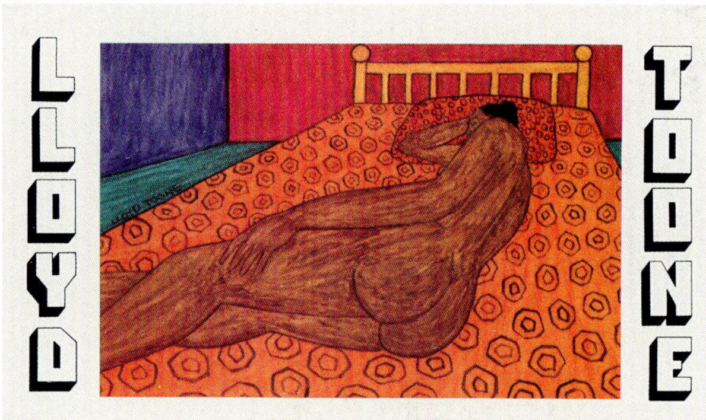

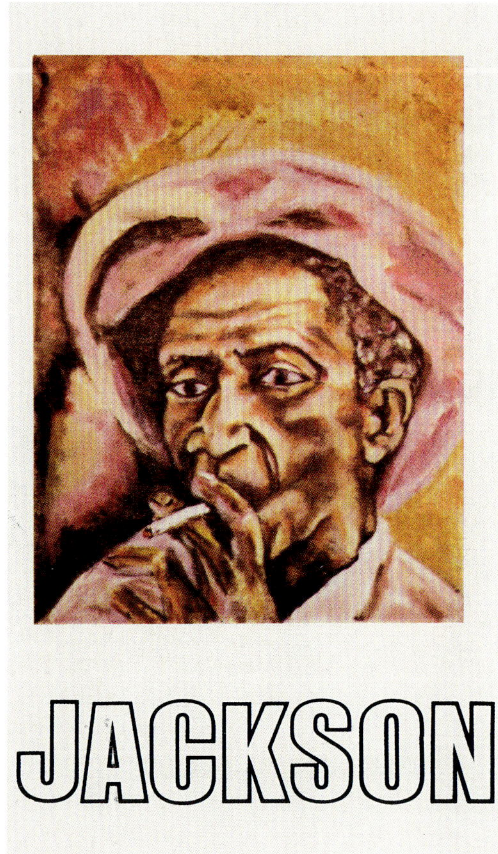

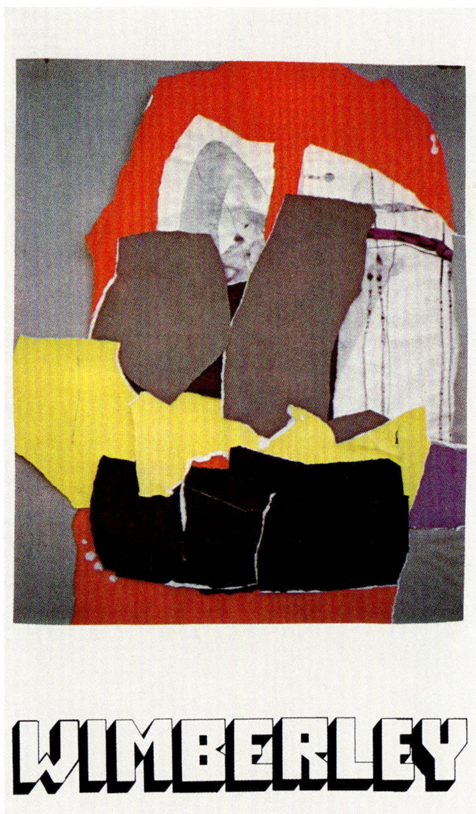

FEB 22–MAR 16, 1974
Lloyd Toone: New Works

MAR 19–APR 9, 1974
Frank Wimberley

APR 12–MAY 3, 1974
Nigel Jackson:
Paintings and Drawings. New Works

1974

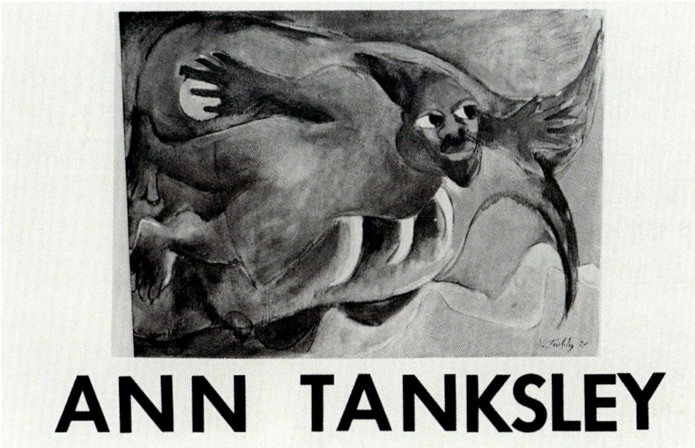

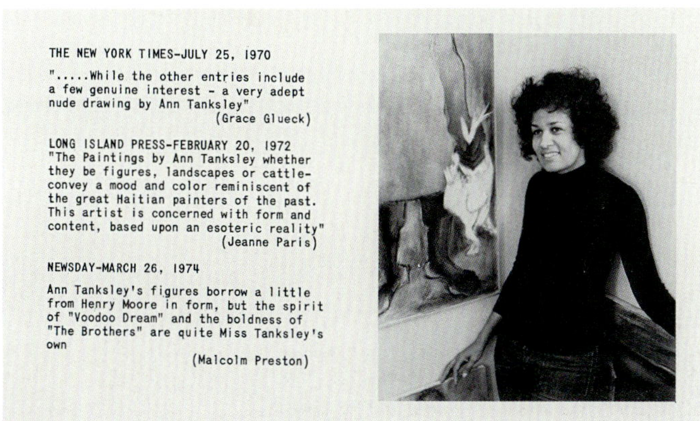

MAY 7–28, 1974
Ann Tanksley: Paintings, Drawings, and Prints

MAY 31–JUN 23, 1974
The Photography of Chester Higgins, Jr.

These are emotional images, not at all dispassionate, but the photographer rarely slips into sentimentality or cliche. Nor does he force his subjects, or his images, to fit into a single overriding visual style. The consistency of these photographs is not one of graphics, but rather of gentleness, warmth, and precise responsiveness to the uniqueness of human beings.

—A.D. Coleman, *The New York Times*, June 16, 1974

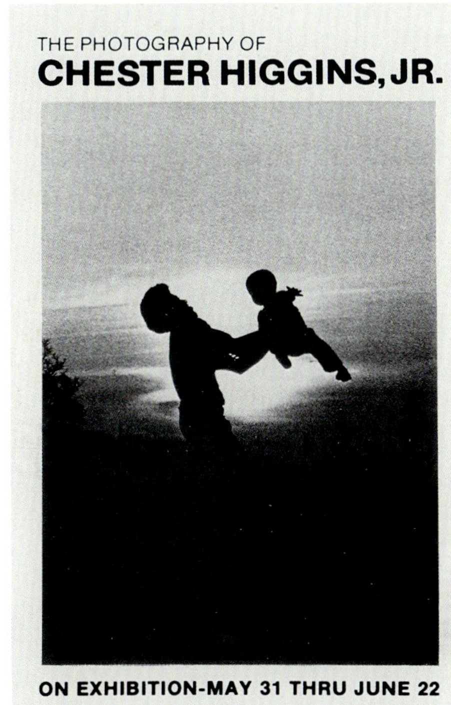

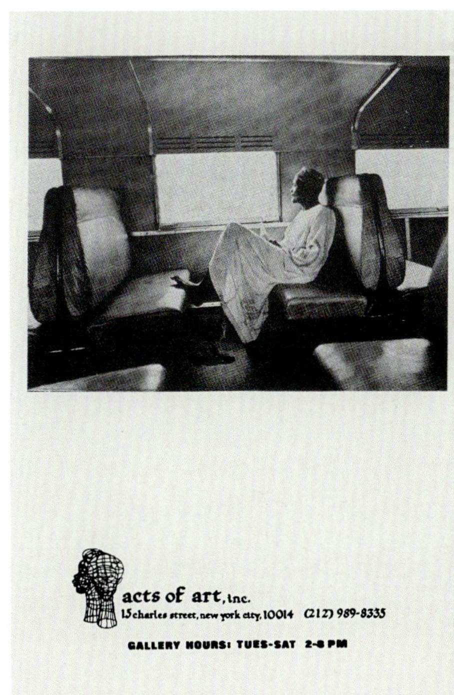

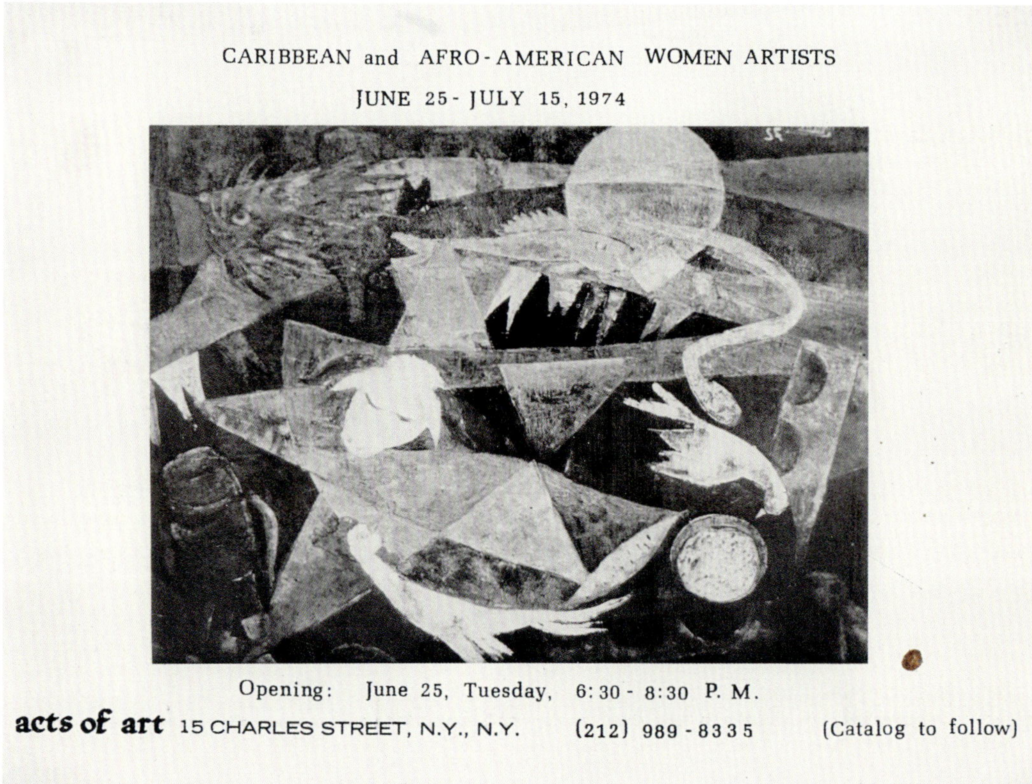

JUN 25–JUL 15, 1974
Caribbean and Afro-American Women Artists

Rose Amelia Auld, Tamara Baussan, Valerie Bloomfield, Star Bullock, Rose-Marie Desruisseau, Gloria Escoffery, Marie-José Gardere, Edith Hollant, Georgia Mills Jessup, Barbara Jones, Loïs Mailou Jones, Gizou Lamothe, Elzire Malebranche, Edna Manley, Michèle Manuel, Claude Maximilien, Valerie Maynard, Judy McMillan, Eva Hamlin Miller, Gilda Thebaud Nassief, Andres Georges Naude, Seya Parboosingh, Hope Parchment, Delilah Pierce, Micheline Prezeau, Faith Ringgold, Maud Gerdes Robart, Malkia Lucille Roberts, Doris Rogers, Heather Sutherland, and Luce Turnier

The exhibition focuses on the achievements of women artists of the Caribbean and Afro-American women artists. Works were selected after a year of survey conducted as a research project for the archives of Howard University in Washington, D.C. The works on view are but a sampling of the vast field yet to be explored. It is evident, however, that this selected group of artists prove the strength of the creativity possessed by women artists regardless of race or origin. The variety of subjects displayed in the show substantiate the fact that there is no limit to the contribution women artists can make to the visual arts. No longer need they be excluded from the art world and isolated from each other. In my opinion, women must work together to find their own structure and imagery. The bringing together of this cross-section of creative work from here and abroad establishes a bind which affirms and supports the importance of the "woman artist."

—Loïs Mailou Jones, exhibition catalogue, June 1974

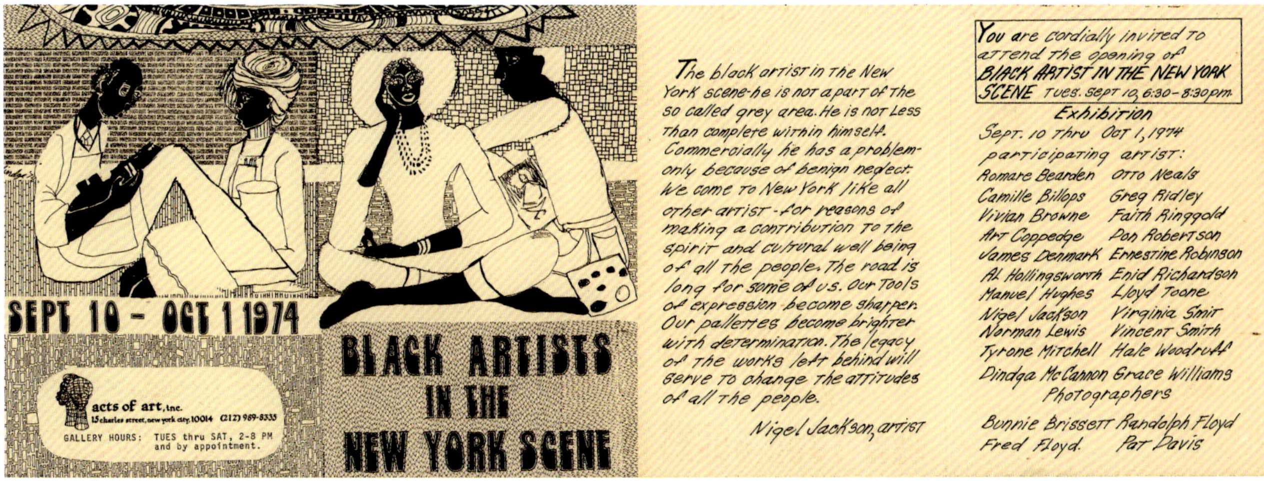

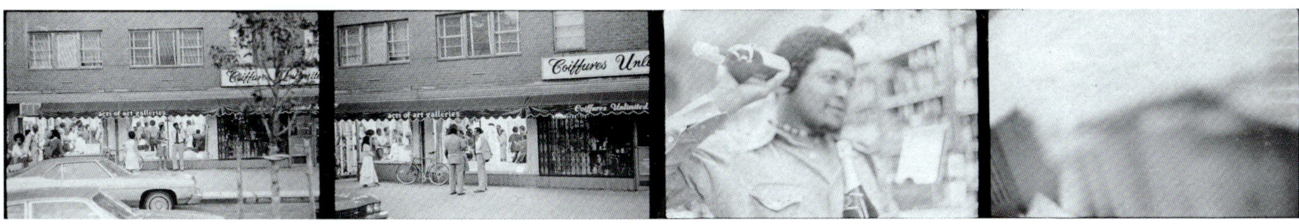

SEP 10–OCT 1, 1974
Black Artists in the New York Scene

Romare Bearden, Camille Billops, Bunnie Brissett, Vivian Browne, Arthur Coppedge, Pat Davis, James Denmark, Fred Floyd, Randolph Floyd, Alvin Hollingsworth, Manuel Hughes, Nigel Jackson, Norman Lewis, Dindga McCannon, Tyrone Mitchell, Otto Neals, Enid Richardson, Gregory Ridley, Faith Ringgold, Don Robertson, Ernestine Robinson, Lloyd Toone, Virginia Smit, Vincent Smith, and Hale Woodruff

Black Artists in the New York Scene *has 28 producers of aesthetic "dy-no-mite"... These artists represent a variety of styles but they share one determination—that Black artists be recognized!...New York has been like a magnet drawing these talented artists from all over the world to "make a contribution to the spirit and cultural well being of all the people." As Jackson says, "the road is long for some of us." It is up to all of us AND our cultural institutions to see that these artists and galleries like Acts of Art, Cinque, Genesis II, Storefront Museum, Sunday Gallery, Melca, and Aub-Ray are not detoured by lack of funds. The road for Black artists is rocky enough.*

—Melvin Tapley, *New York Amsterdam News*, September 14, 1974

1974

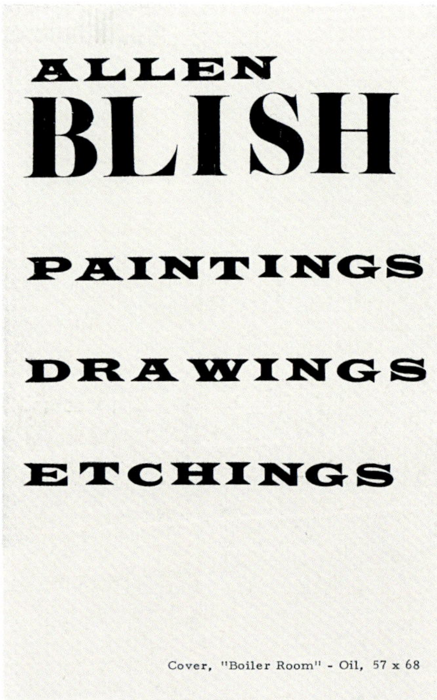

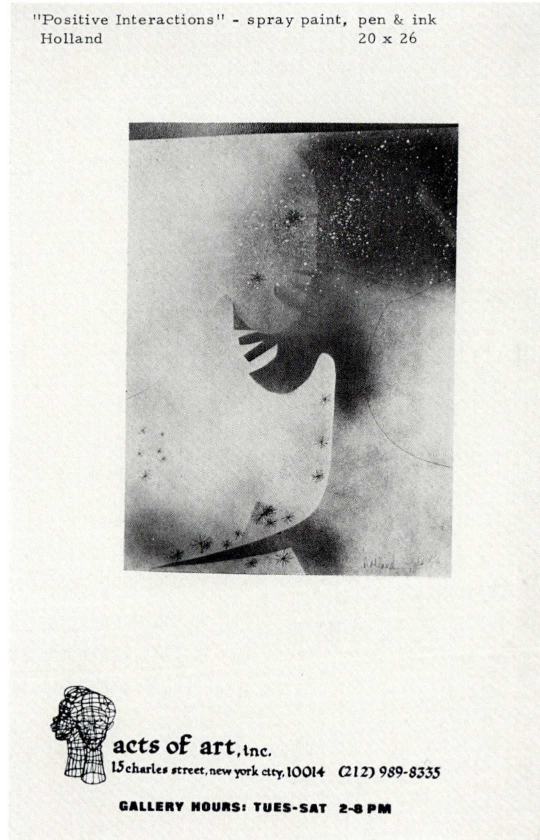

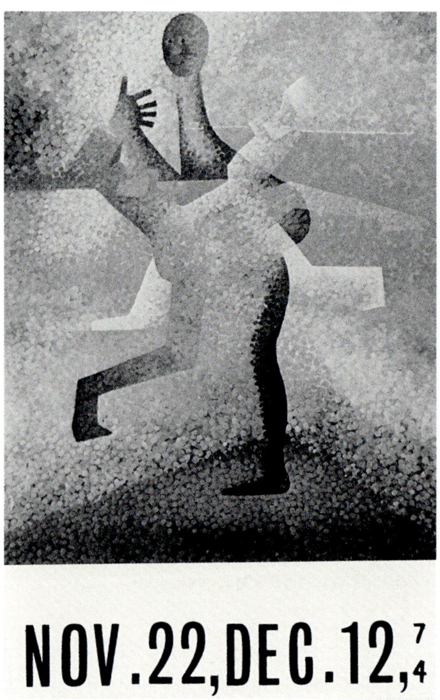

OCT 27–NOV 19, 1974
Carlton Holland and Grace Williams

Although four seasons ago, Grace Williams was not selected to participate in the exhibition Rebuttal to the Whitney's Museum's Black Show, *she has since changed mediums and developed her art with confidence and awareness. Her assemblages are in painted glass and mirrors with objects, evoking strong emotion and feeling of the rich cultural heritage which is always one of the underlying forces in her work….Mr. Holland's sensitive use of spray paint and pen and ink indeed is to be encouraged. His works elicit feelings of delicacy, illusion, sophistication and elegance as well as deep negritude….The exhibit promises to be beyond the stage of interesting.*

—*The Black American*, November 1974

NOV 22–DEC 12, 1974
Allen Blish: Paintings, Drawings, Etchings

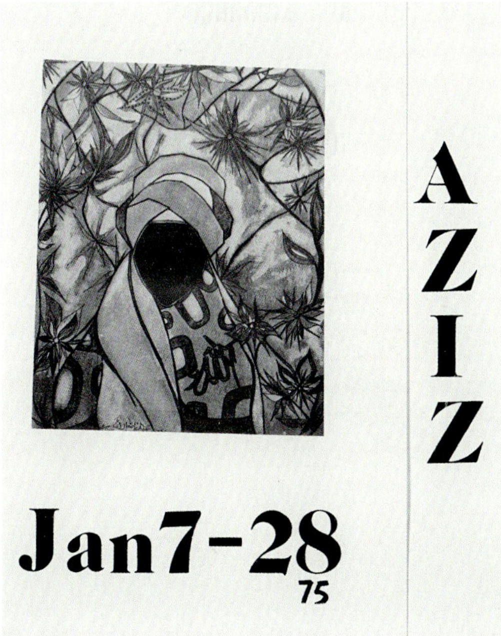

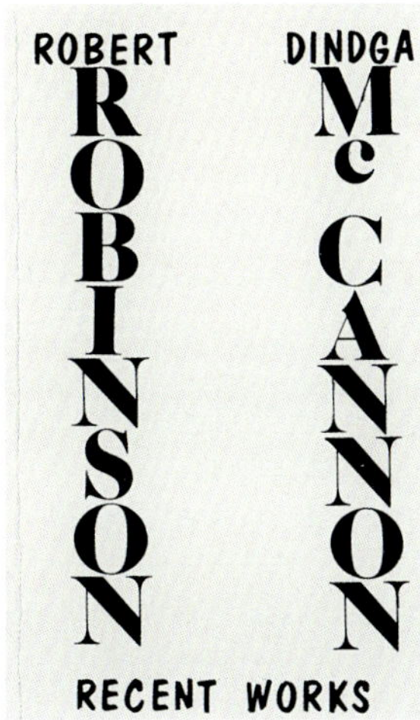

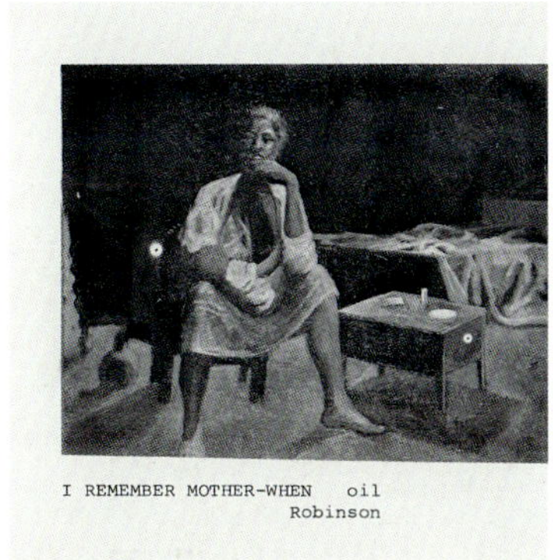

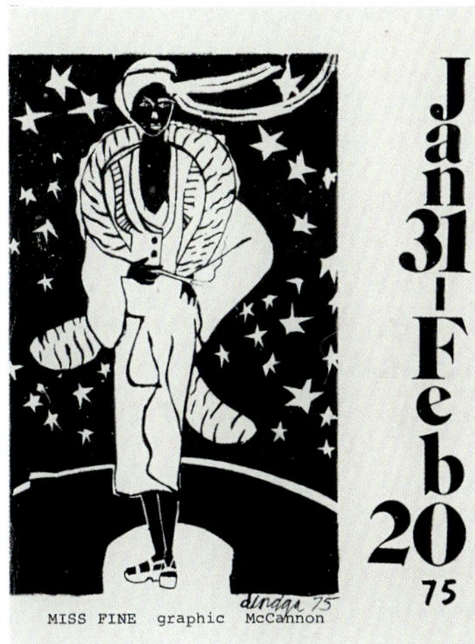

JAN 7–28, 1975
Abdullah Aziz: Oils and Graphics

Abdullah Aziz has often been spoken of as the consummate artist. His work encompasses many dimensions of artistic endeavor. Indeed it attests to that ability of creativity to capture the dignity, grace, beauty and spiritual vitality of African people throughout the world. The vivaciousness of his colors portrays that ever-present quality of life so much a part of traditional and contemporary African people.

—*The Black American*, January 1975

JAN 31–FEB 20, 1975
Dindga McCannon and Robert Robinson: Recent Works

Back in 1969, Robert Robinson presented himself with certain credits...he had studied with, and was encouraged by Gil Edwards at a community center in Harlem. Robinson had been exhibiting in the Greenwich Village Outdoor Art Show and had won several honorable mentions and awards....Dindga McCannon has committed her artistic efforts on a community level. She was commissioned by the New York State Council on the Arts to paint a block-long mural in Harlem. In addition to bringing her art into the community, she has also ventured out in an attempt to create an understanding of her ethnic background—to present her work on a worldwide level.

—*The Black American*, February 1975

1975

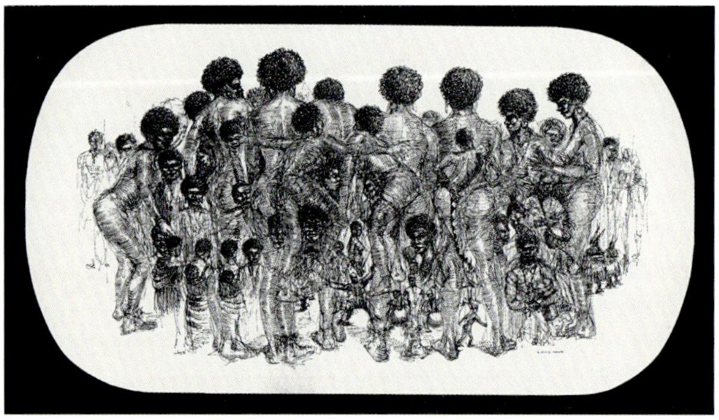

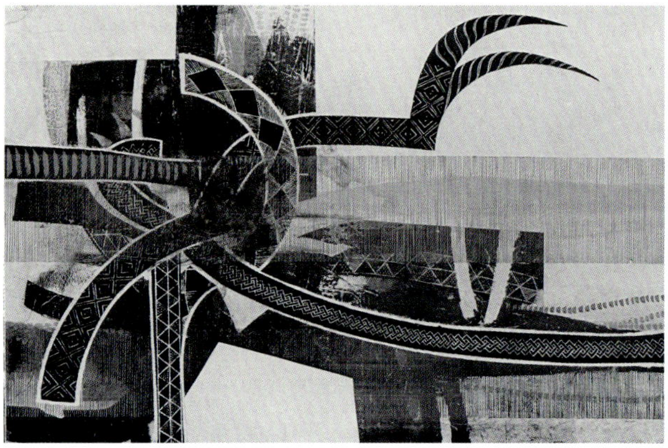

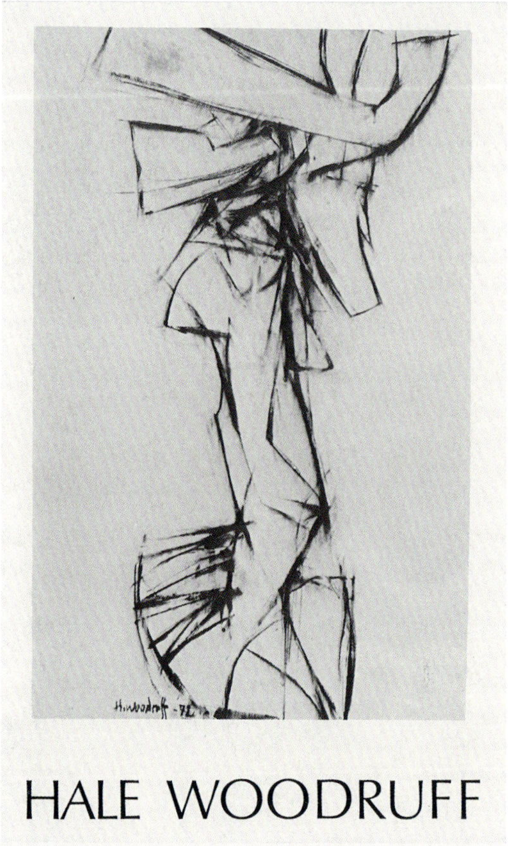

FEB 22–MAR 15, 1975
Gil Edwards: Drawings and Watercolor -In Retrospect-

MAR 24–APR 8, 1975
Harlan Jackson

APR 17–MAY 3, 1975
Hale Woodruff

Hale Woodruff is in his seventies and still going strong. At one time he was considered part of the "outhouse school" because he stressed the importance of painting what one knew. In his own case this included the outhouses which dotted his native Georgia landscape. He has been painting abstractly for the last fifteen years. His canvases are either abstractions of things he has observed such as a playground rendered as floating masses of lines in a colored field or completely abstract works.... The imaginary figures, such as a monkey man, are made up of a rigorous scaffolding of lines which dig the figure out of space and construct it much like building sculpture.

—Ann-Sargent Wooster, *The Villager*, April 17, 1975

MAY 6–27, 1975
Ben Jones

1975

THE COLLECTION

A SPECIAL EXHIBITION

SEPTEMBER 19 THRU OCTOBER 20, 1975

Presenting a broad range of challenging works, sculpture, drawings and prints. This exhibition will become a reference source for years to come. Art lovers are invited to capitalize on its immediate impact and on its longevity.

Benny Andrews
Allen Blish
Kay Brown
James Denmark
Gil Edwards
Reggie Gammon
Lester Gunter
Leon Hicks
Chester Higgins
Nigel Jackson
Phillip Martin
Ademola Olugebefola
Enid Richardson
Faith Ringgold
Robert Robinson
Ed Salter
Phillippe Smith
Vincent Smith
Ann Tanksley
Robert Threadgill
Lloyd Toone
Walter Williams
Frank Wimberley

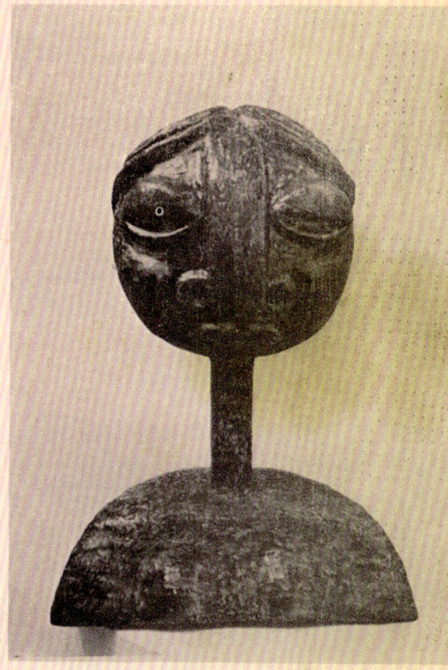

PROUD MARY by Lloyd Toone

JUN 9–21, 1975
Eldridge Suggs III

JUN 24–JUL 18, 1975
James Denmark

SEP 19–OCT 20, 1975
The Collection

Benny Andrews, Allen Blish, Kay Brown, James Denmark, Gil Edwards, Reginald Gammon, Lester Gunter, Leon Hicks, Chester Higgins, Nigel Jackson, Phillip Martin, Ademola Olugebefola, Enid Richardson, Faith Ringgold, Robert Robinson, Ed Salter, Philippe Smith, Vincent Smith, Ann Tanksley, Robert Threadgill, Lloyd Toone, Walter Williams, and Frank Wimberley

On September 19th, a special exhibition, THE COLLECTION *will open at acts of art. This show will feature such works as "Proud Mary" by Lloyd Toone, "Head with a Fantastic Hat" by James Denmark and the unique work of Philippe Smith. Mr. Smith's ingenious method of integrating stone with wood will delight the most demanding of art lovers.* THE COLLECTION *is a display of 50 works by 23 artists—Benny Andrews, Robert Threadgill, Reginald Gammon to name a few. This exhibition will bring to the public the creative achievements of artist exhibitors over the past six years. A special thanks to the friends of acts of art for their continued support.*

—Press release, September 1975

The Black Emergency Cultural Coalition

ANSLEY BROWNING

New York City emerged as a center for Black artistic activism in the late 1960s. Despite the proximity of the city's major museums to Harlem—a national hub for Black expression—most museum collections reflected only the white art historical canon.[1] Works by Black artists constituted less than one percent of these museums' American art collections.[2] Their exhibition history was equally dismal: before 1968, there had not been a single one-person exhibition devoted to a Black artist at the Metropolitan Museum of Art or the Whitney Museum of American Art, and only two such exhibitions had occurred at the Museum of Modern Art.[3] When exhibitions of Black artists were mounted, they were typically held in community spaces or Black-owned galleries; the press paid them little attention. Those that the press did acknowledge were derided for being sociological, derivative, and niche. Works by Black artists were continually tested against white expectations of art, failing for being too representational or—if abstract—not being Black enough. Denied exhibition space, representation in fine arts collections, and attention in critical art analyses, Black artists found their achievements silenced and their roles erased from the narrative of American art history. These injustices served as a rallying cry that led to the formation of the Black Emergency Cultural Coalition (BECC); the organization's interventions in the late '60s and early '70s provided a paradigm of art activism for later activist movements and discredited the notion many institutions were hiding behind—the nonexistence of Black artists.

Many of the artists who would form the BECC were first drawn together in protest of the Whitney Museum's exhibition, *1930s: Painting and Sculpture in America* (1968). Curator William Agee chose to put forth a revisionist view of the decade, prioritizing abstraction over the social realist works included in the show, as an attempt to shift the narrative of American art during the 1930s. Although the Whitney held works created by Black artists in the '30s, each of the eighty artists included in the exhibition was white. Museum director John I. H. Baur defended Agee's decision, claiming Agee chose the "best" work and didn't consider race as a qualifying factor—the implication being that Black art did not feature among the "best" work of the 1930s.[4] These sentiments reflected the attitudes of most institutions when it came to representing Black art and artists. Activists responded by showing rather than telling. A group of thirty artists and arts professionals picketed the exhibition, criticizing the show, its curator, and the museum director, while also advertising their rebuttal show at the Studio Museum in Harlem: *Invisible Americans: Black Artists in the '30s* (1968). The rebuttal exhibition established a canon of Black artists active during the 1930s, highlighting a lacuna present not only in the Whitney's exhibition but also in the greater art world of the 1960s. Although these

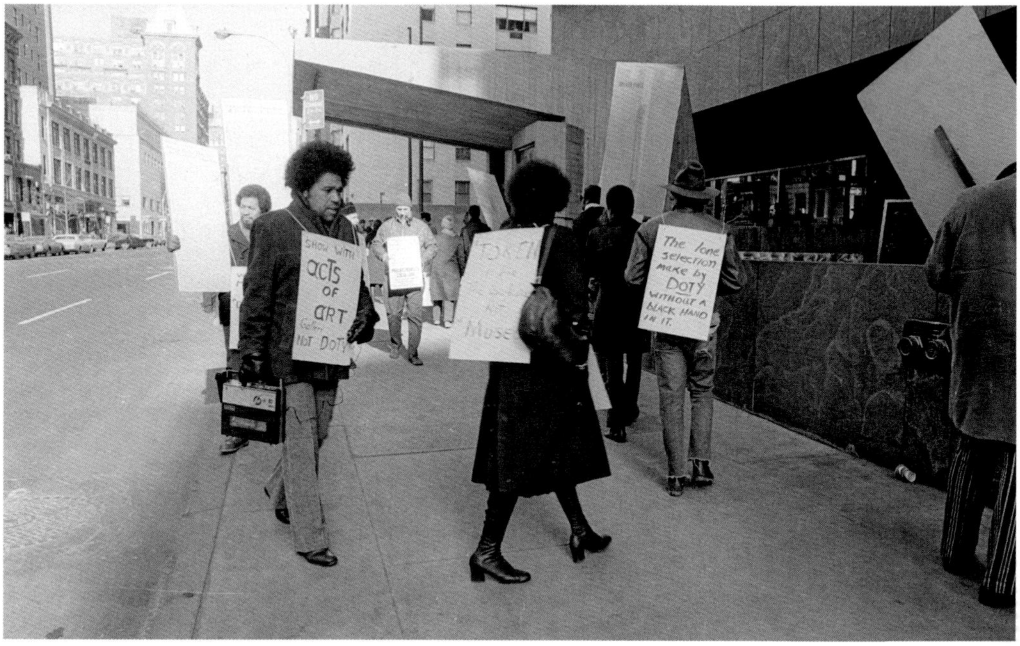

Nigel Jackson (left) and Vivian Browne (center) at the Black Emergency Cultural Coalition protest at the Whitney Museum of American Art, New York, January 31, 1971

artists and arts professionals had yet to formally name themselves, they began to stoke public opinion in order to pressure museums into action.

The Black Emergency Cultural Coalition officially established itself three months later on January 9, 1969, in direct response to the Met's exhibition, *Harlem on my Mind: The Cultural Capital of Black America, 1900–1968*.[5] The show was the museum's first attempt to address Black audiences in its one-hundred-year history and stemmed from a push by director Thomas Hoving for the museum to be more active in social issues. Despite the rich history of art in Harlem, the curator Allen Schoener organized an exhibition that included neither painting nor sculpture, instead featuring primarily photojournalist works hung without any credits or attribution to prevent viewers from seeing them as art pieces.[6] The photos—presenting Harlemites, views of the neighborhood, and famous figures —were taken mostly by white photographers, further placing control of Harlem's image in the hands of outsiders.[7] This sociological approach was decried by advisors and the Harlem community and the exhibition fell flat among art critics. The newly named BECC picketed the show's opening reception; their signs bore slogans attacking Hoving and the inaccurate portrayal of Harlem's history.[8] The decision to protest on the front steps of the Met ensured they were visible to the general public and the press. The appeal to a broader public was furthered by the willingness of artists like Benny Andrews and Romare Bearden to lay bare their dealings with museum officials in the press, thereby exposing the hypocrisy they faced. Thus, public opinion became an integral force in the push for desegregation within the museum. This allowed the BECC to demand meetings with museum officials who were eager to undo the bad publicity of *Harlem on My Mind*. Hoving promised a follow-up exhibition—to be organized by James Sneed, the director of the Harlem Art Gallery and an advisor for *Harlem on My Mind*—which never materialized.[9]

By February 7, 1969, the BECC had grown significantly, prompting a formal meeting to establish a stable organizational structure.[10] Benny Andrews and Cliff Joseph were appointed co-chairs with Russell Thompson serving as treasurer. Vivian Browne, Reginald Gammon, and Lynn Bowers joined them on the executive committee responsible for direct communication with officials at both the Met and later at other institutions.[11] This structure clarified responsibilities and shielded the roughly 150 members from potential repercussions often faced by prominent figures.[12] The BECC's frustration with the major institutions' lack of support was compounded by what they saw as the museums' biased agenda favoring white perspectives over those of Black experts. According to Cliff Joseph, the group aimed to expose this hypocrisy and positioned itself as a watchdog organization dedicated to advocating for the rights and aspirations of individual artists and the broader community.[13] Believing that Black artists should speak for themselves and address issues relevant to Black art, membership was eventually restricted to individuals who identified as Black artists. Associate members included Black experts, sympathetic white artists, and non-professional Black creatives. Funding primarily came from member contributions although some donations were also received from foundations. The BECC was cautious about accepting large sums, however, fearing that doing so might compromise their independence as had happened with other civil rights organizations in the past. Committed to "vigorous and relentless" protest, the BECC turned its attention back to the Whitney, which was eager to repair its reputation after the protest of the prior year.[14]

The museum entered into negotiations with the BECC, which penned a list of demands: the Whitney would produce a major exhibition of Black artists, plus five annual one-man shows for Black artists in the first-floor gallery; and commit to greater representation in the annual painting and sculpture exhibitions, greater representation of Black artists in the collection, and an increase in Black professionals on staff and purchasing and selection committees. In preliminary talks, the BECC negotiated the opening of a major exhibition, *Contemporary Black Artists in America*, and secured a commitment that every other show in the first-floor gallery would feature a Black artist. As communication developed between the two parties, Baur made verbal promises, but internal communications suggest that he had no intention to fully commit to the BECC's demand for a Black curator.[15] This was cemented when Baur chose Robert M. Doty to curate the survey exhibition—a white curator with no history of engagement in art by African American artists. Although Doty did visit Black artists' studios, he did so with a particular idea of Black art that fit stylistically within an already established canon of New York abstraction.[16] Once it became clear that there would be no Black voice or vision to lead the show, the BECC shifted from the role of collaborator to that of agitator.

With the aid of arts journalist Grace Glueck, who had reported on the responses to *1930s: Painting and Sculpture in America*, *Harlem on My Mind*, and the initial announcement of *Contemporary Black Artists in America*, the BECC published a letter addressed to Baur condemning the show and announcing their intention to protest. Like their previous engagements with museum officials, what evolved was a public debate. The BECC criticized Baur for failing to uphold his verbal agreement to hire a Black curator and questioned the authenticity of an exhibition of Black artists chosen by a white curator. Baur responded that the museum had never promised to hire a curator but only to consider Black candidates should a position open. Both he and Doty insisted that the museum had kept its promise to consult Black experts, noting that Doty was in communication with artist and

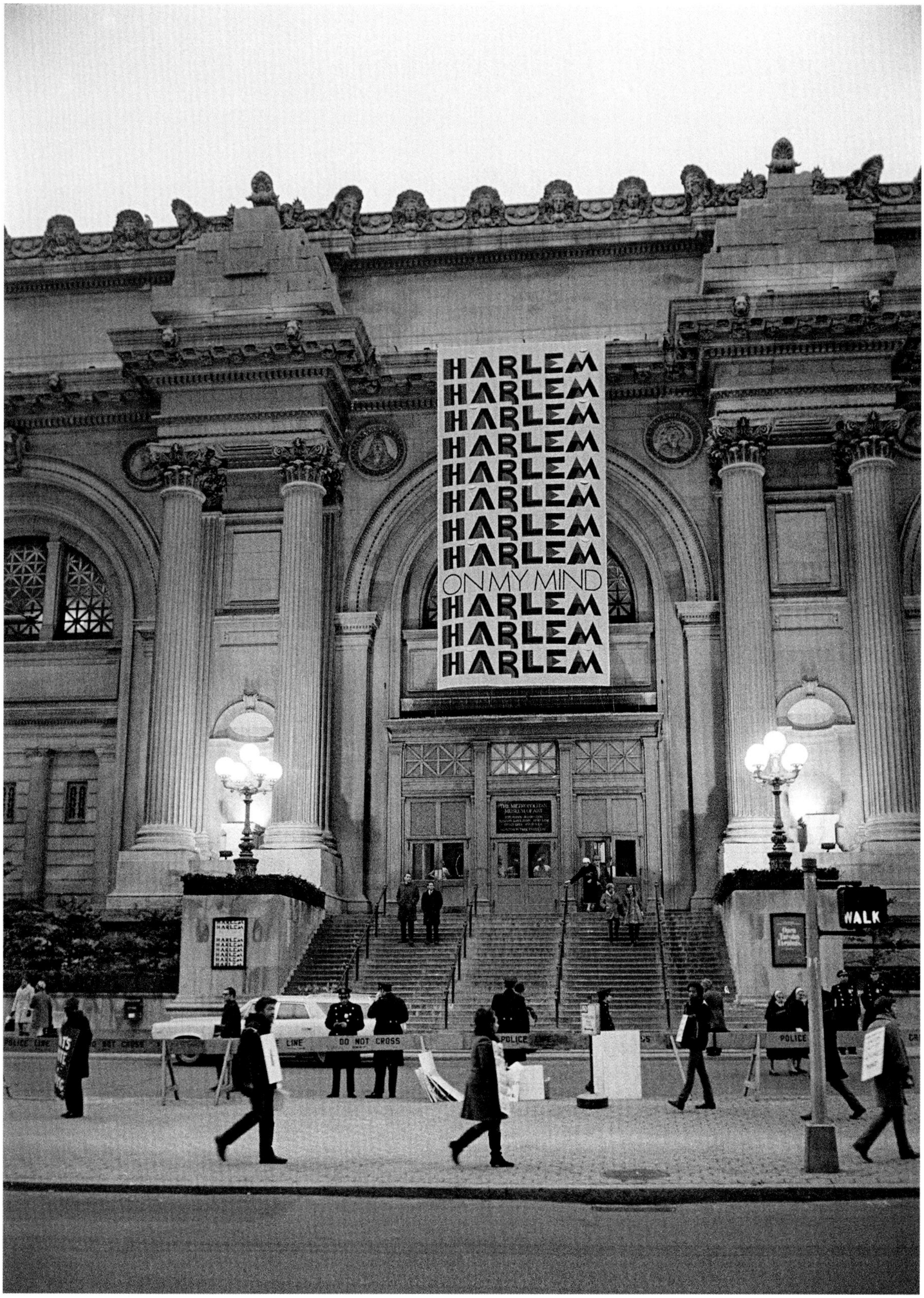

Demonstrators picket outside the Metropolitan Museum of Art in New York in response to the exhibition *Harlem on My Mind*, January 16, 1969

scholar David Driskell, the head of the Fisk University Art Department, throughout the development of the exhibition. However, accounts from other Black experts and artists contacted by Doty describe him as more concerned with confirming his vision than in expanding it.[17] The BECC picketed the Whitney in January 1971 with signs condemning the exhibition, the museum, and Doty by name, alongside signs advertising a rebuttal show to open the same evening at the Acts of Arts Gallery in Greenwich Village. The public debacle was exacerbated by the withdrawal of fifteen artists from *Contemporary Black Artists*—two of whom chose to show, instead, in Acts of Art's exhibition, *Rebuttal to the Whitney Museum Exhibition: Black Artists in Rebuttal*. Four months later, on April 6, 1971, the two exhibitions opened. At the Whitney, a show focusing on abstraction was framed by Doty in the foreword as Black artists choosing freedom over the mandate that they create "art that expresses Blackness."[18] At the Acts of Art Gallery, a stylistically diverse vision asserted that Black artists cannot be confined to a single narrative—particularly one dictated by a white art canon that had up until then classified Black artists as "unskilled, unsophisticated, prehistoric and primitive."[19]

Some six months after the *Rebuttal* exhibition, in the wake of the Attica uprising in September 1971, the BECC's attention shifted from its campaign against Black exclusion in the white-dominated art world to the Prison Arts Exchange program launched by Andrews and Joseph in November that year. The program brought working artists into prisons to foster the artistic and literary expression of incarcerated people through art and writing classes; it remained the primary focus of the group until their dissolution in 1982. Although the BECC's work against New York's museums was relatively short-lived, its actions established a model for future protests. Later, groups like the AIDS activist group ACT UP would take up their strategies including the photo-op and coordination with the press to ensure widespread publicity for each of their protests. Most importantly, the BECC inserted the Black voice into the art world in arguably the most important city for art in the latter half of the twentieth century.

NOTES

1 This claim is based on collection data drawn from the Guggenheim Museum, the Metropolitan Museum of Art, and the Whitney Museum of American Art.

2 At the Metropolitan Museum, only ten out of 1,200 works; at the Museum of Modern art only twelve out of 450. "Object: Diversity," *Time Magazine*, April 6, 1970, accessed September 20, 2024 <https://time.com/archive/6877086/art-object-diversity/>.

3 These facts are reported in Bridget R. Cooks, "Black Artists and Activism: Harlem on My Mind (1969)," *American Studies* 48, no. 1 (2007): 7; and Caroline V. Wallace, "Exhibiting Authenticity: The Black Emergency Cultural Coalition's Protests of the Whitney Museum of American Art, 1968–71," *Art Journal* 74, no. 2 (2015): 16. The Museum of Modern Art exhibitions of Black art are discussed at length in Darby English and Charlotte Barat, eds. *Among Others: Blackness At MoMA* (New York: The Museum of Modern Art, 2019).

4 Susan E. Cahan, *Mounting Frustration: The Art Museum in the Age of Black Power* (Duke University Press, 2016), 130–32.

5 The original meeting took place in Benny Andrews's studio while attendees created signs for the coming protest. Artists present at the meeting included: Benny Andrews, Reginald Gammon, Ed Taylor, Romare Bearden, Henri Ghent, Ray Saunders, Mahler Ryder, Calvin Douglass, Bill Durante, Norman Lewis, Leroy Henderson, Vivian Browne, Wes Swint, Raymond Andrews, Russ Thompson, Nigel Jackson, and Ann Carter. Benny Andrews, "Pies in the Sky," *Artworkers News* (New York: Foundation for the Community of Artists), December 1980: 11.

6 Cahan, *Mounting Frustration*, 80–81.

7 James Vanderzee and Gordon Parks—two Black photographers famous for their photos of Harlem—were included in the exhibition. However, without proper credit given, the show had no significant impact on their success or the success of Black photography in general.

8 Bridget R. Cooks, "Black Artists and Activism: *Harlem on My Mind* (1969)," *American Studies* 48, no. 1 (2007): 24.

9 In his entry on April 17, 1970, Benny Andrews describes why the BECC disagreed with the Met's choice of James Sneed, Carroll Greene, and Romare Bearden as the selection committee: Sneed because of his involvement with *Harlem on My Mind*; Greene because Andrews felt that he wasn't qualified to speak on art past 1950, thus he did not represent contemporary art; and Bearden because he resented the idea of only letting artists curate shows instead of hiring a Black expert (although Greene was an experienced curator, not an artist). See Andrews, "Pies in the Sky," 12.

10 JoAnn Whatley, "Meeting the Black Emergency Cultural Coalition," *ABA: a journal of affairs of Black artists* 1, no. 1 (1971): 6.

11 These officers reflect reporting from Whatley's article. However, according to Andrews's journals and Wallace's essay, in the early stages of the group the co-chairs were Andrews and Henri Ghent, with Ghent being responsible for most of the communication between the BECC and the Whitney. Additionally, although they had a formal committee, at times members outside the leadership committee would join on official meetings (such as when Mahler Ryder joined in on the May 1, 1969 meeting with Baur; or when Frank Sharpe joined September 11 and 18, 1969 meetings). See Cahan, *Mounting Frustration*, 134.

12 Benny Andrews alleges that museums would reach out to the galleries of protesters and advise that if they did not drop the member the other artists the galleries represented would be negatively affected. See Andrews, "Supplement: What is the Problem?" *Art and Artists*, February 1986: 18.

13 Whatley, "Meeting the Black Emergency Cultural Coalition," 8.

14 Whatley, "Meeting the Black Emergency Cultural Coalition," 9.

15 Cahan, *Mounting Frustration*, 134–36.

16 In the penultimate paragraph of his introductory text, Doty lists Richard Hunt, Barbara Chase-Riboud, Daniel Johnson, Melvin Edwards, William Henderson, and Frank Bowling and frames their artistic progression overcoming representations of the Black experience in favor of exploring the "universal canons of visual arts." For each artist, Doty celebrates their shift toward abstraction and works without content or narrative. Robert M. Doty, *Contemporary Black Artists in America* exhibition catalogue (New York: Whitney Museum of American Art, 1971), 12.

17 Samella Lewis, a professor at Scripps College and co-editor with Ruth Waddy of *Black Artists on Art*, described Doty as fixed in his own philosophy of art, stating that he didn't seem to be looking for new artists. Artist Vivian Browne's account also supports this assertion, describing Doty's visit to her studio as abrupt and dismissive. See Cahan, *Mounting Frustration*, 138.

18 Doty, *Contemporary Black Artists in America*, 12.

19 Oakley N. Holmes, "Forward," in R*ebuttal to the Whitney Museum Exhibition: Black Artists in Rebuttal*, exhibition catalogue (New York: Acts of Art Gallery, 1971), 3.

Rebuttal to the Whitney Museum Exhibition

BRIANNA GOLUB

Acts of Art made its most significant impact, both in the moment and historically, as the venue for *Rebuttal to the Whitney Museum Exhibition: Black Artists in Rebuttal*, the 1971 counter-exhibition to the Whitney Museum of American Art's controversial show, *Contemporary Black Artists in America*. In collaboration with the Black Emergency Cultural Coalition and with endorsements by Black arts professionals across the United States, Acts of Art Gallery assembled the work of fifty diverse Black artists in this direct response to the white-curated selection of art on view at the Whitney. Although the gallery had already been in operation for a year and a half when the *Rebuttal* opened, the exhibition publicly solidified the gallery as a space by and for Black artists; in this way, Acts of Art was instrumental in the fight for proper representation of Black voices in the arts and in the broader cultural landscape of early 1970s New York.

The Whitney first raised serious concerns among the Black arts community after utilizing exclusionary curatorial tactics in their 1968 exhibition, *The 1930s: Painting and Sculpture in America*; out of the more than eighty individuals represented in the show, not a single artist of the African diaspora in the Americas was included. Realizing that the time had never been so dire for Black voices to speak out against some of the United States' most lauded, white-run institutions—like the Whitney—artist Benny Andrews, critic Henri Ghent, and Harlem Cultural Council executive director Edward K. Taylor would go on to form the Black Emergency Cultural Coalition (BECC), with artist Cliff Joseph later joining Andrews as co-chair. As a direct response to initiatives undertaken by the BECC, executive and curatorial leaders at the Whitney agreed to meet with the coalition's leadership to discuss programming that would respond to the demands of a community of Black artists. After months of back-and-forth meetings and correspondence with the BECC, the Whitney agreed to mount an exhibition "by Black artists" within the next year.[1] The show, entitled *Contemporary Black Artists in America*, was ultimately organized by a white curator, Robert Doty, which blatantly ignored the BECC's "minimal demands" for the inclusion of Black curators and other arts professionals in the organizing of an exhibition of Black artists.[2]

In the midst of the Whitney and the BECC's failed negotiations, Andrews, Joseph, and other prominent coalition members made arrangements behind the scenes to organize a rebuttal exhibition of Black artists, many of whom had been overlooked and disregarded by Doty. As one of the only Black-owned and run commercial art galleries in New York located outside of Harlem, Acts of Art

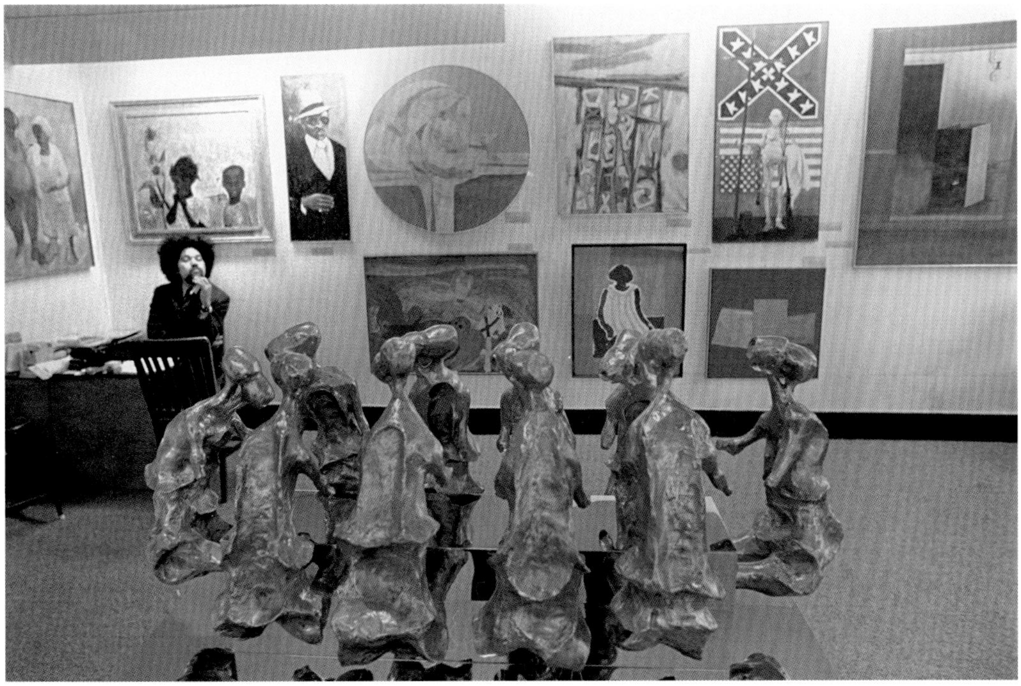

Nigel Jackson, owner of Acts of Art, 15 Charles Street, pictured here inside the gallery's exhibition, *Rebuttal to the Whitney Museum Exhibition*, April 7, 1971

became the venue for the proposed show. Andrews had previously given his support to the gallery by providing owner Nigel Jackson with a selection of his works for Acts of Art's inaugural exhibition in October 1969 and mounting his own one-person exhibition there in October 1970. Andrews was known in the mainstream art world well before the gallery's inception, and he hoped his involvement would boost its visibility as a venture supporting Black artists. In the months leading up to the opening of the Whitney's *Contemporary Black Artists in America* in April 1971, fifteen of the artists slated to appear in the exhibition dropped out in protest.[3] Two of these individuals, Betty Blayton-Taylor and Richard Mayhew, chose instead to participate in Acts of Art's *Rebuttal to the Whitney Museum Exhibition.*

The two exhibitions opened simultaneously on April 6, 1971. Writing in the *Chelsea-Clinton News*, critic Z. D. Allen described the evening at Acts of Art, reporting on a crowd that "overflowed ...with painters, actors, their friends and some press. Even some artists who were showing at the Whitney were there."[4] Charles Wright of *The Village Voice* reviewed the two shows together and ended by recounting his conversation with a Black museum guard uptown at the Whitney: "There was a large Black crowd at the opening and 'everything went along smoothly,' he told me. 'I'm glad of that.'"[5] There was notable press coverage of both events; John Canaday of *The New York Times* wrote that *Contemporary Black Artists in America* was "not very Black and not very good" and that Acts of

Art's *Rebuttal* was "somewhat Blacker and much spottier."[6] Highly critical of the intentional identification of the exhibiting artists as "Black," Canaday closed his scathing review by stating "With any luck—or, better yet, with any common sense—these may be the last shows in which we will be forced to think of an artist's color as a factor in his accomplishment." The sentiment, that "art has nothing to do with color"[7]—to quote the Whitney's director John I. H. Baur—was a significant point of contention in many of the conversations about the two exhibitions. Questions lingered as to what constituted "Black" art and whether or not an artist's ethnic origin and identity should even be examined in relation to their artistic output in the first place. Canaday's stance—and Baur's—failed to address the core sociopolitical implications of the inadequate representation Black artists and arts professionals had faced historically; the tacit yet clear message of their shared argument was that what had led to the wholesale exclusion of Black artists was an aesthetic failure on the part of the artists themselves.

The Whitney's *Contemporary Black Artists in America*, the BECC's response in the press and on the picket line, and the *Rebuttal* at Acts of Art amplified the divisions between Black artists both within and beyond the exhibitions. Some fully supported the protest politics of the BECC while

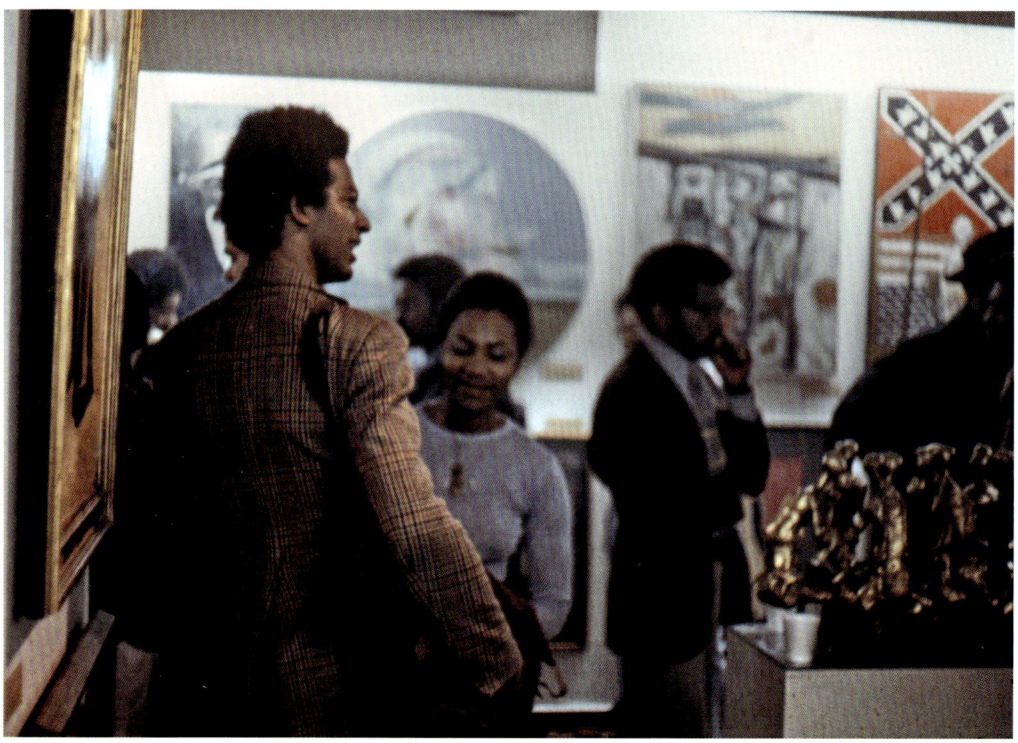

Opening reception, *Rebuttal to the Whitney Museum Exhibition* at Acts of Art, April 6, 1971

others opposed the protests and their visibility. The prospects of becoming embroiled in the larger sociopolitical conversations that extended far beyond the visual arts surrounding Black representation in America deterred some artists from supporting either show. A number of artists included in the Whitney's show did not want to pull their work out as they saw it as one of their only chances to have their work recognized by a major American cultural institution.[8] In a letter written in response to the BECC's call to postpone or otherwise cancel the show, Baur asserted that there were "Black artists…counting on this opportunity for…critical recognition which we hope and believe the show will bring them" and declared that the BECC's decision to denounce the exhibition was "an act of open hostility to those Black artists who do not happen to share [the BECC's] position."[9] Still others, like the seven well-established artists who published an open letter explaining their reasons for not participating in *Contemporary Black Artists in America*, did not offer express support for the BECC or the *Rebuttal*, but nevertheless put the blame squarely on the Whitney. Publishing their views in *Artforum* in May 1971, these artists wrote: "We say that the Whitney Museum has anti-curated its survey which results in misrepresenting and discrediting the complex and varied culture and visual history of the African American."[10]

The Whitney controversy and the *Rebuttal* brought a good deal of attention to the Acts of Art Gallery and its owner Nigel Jackson, who tended to downplay the *Rebuttal*'s political challenge to focus on the exhibiting artists and the value of their work. He told Mel Tapley of the *New York Amsterdam News* that the goal of the *Rebuttal* was to "represent the feeling of Black culture through the eyes of Black people,"[11] and insisted to Cheryl Bentsen of *Newsday* that despite the *Rebuttal*'s title, "I'm not anti-anybody. The world is open and I will participate in anything as long as I can enter the front door and we are proud together."[12] If the moment was marked by divisions, *Rebuttal* was also lauded as a substantial display of solidarity by a diverse community of Black artists exhibiting their art on their own terms. The *Voice*'s Charles Wright wrote of the artists assembled in the *Rebuttal*, "I am proud of them," even as he expressed his "regret that all of the Black artists could not have exhibited together. But that is the price one pays for being Black and an artist in America."

The participating artists of *Rebuttal* worked primarily in the mediums of painting, drawing, collage, and sculpture; a full list of artists and images of their submissions were detailed in the exhibition catalogue produced by Acts of Art sometime after the initial April 6 opening.[13] It is not known how many works were sold during the opening night or overall run of the exhibition which spanned just a little over a month. With a closing date of May 10, 1971—six days prior to the end of *Contemporary Black Artists in America*—it seems that the Act of Art exhibition was financially successful: Jackson later remarked in an interview that "many of the artists who showed in the *Rebuttal* made some money."[14] Benny Andrews's contribution, *American Gothic* (1971), would be sold by the artist to the Metropolitan Museum of Art in 1989—almost two decades later[15]—making it the only known work included in the *Rebuttal* that ended up in one of the institutions that were the BECC's targets. Many of the other works are in private hands or are now lost, existing only in the black-and-white images in the gallery's catalogue. Much in the same way that it was the hope of the artists of *Rebuttal* to exhibit their art as representative of their own lived experiences as Black persons—preserving what was lost in the Whitney's decisively white-washed exhibition—it is vital that these artists' contributions to *Rebuttal* and to Acts of Art are not forgotten.

NOTES

1 Grace Glueck, "Whitney Museum Plans Show By Black Artists for Next Year," *The New York Times*, October 2, 1969, p. 53. Glueck became something of a default—albeit involuntary—interlocutor between the Whitney and the BECC during this time.

2 Harry S. Huggins, "Acts of Art Statement," *Rebuttal to the Whitney Museum Exhibition*, exhibition catalogue (New York: Acts of Art Gallery, 1971), unpaginated.

3 Grace Glueck, "15 of 75 Black Artists Leave As Whitney Exhibition Opens," *New York Times*, April 6, 1971, p. 50. Notably, artist Romare Bearden would also go on to withdraw his work from the show after it opened.

4 Z.D. Allen in the *Chelsea-Clinton News*, April 15, 1971, reprinted in *Rebuttal to the Whitney Museum Exhibition* catalogue, unpaginated.

5 Charles Wright, "Paint Art Racist," *The Village Voice*, April 15, 1971, p. 20.

6 John Canaday, "Black Artists on View in 2 Exhibitions," *New York Times*, April 7, 1971, p. 52.

7 Grace Glueck, "1930's Show at Whitney Picketed by Negro Artists Who Call It Incomplete," *New York Times*, November 18, 1969, p. 31. Baur repeated his position in subsequent interviews and responses to both the BECC directly and to *The New York Times.*

8 In Grace Glueck, "Black Show Under Fire at the Whitney," *New York Times*, January 31, 1971, p. D25.

9 As stated in a letter from John I. H. Baur to the BECC, February 19, 1971. The Whitney Museum of American Art, Frances Mulhall Achilles Library and Archives, New York, NY; Records of the Office of the Director, Series II: John Baur, box 6, folder 22.

10 The signers of this open letter included artists John Dowell, Sam Gilliam, Daniel Johnson, Joe Overstreet, Melvin Edwards, Richard Hunt, and William T. Williams. For a complete list of supporting artists, see: "Politics," *Artforum*, vol. 9, no. 9 (May 1971): 12.

11 Tapley, Melvin, "Racism Charged Against Museum," *New York Amsterdam News*, April 10, 1971, p. 1.

12 Bentsen, Cheryl, "Life in the Back Of the Gallery," *Newsday (Nassau Edition)*, May 10, 1971, p. 27A.

13 Acts of Art's *Rebuttal to the Whitney Museum* is available digitally at <actsofartproject.org>.

14 Nigel Jackson, December 1, 1972, Camille Billops and James V. Hatch archives, MSS 927, Series 6: Oral History Interviews, box 4, folder 441, Stuart A. Rose Manuscript, Archives and Rare Book Library, Emory University, Atlanta.

15 The date of the sale is indicated by The Metropolitan Museum of Art's provenance entry on Andrews's *American Gothic* (1971) as 1989.

Raven Art Rap

EVE ARBALLO & ERIN CHASE

Emblazoned across the front page of the second and final issue of the eight-page tabloid *Raven Art Rap*, an announcement reads: "Last Complimentary Edition! Subscribe!!" The first and penultimate issue of the paper, published by co-founder of Acts of Art Nigel Jackson, was dated April 1, 1971—a few days before the opening of the gallery's *Rebuttal to the Whitney Museum Exhibition: Black Artists in Rebuttal*. The second was released on June 1, a few weeks before *Where We At: Black Women Artists 1971* opened. Despite Jackson's aspirations for an ongoing bimonthly periodical, the second edition proved to be the last, likely for financial reasons. Through interviews, profiles, reviews, essays, advertisements, letters, and listings focused on Black art and culture, *Raven Art Rap* set out to be a powerful voice for promoting and unifying contemporary Black artists.

Both issues of *Raven Art Rap* feature a "portrait" column penned by Betty Powell spotlighting notable Black artists. Powell begins her "Portrait of James Denmark" in volume 1, number 1, by noting the "qualities of strength and purpose" that characterize Denmark's art and person, which together are an "affirmation of Black dignity."[1] Powell affectionately refers to the artist as "Jim," recounting his struggles for artistic education amid prejudice. According to Powell's profile, Denmark emphasizes the spiritual and psychological depth inherent in Black life which Powell considers crucial for Black artists to express authentically. In volume 1, number 2, Powell delves into Hale Woodruff's artistic journey, beginning with his childhood love of drawing and detailing his job as a political cartoonist and later as a young painter in Paris and Mexico, where he studied fresco painting with Diego Rivera. Powell recounts Woodruff's noteworthy accomplishments, including his Harmon Foundation prize in 1926 and his influential two-decade teaching career at New York University. The piece concludes with Woodruff discussing the need for Black critics to write and think about Black culture.

To encourage Black critics, *Raven Art Rap* included a column for exhibition reviews. In the inaugural issue, Michele Wallace, a Black feminist author and critic and the daughter of artist Faith Ringgold, reviews the exhibition *Black is a Color* organized by Nigel Jackson. Wallace highlights that the representation of women in the show was "as close to fifty percent representation as any Black art show I've ever seen"[2]; of the seven artists included, three were women: Vivian Browne, Dindga McCannon, and Enid Richardson Moore. Her critique of all the artists was candid and sometimes cutting. While she dismissed Browne's landscape paintings with the blunt assessment that abstraction and impressionism were "dead," she praised Browne's etchings *Two Men* and *Warning*, writing that they presented true-to-life situations that would be recognized by Black viewers. Overall, Wallace "found the work of the women artists filled with more delightful implications as to what the future of Black art will be about." The second issue reprinted a review by Z.D. Allen from the *Chelsea-Clinton News* of the *Rebuttal to the Whitney Exhibition* at Acts of Art. In a headnote to the review, it is noted that while the *Chelsea-Clinton News* was not a paper based in the Black community, it had chosen a

RAVEN art rap

VOLUME I NO. 2 © NEW YORK, JUNE 1, 1971 20¢

Portrait of

HALE WOODRUFF

by Betty Powell

His paintings reverberate with color and abstract form used in a uniquely forceful and effective manner. They surge from the canvases to pursue you with their originality and with the affirmation of the painter's rarely found quality of great power within a fineedged sensitivity. The viewer does not wonder then that the creator of these works, Hale Woodruff, is widely acclaimed and respected as one of the foremost black artists in America today. One does wonder, however, as we so often do about the creatively gifted, how the development of these natural yet extraordinary talents began and how they were integrated into the life of the artist.

Mr. Woodruff's career began inconspicuously enough in his early childhood when there was time spent alone during which he entertained himself with drawing and doodling. This quite normal activity of an only child would, however, manifest itself as a real talent when young Woodruff became the cartoonist for his high-school newspaper. Mr. Woodruff recalls that there was no regular art course in the public schools of Nashville, Tennessee where he was reared, but that he did a lot of drawing in school nonetheless. He used to copy pictures out of the history books, especially the ancient history ones. Becoming cartoonist for the school paper spurred him on, and while working hard as a waiter after school young Woodruff would come home and draw late into the night. Another source for his drawings were pictures from the big family Bible and the lush pen and ink drawings of Gustave Dore to which Woodruff was greatly attracted. Finding any sort of acknowledgement encouraging at that age, Woodruff also painted the most artistic, crowd-drawing menus in town on the window of the restaurant where he worked.

Determined to undertake the serious pursuit of art studies, Hale Woodruff went off to Indianapolis, Indiana after finishing high school in 1918. There he studied at the John Herron Art Institute. This was his first formal art training and the aspiring young artist truly reveled in this period of growth. A job was necessary also in order to survive, so Woodruff began in the early 1920's to do political cartoons for the local "colored" newspaper, The Indianapolis Ledger. His cartoon drawings protested the lynchings, segregation and other injustices and cruelties inflicted upon the black communities of that era. He engaged in this work for several years while still studying art, painting obsessively, and nurturing the desire to become someday a truly great landscape painter.

In 1926 the first notable recognition of his talent came from the art world when Hale Woodruff received a bronze medal for his participation in the Harmon Foundation national black art competition. This was quite a personal and historical event, for up to this time--

(Continued on page 3)

NEWS ITEM...

Another step away from free expression in this country has been taken. The Judson Three (Faith Ringgold, a black woman artist is one of them) were found guilty of a "desecration of the flag" charge in the State courts (New York) on Friday, May 14, 1971. They were arrested on Friday, November 13, 1970 because of their alleged involvement with the People's Flag Show held at the Judson Memorial Church during the week of November 9th. They were taken into custody by representatives of the Distric Attorney's Office and the show was officially closed by the police.

Hopefully, the Judson Three will go on to the Supreme Court to test the constitutionality of the "desecration of the flag" law. As things stand now, the flag is a fetish in this country that all are forced to respect by the government.

Faith Ringgold is quoted as saying:

"The flag is the only truly subversive and revolutionary abstraction one can paint."

LAST COMPLIMENTARY EDITION! SUBSCRIBE!!

REVIEWS

The review reprinted here of the Rebuttal to the Whitney Exhibition appeared in the Chelsea-Clinton News, Thursday, April 15, 1971. Given the issues surrounding the exhibition it is note-worthy that this publication, which is not based in a predominently black community, had the awareness to enlist the talent of a black critic to review the exhibition.

By Z. D. ALLEN

"I'm showing the real stuff and they're showing a watered down standard," said Nigel Jackson of Acts of Art gallery, currently housing the "Rebuttal to the Whitney Museum Exhibition." Both exhibitions previewed April 5th and opened the following day.

The Whitney, allegedly showing a "national representation of black artists," has incurred the disfavor of a large segment of this country's community of black artists. Hence the rebuttal.

Acts of Art, a small Village gallery run and owned by a black painter who lives in Chelsea, overflowed preview night with painters, actors, their friends and some press. Even some artists who were showing at the Whitney were there the night of the preview.

Black art is something done from the black experience-it's not the media but the message that counts. Standing on the auction block, being sold to the highest bidder, sharing crowded crumbling tenements with rats and roaches and ever

(Continued on Page 2)

Front page of *Raven Art Rap* 1, no. 2 (June 1, 1971)

Black critic to review the *Rebuttal*. In her review, Allen endorses Jackson's efforts to convey the Black experience, contrasting it sharply with his critique of the Whitney's exclusionary practices. One gets the sense that Nigel Jackson walked Allen through the exhibition considering the number of direct quotes attributed to him. Jackson says that "the path to freedom is in the culture…to let the Whitney exhibition go unanswered, we're saying it's alright for Doty to tell <u>me</u> about <u>my</u> poverty and <u>my</u> background."[3] Allen concludes the review with a thought from Jackson about how the conflict with the Whitney Museum exemplified a larger issue in society: that of the co-opting of Black culture, slang, and art by white people.

The "Letters to the Editor" column served as a space for discussing Black cultural events. The first issue featured a questionnaire by Hans Bhalla, chair of Spelman College's art department along with responses from artist Leon N. Hicks. Issue two covered an exhibition of incarcerated sculptor James Lightbourne at the Countee Cullen Library and the *Rebuttal to the Whitney Museum Exhibition* at Acts of Art, ending with a letter from Oakley Holmes, Jr., a painter, sculptor, and art historian. Tecla Selnick's letter on Lightbourne asserts his innocence and criticizes the art establishment for being money-driven and disconnected from everyday life. Comments on the *Rebuttal* show come as letters from students of the Ocean Hill-Brownsville district of Brooklyn, who were given a tour of the exhibition by Nigel Jackson. One student remarked that Jackson's explanations helped them understand the artworks, particularly the paintings *Superman* (1966) by Cliff Joseph and *Monk's Letter* (c. 1971) by Frank Wimberley. In his letter to the editor, Holmes criticizes the historically passive response of white institutions to changing canonical artworks, writing, "We have tried in vain to get all major media to include us and give us the exposure we never had in this country."[4]

Nigel Jackson's editorial column, "Nigel Raps," appeared in both issues as a platform for his thoughts and opinions. In volume 1, number 1, he discusses the responsibilities of Black art and artists, restating the intention of the *Raven Art Rap* to be an instrument for bringing Black artists together. He stresses the importance of educating the public about the significance of Black culture in American life and advocates for unity among Black artists in order to establish a robust marketplace. In volume 1, number 2, Jackson criticizes the paternalism of the white establishment and its appropriation of Black culture—from music to food and fashion. Despite this, he writes that he believes in the leadership of Black aesthetics, asserting that Black creativity is foundational to American art. He ends with a broad call for subscriptions to *Raven Art Rap*, and with a very generous sentiment on unity and difference: "We may have different views on art and what's Black and what's Black art, but that's what makes it interesting and vibrant and alive—and that's why we all need each other, whatever our views."

Both issues include a column that focuses on the collections and preferences of Black art collectors. The first column in issue one features Jacqueline Hedrick, a New York City English teacher studying dance, who discusses her motivations for collecting art, details about some of the artworks she owns, and her thoughts regarding the scarcity of Black collectors. With her dance background, she prefers "forms" to abstraction and her collection includes figurative work by Acts of Art artists Enid Richardson Moore and Lester Gunter. She attributes the scarcity of Black collectors to the demands of daily life and a lack of familiarity with art. In the next issue, Joanne Anntonovich profiles Harlem residents Frank and Fay Leeper whose collection evolved from travel souvenirs to contemporary art.

Initially, the Leepers amassed "things" to occupy space, but their evolution into genuine art collectors was signified by their support of Acts of Art. There the Leepers began to collect contemporary works reflecting current social and political issues with a particular focus on championing the art of Black artists. Anntonovich highlights artworks from Acts of Art's represented artists, such as Richardson Moore, Denmark, Moses Groves, Pat Grey, and Jackson, among others.

Alongside the columns detailed above, there were other pieces of note that speak to *Raven Art Rap*'s mission to unite and fortify the Black contemporary art scene in New York. In the first issue, following the opening of *Contemporary Black Artists in America* at the Whitney, there is an essay by Harry Huggins titled "Whitney vs. Whitney," which recounts the missteps the Whitney Museum made in pursuing its survey exhibition. Huggins repeats the BECC's charge that the Whitney's white curator, Robert Doty, did not effectively consult with Black curators and art professionals within the Black community. The museum was "less concerned with presenting America's multi-cultural heritage than with defending an exhausted Western aesthetic." Huggins applauds the artists who pulled out of the Whitney's exhibition and those who joined the Acts of Art community for the *Rebuttal* exhibition. In the second issue, there is an interview with the Studio Museum's then-director Ed Spriggs conducted by Gary Gilchrist. Their conversation ranges from the Studio Museum's financial status and funding to the possibility of a future permanent collection. Gilchrist describes Spriggs as "an idealist, in a sense," for his support of "artists who are not concerned with making a living off their work," but are instead "concerned with the dissemination of their work to their people." The interview concludes with Spriggs considering the possibility that museums may not be necessary in the future: "In a hundred years, museums may not be necessary at all. That is—houses of art—may not be necessary at all in a hundred years."[5]

While *Raven Art Rap* had a brief lifespan of only two issues, it remains a valuable art historical document for its contribution of original thought and as a time capsule for how artists, critics, gallerists, collectors, and viewers of art were thinking about and deeply considering Black art and aesthetics. Despite the fact that so much remains unknown about the publication—including its print run and how widely it circulated—*Raven Art Rap* underscores Acts of Art's mission to be a center for the Black arts movement downtown and to create a space where Black thought could be disseminated. However briefly, *Raven Art Rap* successfully achieved Nigel Jackson's vision of a platform to "fill the need for communication between Black artists."[6]

NOTES

1 Betty Powell, "Portrait of James Denmark," *Raven Art Rap* 1, no. 1 (April 1971): 1.

2 Michele Wallace, "Reviews: Black is a Color," *Raven Art Rap* 1, no. 1 (April 1971): 7.

3 Nigel Jackson quoted in Z.D. Allen, "*Rebuttal to the Whitney Exhibition*," exhibition review, *Chelsea-Clinton News*, reprinted in *Raven Art Rap* 1, no. 2 (June 1971): 2.

4 "Letters to the Editor," *Raven Art Rap* 1, no. 2 (June 1971): 5.

5 Gary Gilchrist, "Ed Spriggs Interviewed by Gary Gilchrist," *Raven Art Rap* 1, no. 2 (June 1971): 6.

6 Nigel Jackson, "Nigel Raps." *Raven Art Rap* 1, no. 1 (April 1971): 4.

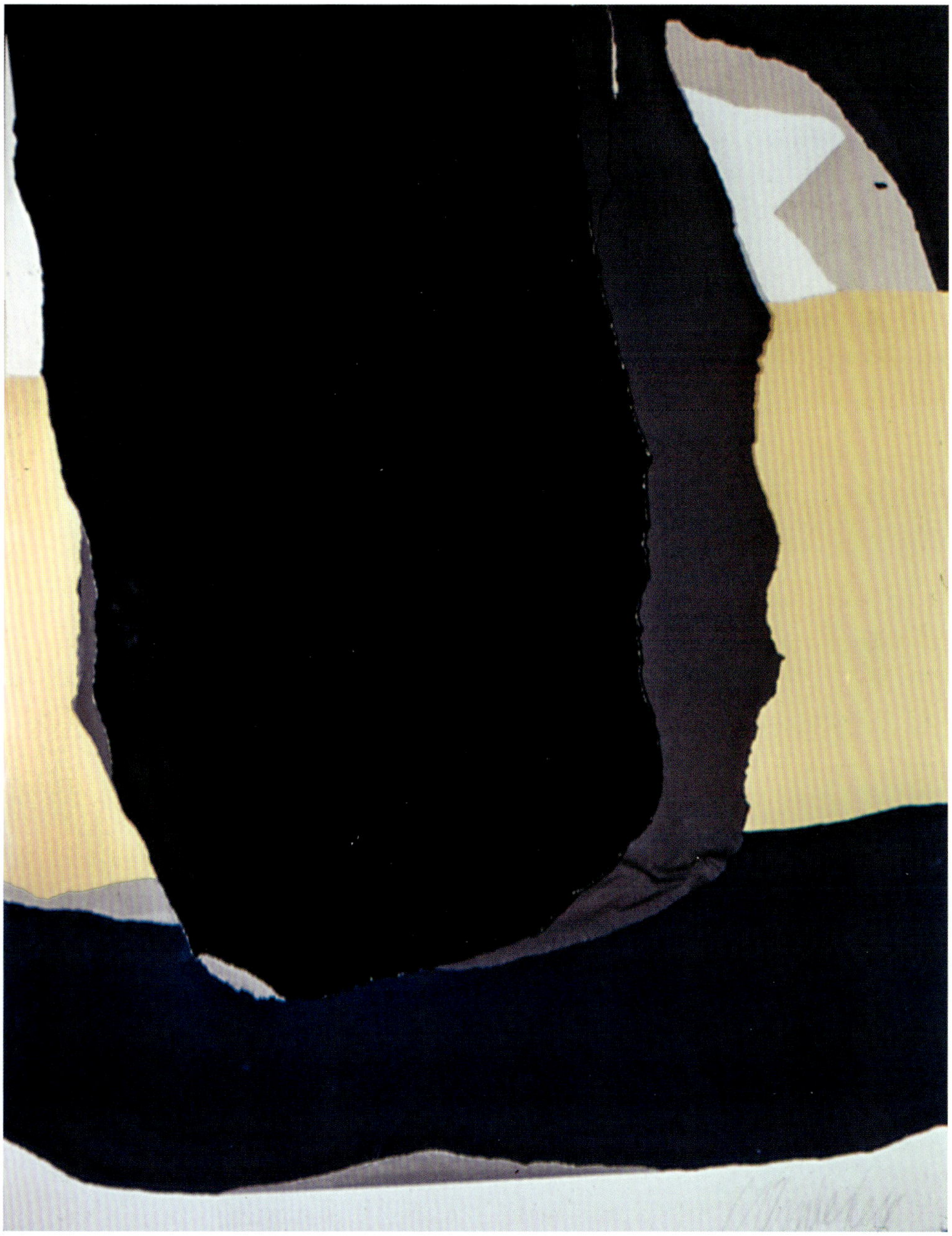

Frank Wimberley, *Monk's Letter*, c. 1971. Mixed media; 40 × 50 inches

Tecla Selnick, James Lightbourne, and the BECC's Prison Arts Program

KAREWITH CASAS & GRACE SANABRIA

In October of 1971, Tecla Selnick opened a solo exhibition at Acts of Art Gallery; in the gallery's six-year history, she was the only white artist to be afforded the opportunity. The exhibition was billed as a retrospective of Selnick's career and included artworks spanning forty years. Selnick was a longtime resident of East Harlem, and the paintings, drawings, and sculptures she exhibited at Acts of Art—portraits of the neighborhood's residents—reflected her engagement with the community. In the exhibition brochure, she writes of the inspiration she draws from "the streets, my street, wherever people gather. Children on park benches, youth—their life in movement, eyes, and songs, and drums."[1] Her involvement with her community extended beyond representation and into political activism. Selnick was involved in many leftist and Black nationalist causes and contributed illustrations for communist and feminist publications. Her exhibition at Acts of Art was dedicated to the late James Lightbourne, who had passed away in August of that year; the show also included portraits of Lightbourne at work. Selnick had been an outspoken and public advocate for Lightbourne during the two years that he was unlawfully imprisoned without having faced trial. In the exhibition booklet, Selnick poses Langston Hughes's famous question, "What happens to a dream deferred?"; a potent question in light of Lightbourne's subjugation within the carceral system and his tragic death at the age of twenty-seven.

Accused of the murder of a Lower Manhattan merchant during an attempted robbery, Lightbourne spent twenty-nine months awaiting trial in the Tombs, the Manhattan Detention Complex at 125 White Street. Against the recommendation of his court-appointed attorney and despite pressure from the District Attorney's Office, Lightbourne refused to plead guilty to the murder charge and maintained his innocence during his stay at the Tombs. He was finally released in April of 1971. This clear violation of Lightbourne's constitutional right to a speedy trial was not an isolated incident but reflected a widespread issue within New York's justice system. During the campaign led by Lightbourne's family and supporters to address his case, William vanden Heuvel, the Chairman of the New York City Board of Corrections, told *The New York Times* that the Board was aware of 706 prisoners who had been incarcerated in the Tombs for over six months while awaiting trial.[2] This was not Lightbourne's first experience with the inequity and failures of the justice system. In 1965, he had been convicted in a burglary case and sentenced to two and a half years in prison only to see his conviction finally reversed by an appellate court after he had served his full sentence.[3] By the time he passed away at twenty-seven years old, Lightbourne had spent almost five years of his life wrongfully imprisoned. The circumstances surrounding his death were suspicious. The coroner

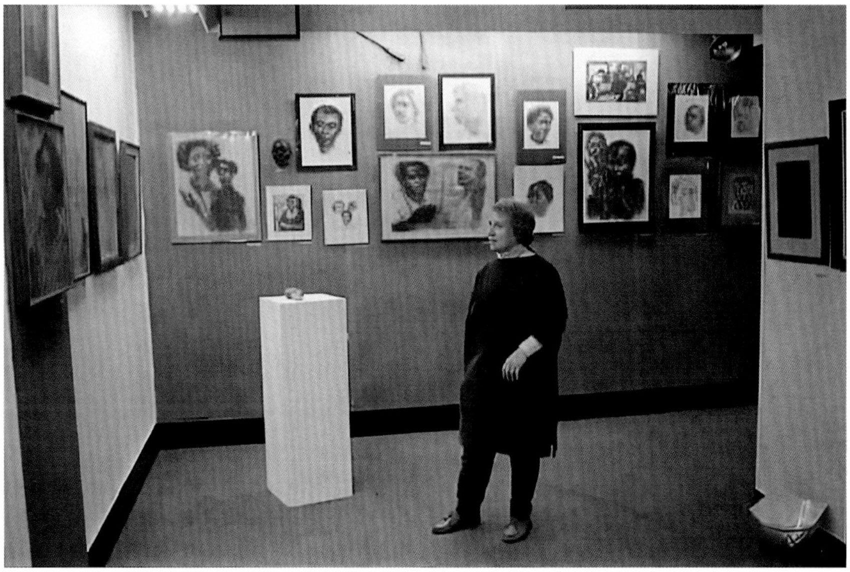

Tecla Selnick in her exhibition at Acts of Art Gallery, October 27, 1971

ruled the cause of death was "narcotism," but his family and supporters believed that foul play was involved. The day he was found dead was the same day he was scheduled to file a lawsuit against New York City for false arrest and malicious prosecution.[4]

During his first period of incarceration, Lightbourne began to make sculpture. He fashioned tools out of bones left over from meals and employed them in sculpting figures with papier-mâché made of old newspapers and soap. His subjects were drawn from Black life, with the emotiveness of many of his figures alluding to his own experiences of systemic oppression. In one work, the head of a man appears to cry with his eyes closed in agony and his mouth fixed open as though he is yelling out. In another bust, a woman leans her head to the side. Her eyes are closed serenely, and her lips are puckered, forming a kiss. She appears blissful and at peace, in stark and ironic contrast to the words that are plastered all over her. Lightbourne clipped newspaper headlines bearing the words "Arrested," "Captured," and "Accused" to adhere to her neck and chest. Across her head a single clipping reads: "Black." The work addresses the societal collusion in the media-led sensationalization that led to the disproportionate and often—as in Lightbourne's case—wrongful imprisonment of Black men. In February of 1971, while he was still awaiting trial in the Tombs, Lightbourne's sculptures were exhibited at Countee Cullen Library in Harlem where Selnick had shown years earlier with fellow artists Benny Andrews and Alice Neel. The exhibition was organized in collaboration with a committee of supporters working to publicize Lightbourne's case including Selnick, the actors Ossie Davis and Ruby Dee, union organizer Edna Slatkin, Harlem Cultural Council leader Edward K. Taylor, and the historian John Henrick Clarke.

Just a month after Lightbourne's passing, the uprising at Attica Correctional Facility occurred in western New York. On September 9, 1971, tensions at Attica peaked and over a thousand of some twenty-two hundred men incarcerated in the severely overcrowded facility rose up against the prison's guards. The inmates initiated a hostage negotiation that ended after four days when New York State and local police infiltrated the facility, killing thirty-three inmates and ten of the forty-two guards who were being held as hostages.[5] Lightbourne's case and the Attica Prison Uprising became catalyzing events for the Black Emergency Cultural Coalition (BECC). In the wake of these events, Benny Andrews and Cliff Joseph began to focus the organization on the carceral conditions and treatment of inmates of color, acknowledging incarcerated people as an important part of the Black community. Andrews and Joseph addressed Lightbourne's death directly in a BECC letter imploring artists to join them in teaching art in prisons: "The power of artistic expression as a means of radical communication, cannot be denied. The right of our brothers and sisters in prison to comment creatively on the oppressive system which subjects them to an unrelenting nightmare of inhuman brutal treatment, must be secured."[6] The political and emotional expression that was exhibited in Lightbourne's work exemplified the necessity for the incarcerated to be given the time, space, and material to address their own experiences and circumstances through creativity. The BECC emphasized the need for people like Lightbourne—who are stripped of their rights by being detained and alienated from society—to have a creative outlet to communicate the injustice and inhumanity of the prison system in the United States.

In September 1971, two months after the Attica uprising, Andrews visited the Tombs and held his first drawing session there. This was made possible through arrangements by Herman Green, the correctional officer in charge of the prison library and the arts and crafts program. Andrews was also assisted by the Museum of Modern Art's Junior Council, which helped supply $400 worth of art materials. This was the starting point of what would become known as the BECC's Prison Arts Program. The Prison Arts Program's first session was a success, and a second class was held soon after. At this class Joseph was accompanied and assisted by two artists, the sculptor Camille Billops and the painter Rudolph Baranik, as well as Barbara Jacobson, a member of MoMA's Junior Council. In a 1973 article on the program, Andrews wrote,

> The Prison Arts Program serves as an instrument to bridge the gap between the free and the incarcerated. It includes art instruction, various informative art discussions about current activities in the art world and a chance to exchange ideas and experience. The communication that takes place between us (the artists) and the inmates really transcends teaching art: it becomes a human exchange experience, and our being artists quickly becomes secondary.[7]

It was important to Andrews and the other program teachers that the program focused on teaching the fine arts: painting, drawing, and sculpture. The program was not intended as a vocational program that would equip the inmates with skills they could utilize toward employment upon release; rather, it offered time and space for inmates to cultivate a creative outlet that prioritized themselves by utilizing art for expressive purposes. Because of this perceived lack of utility, funding for the program was difficult to come by and it relied on a small annual grant from the National Endowment for the Arts and on the generosity of artists who were willing to volunteer or receive a very small stipend to serve as instructors. Still, the program was a success and by 1981—a decade after the BECC's initial session—prison arts programs were active in forty facilities across twenty states.[8] This small affirmation of humanity was significant in a system that provided very little.

Today, the prison-industrial complex, biased laws, and aggressive policing continue to plague the United States with a disproportionate effect on Black communities. In 2023, The Schomburg Institute for Research in Black Culture, which houses the Black Emergency Cultural Coalition and the Prison Arts Program's archives, hosted the exhibition *Marking Time: Art in the Age of Mass Incarceration*. Curated by Dr. Nicole R. Fleetwood, the exhibition explored the cultural impact of the US prison system through the works of both incarcerated and nonincarcerated artists, foregrounding experiences and themes traditionally excluded from institutional spaces.[9] With the gallery's 1971 Tecla Selnick exhibition, Acts of Art similarly made space for these issues, placing Selnick's portraits of Lightbourne and, with them, the tragic record of injustice the incarcerated sculptor faced on the walls

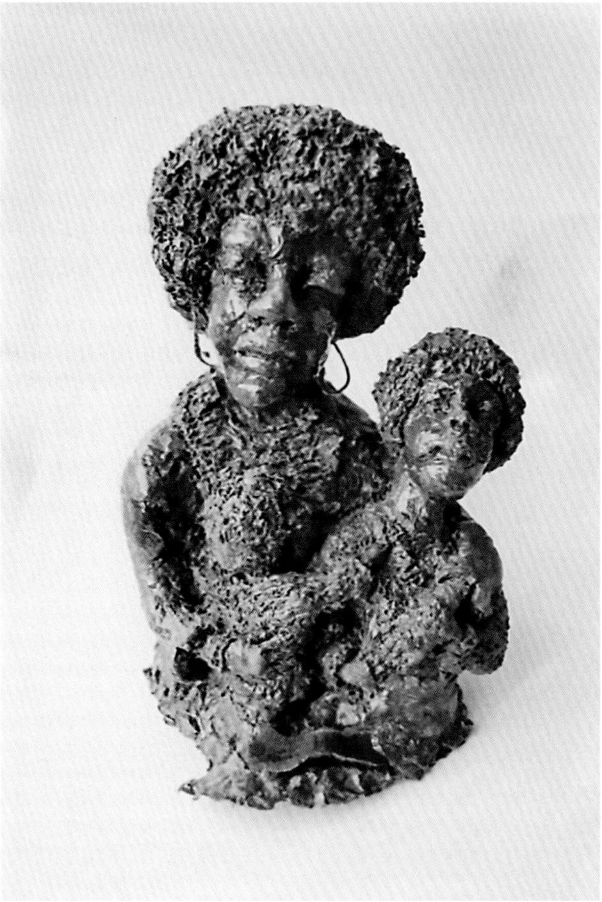

Sculpture by James Lightbourne on display at New York Public Library Countee Cullen Branch, February–March, 1971

of a commercial art gallery and in front of its audiences.[10] The gallery's commitment to platforming artists that engaged with Black issues was a stark contrast to the apathy of the contemporaneous white and Eurocentric commercial gallery model. Acts of Art's highlighting of Lightbourne's story through Selnick, its exhibitions with BECC artists, and fundraising initiatives on behalf of the Tombs 7 and similar causes demonstrate that political and social engagement were throughlines in the gallery's history.[11]

NOTES

1 Tecla Selnick, *Tecla in Retrospect: Forty years of art from the ghettos of the earth*, exhibition brochure published for the exhibition of the same name, Acts of Art Gallery, New York, October 22–November 13, 1971.

2 Charlayne Hunter, "Study is Sought in Delay of Trial," *The New York Times*, February 12, 1971, accessed September 18, 2024 <https://timesmachine.nytimes.com/timesmachine/1971/02/21/91268338.html?pageNumber=27>.

3 Charlayne Hunter, "Innocent Man is Freed After 29 Months in Jail," *New York Times*, April 17, 1971, accessed September 18, 2024 <https://www.nytimes.com/1971/04/17/archives/innocent-man-is-freed-after-29-months-in-jail.html>.

4 As *The New York Times* reported shortly after his death, "[Lightbourne] was scheduled to appear with his lawyers in the City Controller's office on Monday to prepare for a suit against the city for false arrest and malicious prosecution." Martin Gansberg, "Narcotism Kills Negro Sculptor," *New York Times*, August 4, 1971, accessed September 18, 2024 <https://timesmachine.nytimes.com/timesmachine/1971/08/04/79683477.html?pageNumber=22>.

5 Chad Dawkins, "The Emergency Cultural Coalition: Direct Action and Attica Prison," Rose Library News, August 17, 2023, accessed September 18, 2024 <https://scholarblogs.emory.edu/marbl/2022/10/17/the-black-emergency-cultural-coa-lition-direct-action-and-attica-prison/>.

6 Benny Andrews and Cliff Joseph, letter to fellow artists about James Lightbourne, October 7, 1971.

7 Alexandra C. Anderson, "Art from the Inside," *Art in America* 61 (March–April 1973): 14–15.

8 Andrews, Benny, "What's the Assessment of the Prison Arts Program After a Decade?," *American Artist* 45, no. 464 (March 1981): 73–74.

9 The exhibition began at MoMA PS1—a satellite space of the Museum of Modern Art located in Queens—which had associations with the Prison Arts Program from its inception.

10 The *ARTnews* review of Selnick's Acts of Art exhibition notes that she utilized her techniques of fast brushwork and direct application of paint in portraits of Lightbourne included in the show. The critic continues, comparing Tecla's illustrations of Lightbourne with his own work, "His face and the heads he sculpts contain an equal measure of life." Bill Beckley, "Tecla Selnick," *ARTnews* 70, no. 7 (November 1971): 80.

11 The Tombs 7 were inmates in the Tombs who were indicted for their alleged roles in the 1970 prison riots. In 1972, the Prison Justice Committee, which had formed to advocate for the Tombs 7, hosted a benefit for their defense fund at Acts of Art. The artists James Denmark, Ann Tanksley, and Frank Wimberley exhibited with a portion of the sales benefitting the detainees.

The Weusi Artists, Nyumba Ya Sanaa Gallery, and Academy of Fine Arts and Studies

LAURA LUO

The 1960s saw a proliferation of new cultural and political organizations embracing Black nationalist ideologies. As sociologist Alphonso Pinkney has pointed out, regardless of their diverse practices and principles, these organizations shared three key characteristics: Black solidarity, pride in cultural heritage, and self-determination.[1] In this spirit, a large and diverse group of visual artists from the New York metropolitan area came together with the shared goal of elevating and amplifying Black artistic expression to form the Twentieth Century Creators, a precursor to the Weusi Artists. Led by James Sneed (Jemisi Obanjoko) and Malikah Rahman, the Twentieth Century Creators included more than fifty artists; among them were Gaylord Hassan, Mel Green, Taiwo DuVall, Jerry Glib, Alma Mosley, Abdul Rahman, Jokulo Cooper, Frenchie Dickerson, Margaret Christian, Ademola Olugebefola, Bill Howell, Abdullah Aziz, Tony Northern, Perry Cannon, Dindga McCannon, and Grace Joyce. In 1963, the Twentieth Century Creators held their inaugural exhibition at the NAACP's Harlem branch, showing works by community artists from various disciplines. The group took their mission of community engagement and self-determination a step further in 1964, when they staged a major outdoor art exhibition titled *Creative Profile* along 7th Avenue in Harlem, stretching from 127th to 135th Streets. The outdoor exhibition, which ran from October 1964 through February 1965, brought art into the Harlem community in an accessible and immediate fashion.

Within the Black Arts Movement, there was significant and often tense debate between Black artists demanding institutional integration and those who supported cultural separatism. Such ideological divergences ultimately led to the disbanding of the Twentieth Century Creators: some members felt that Sneed was pushing too hard for integration into the white art world. Although the Twentieth Century Creators was short-lived, the artists' spirits and legacy continued to shape the art world in Harlem. In 1965, a segment of the original group reconvened in Harlem and formed a new coalition named the Weusi Artists. Their collective name, "Weusi"—meaning "Blackness" in Swahili—conveyed their clear commitment to affirming and uplifting Black culture.

The new Weusi Artists included Aziz, DuVall, Hassan, Howell, Olugebefola, Rahman, Otto Neals, Okoe Pyatt, Renee Pyatt, and Kay Brown, and established their headquarters at Hassan and DuVall's Studio at 248 West 139th Street. Maintaining the Twentieth Century Creators' mission to introduce "Black Art for Black People," the Weusi Artists continued the tradition of outdoor art

THE WEUSI

WEUSI is a Swahili word meaning Blackness. WEUSI is a Black Organization meaning BLACK ART, BLACK BROTHERHOOD, and developing BLACK UNITY.

BLACK ART: In 1962 a group of black artists united to further the awareness of the black community of Art, Black Art and Culture -- its yesterday, its today and to mold its tomorrow.

BLACK BROTHERHOOD: WEUSI members achieve this and through self awareness, self understanding, self development, and thusly self pride.

BLACK UNITY: Through working together to accomplish common goals the members of WEUSI are understanding and developing black unity.

WEUSI stresses self respect for all men which it believes cannot be achieved unless the man respects himself.

We consider this Gallery -- (The House of Art) a neighborhood center for the enjoyment and education of our brothers and sisters who reside within this block, and the total Harlem Community, as well as for the fulfillment of the Artists and their patrons.

Please visit our new Gallery located within the Heart of Harlem

Gallery Nyumba Ya Sanaa (The House of Art)
158 West 132 Street (off 7th Avenue)
New York, New York Phone: 283-8112

WEUSI MEMBERS:

Ademola Olugebefola
G. Falcon Beazer
Taiwo Shabazz
Abdulah Aziz
Rudy Irvin
Kay Brown
Bill Howell
Muhammad Mufutau
Otto Neals
Ronald Pyatt
Abdul Rahman
Gaylord Hassan
Jim Sepyo

Flyer for Weusi and Nyumba Ya Sanaa, c. 1968

exhibitions and held annual Outdoor Art Festivals from 1965 to 1977.[2] The Outdoor Art Festivals marked the group's agency in placemaking: collaborating with the Black Arts Theatre (BAT), Countee Cullen Library Gallery, Lincoln Community Center, NAACP Offices, Minars Furniture, and various Harlem churches, the Festivals empowered and enlivened the Harlem community through the creation and promotion of Black art, literature, music, and theater. As co-founder Olugebefola recalls, "I remember very fondly how old people and young children would walk up [to the fences] and be amazed that 'you actually painted that'....So that was the joy—to see these old churchwomen's faces and these young kids looking at images of themselves."[3] In addition to the Outdoor Art Festivals, the Weusi Artists also held two annual Black Balls on Christmas night in 1965 and 1966. The Black Ball provided the Harlem community an alternative to the over-commercialization of Christmas and celebrated Afrocentric fashion, music, and dance. More than a social extravaganza, the Black Ball had a lasting cultural significance as it set the precedent for Kwanzaa celebrations initiated by Maulana Karenga in 1966.

In 1967, five members of the Weusi Artists—Aziz, DuVall, Neals, G. Falcon Beazer, and Rudy Irwin (Baba Kachenga)—founded Nyumba Ya Sanaa Gallery, which translates from Swahili to "House of Art." Located in a brownstone at 158 West 132nd Street near 7th Avenue, the gallery opened to the public in the fall of 1967. In the same year, Weusi member Bill Howell opened his own Pamoja Gallery located at 268 Bleecker Street in Greenwich Village. Howell was referred to as the "'soul' owner,"[4] credited with bringing Weusi's spirit downtown.[5] As the Weusi's brick and mortar spaces took shape uptown and downtown, the coalition's membership grew as well. In 1968, the gallery became a full cooperative involving the entire Weusi Artists roster and was renamed the Weusi Nyumba Ya Sanaa Gallery. That year the coalition welcomed new members Muhammad Mufutau, Nii Ahene Mettle Nunoo, James Phillips, James Sepyo, and Ed Sherman. Though it was a commercial space, the Weusi Nyumba Ya Sanaa Gallery was run exclusively by artists. The diverse group of artists included painters, sculptors, printmakers, muralists, and illustrators who collaborated closely not only on the business side but also in their creative processes. McCannon—who joined the Weusi at age eighteen—describes how the Weusi artists fundamentally shaped her early artistic training: "I met this group of Black artists and it was perfect timing....they showed me stuff like where to buy paint...how to stretch a canvas, etc. The basic stuff that most visual artists need to know."[6] Brown, who worked as an apprentice at Weusi's printmaking workshop, found her works anchored in "the cultural and sociopolitical views embraced by the group."[7]

In 1969, the Weusi once again expanded its programming to become the Weusi Nyumba Ya Sanaa Gallery and Academy of Fine Arts and Studies. This iteration functioned as a culturally affirming organization dedicated to uplifting Black art, Black brotherhood, and Black unity.[8] The gallery took on the responsibility of furthering community awareness of the scope and depth of the fine arts in addition to more popular music and theater arts. More importantly, the gallery established a creative hub that nurtured Black artists across New York City and provided them with stability and visibility. The gallery gave many artists their first opportunity not only to show in a professional gallery but also to show in Harlem. Faith Ringgold's show in 1972 at the Weusi Gallery Ya Sanaa was one of her first exhibitions in the Harlem community. Ben Jones held his first show in New York City at the gallery in 1972 before having a solo exhibition at the Studio Museum in 1973.

The gallery served as an important node in the Black Arts Movement, fostering camaraderie and solidarity among different artists' groups. In 1971, Weusi members Brown and McCannon, along with eleven other artists including Ringgold, Carol Blank, and Pat Davis, formed Where We At (WWA), one of the first collectives for Black female artists. Following its inaugural exhibition at Acts of Art in summer 1971, WWA installed its second exhibition *Cookin' and Smokin'* at the Weusi Nyumba Ya Sanaa Gallery in the winter of 1972. The collaboration between Weusi and WWA was fruitful: in February 1985, *Close Connections* opened at the 1199 Gallery in midtown featuring sixteen WWA artists and eight Weusi artists whose works covered a wide spectrum of themes and concepts. WWA artists and Weusi member Neals collaborated again on the exhibition brochure for *She Is*, a traveling exhibition celebrating the oeuvre of Onnie Millar, one of WWA's original members. WWA's founding member Brown considered the bond between Weusi and WWA "particularly meaningful because it finally made clear that a cooperative spirit existed between women artists and their male counterparts."[9] Weusi members were also actively involved in the programming at Acts of Art Gallery, creating an active uptown-downtown dialogue. In 1971, Weusi members Olugebefola, McCannon, and Phillips were among the artists who participated in *Rebuttal to the Whitney Museum Exhibition*, the influential group exhibition organized by the Black Emergency Cultural Coalition and Acts of Art. From 1971 to 1975, Acts of Art's Nigel Jackson organized eight more solo and group exhibitions that involved Weusi members including Olugebefola, McCannon, Neals, and Aziz.

The Academy transformed the Weusi into a comprehensive educational institution that served the community. Under the directorship of Pyatt, the Academy launched a campaign to raise awareness for Black art on university and college campuses in Harlem and beyond. The Academy organized traveling exhibitions and printmaking workshops in local schools, churches, and community centers. Beyond Harlem, Weusi artists Beazer and Olugebefola designed and taught a course in contemporary Black art at Wesleyan University in 1972. During this period, the Weusi artists created over five hundred woodcuts, etchings, monoprints, serigraphs, and lithographs as covers and illustrations of educational publications. The reproducibility and accessibility inherent to printmaking enabled these works to disseminate widely, exposing many educators and students nationwide to contemporary African American art for the first time. The Academy played an instrumental role in educating the general public about fine arts and in writing Black art history as Weusi artists toured and lectured throughout the country.

The Academy also fostered active communication and collaboration across the various theater, visual arts, and music communities in Harlem. The Weusi had a long history of active participation in theater, as most Weusi artists came from backgrounds of theater set design. From 1969 to 1973, the New Lafayette Theatre and the Weusi collaborated closely on the production of eight plays, four issues of *Black Theatre* magazine, two full-length films, two in-theater murals, and other artistic and intellectual activities. In 1978, Weusi artists Sepyo, Olugebefola, Rahman, and Aziz co-founded the National Arts Consortium with Hazel Bryant, founder of the Richard Allen Center for Culture and Art, and Rod Rodgers, director of the Rod Rodgers Dance Company. The consortium produced the

Centerfold, *Weusi Resurrection*, exhibition brochure,
Studio Museum in Harlem, November 15, 1970 to January 31, 1971

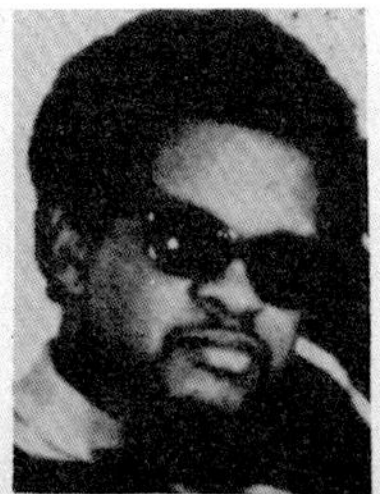

RUDY
IRVIN

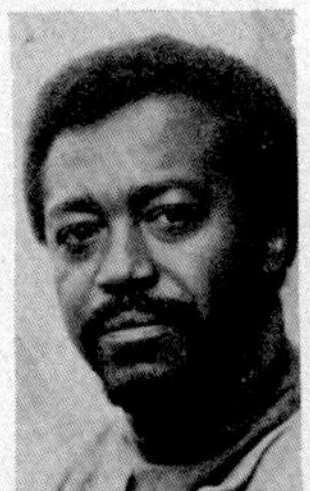

OTTO
NEALS

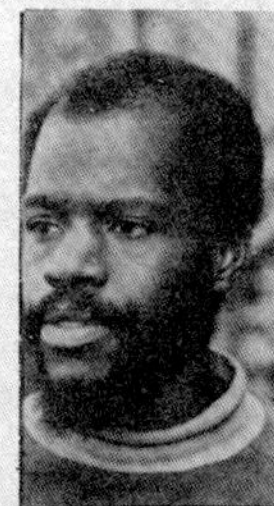

GAYLORD
HASSAN

IMAGINATION IS THE SEED
OF PROGRESS

WE PLANT AND CULTIVATE
THIS SEED
IN A GARDEN OF TRUTH

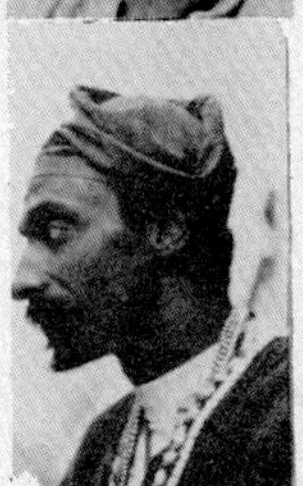

JIM
SEPYO

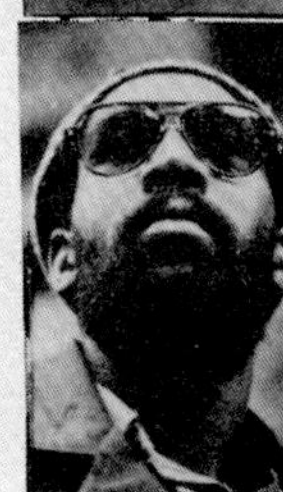

RONALD
PYATT

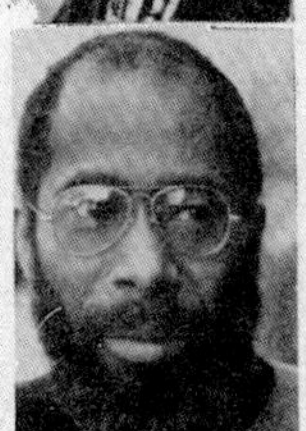

G. FALCON
BEAZER

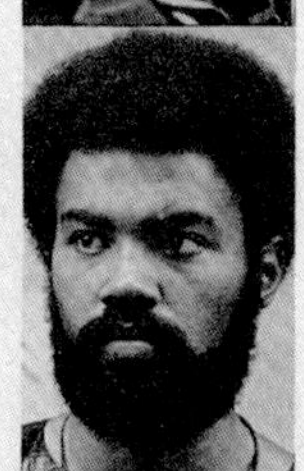

BILL
HOWELL

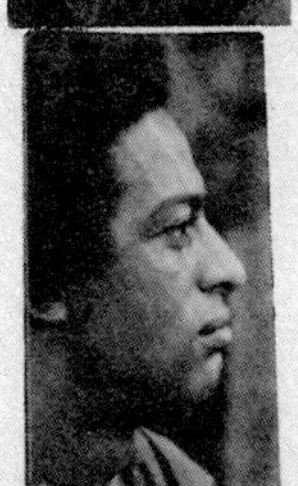

JIM
PHILLIPS

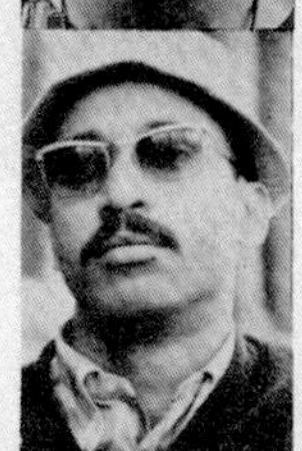

TAIWO
SHABAZZ

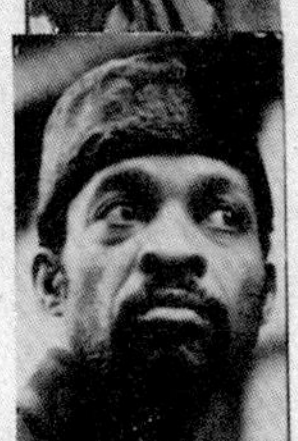

MUHAMMAD
MUFUTAU

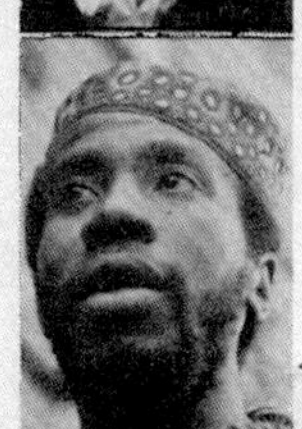

ADEMOLA
OLUGEBEFOLA

WEUSI
NYUMBA
YA
SANAA

GALLERY AND ACADEMY OF ARTS AND STUDIES
158 W. 132ND ST. HARLEM
PHONE–(212) 283-9475

WOODCUTS–OILS–LITHOS– POSTERS
EXHIBITIONS– BROCHURE AVAILABLE

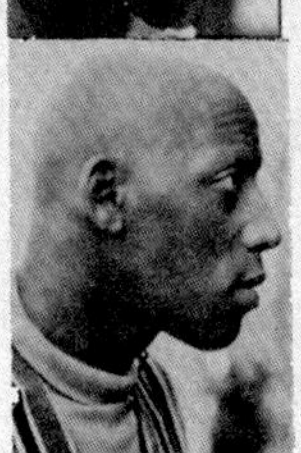

ABDUL
RAHMAN

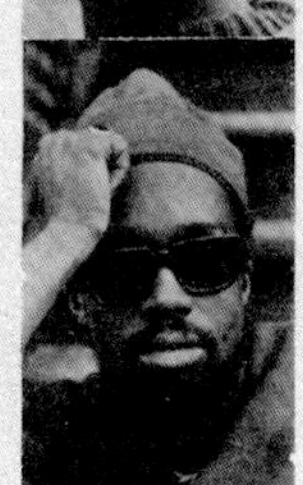

ABDULLAH
AZIZ

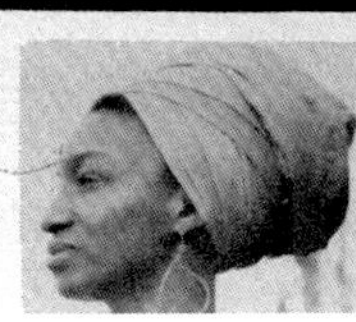

KAY
BROWN

First Black Theatre Festival at Lincoln Center for the Performing Arts. In addition to the theater community, the Academy also attracted musicians, poets, creatives, and scholars from around the world, becoming the "Black Mecca."[10]

The Weusi Nyumba Ya Sanaa Gallery and Academy of Fine Arts and Studies played a pivotal role in shaping the cultural landscape of the 1960s and 1970s. From Twentieth Century Creators to the gallery and academy, the Weusi evolved and renewed itself with vitality and multiplicity. By centering African identity, challenging institutional biases, and empowering their local community, the Weusi artists made an indelible mark on the trajectory of the Black Arts Movement and its lasting legacy. Echoing what writer Freida Jones describes as the functions of an art organization, the institutions Weusi built truly functioned as "a vehicle of social and political thought, germinator of cultural institutions, and a forum for Black art professionals and thinkers."[11]

NOTES

1 Alphonso Pinkney, "Contemporary Black Nationalism," in *Black Life and Culture in the United States*, ed. Rhoda Goldstein (New York: Thomas Y. Crowell, 1971), 246.

2 Kay Brown, "The Weusi Artists," *Nka: Journal of Contemporary African Art* 30 (Spring 2012): 61.

3 Ademola Olugebefola, in "When that Time Came Rolling Down, panel I," *Artist and Influence*, unnumbered (1985): 129. Panel at the James Hatch and Camille Billops loft, New York, March 25, 1984.

4 Bobbie Barbee, "New York Beat," *Jet*, October 12, 1967, p. 64.

5 Nathaniel G. Nesmith, "Doing It His Way: Ademola Olugebefola's Long and Varied Career in the Arts," *New England Review* 42, no. 3 (September 2021): 139.

6 Dindga McCannon, "An Oral History with Dinga McCannon by Philip Glahn," interview by Philip Glahn, *BOMB Magazine*, August 1, 2020, accessed September 20, 2024 <https://bombmagazine.org/articles/2020/08/03/dindga-mccannon-by-philip-glahn/>.

7 Kay Brown, "The Emergence of Black Women Artists: The Founding of 'Where We At'," *Nka: Journal of Contemporary African Art* 29 (Fall 2011): 120.

8 The Weusi flyer, circa 1968, 1918–2005, box 4, folder 44. Jeff Donaldson Papers, Archives of American Art, Washington, D.C.

9 Brown, "The Emergence of Black Women Artists," 122.

10 Brown, "Weusi Artists," 64.

11 Freida Jones, "Artists Hold Sixteenth Convention: A NEW ERA OF BLACK ART," *Black View* 2, no. 7 (1974): 15.

Where We At: Black Women Artists 1971

MARY LISETTE MORRIS & NICOLAS POBLETE

Sometime in the spring of 1971, a group of some ten Black women artists met in Dindga McCannon's walk-up apartment on the Lower East Side to discuss their experiences and concerns about the lack and dismissal of women as professional artists in Black art spaces.[1] After a few meetings, the group mounted an exhibition at Acts of Art Gallery titled *Where We At: Black Women Artists 1971*. Adopting the title of the show as its name, Where We At (WWA) quickly blossomed into an art collective—or a "sisterhood"—that continued to show together until 1999.[2] The initial idea for a Black women's art collective developed across events, meetings, and activism related to the Weusi Artists collective in the late 1960s.[3] WWA co-founders Dindga McCannon and Kay Brown were close to the male artists of the collective: McCannon had been taken in by Weusi as a teenager, and Brown would become the first woman to be an official member of the collective in 1968.[4] WWA's other co-founder, Faith Ringgold, exhibited at Weusi's Nyumba Ya Sanaa Gallery in 1969 and met Brown and McCannon around that time. In 1971, the three women posited a potential exhibition entirely dedicated to Black women artists.[5] Three meetings took place between January and March of 1971; during this time, the ten women organically morphed into an art collective with the shared goal of mounting a Black women art show.[6] McCannon, who had exhibited and sold at Acts of Art, suggested that gallery director Nigel Jackson might be willing to host this show.[7] McCannon, Brown, Ringgold, Carol Blank, and Pat Davis went to Jackson and got his blessing "after much persuasion."[8] *Where We At: Black Women Artists 1971* opened on June 22, 1971. The exhibition included the work of thirteen of WWA's members: Brown, McCannon, Ringgold, Davis, Blank, Ann Tanksley, Vivian Browne, Iris Crump, Charlotte Richardson, Jerrolyn Crooks, Mai Mai Leabus, Onnie Millar, and Omolaye.[9]

WWA emerged during the Black Arts Movement, and most—though not all—of its members shared the project of Black representation. The social and political responsibility of the Black artist was a concern for Black women artists, though it was often overshadowed by their basic need to get exhibition opportunities and recognition from their male peers. Jackson opened Acts of Art in October 1969, providing a networking platform and exhibition space for Black artists downtown.[10] Jackson believed that Acts of Art's Afrocentrist curatorial vision was a necessary—though precarious—political tool, and he aimed to cultivate an audience invested in Black art and provide a space to develop a Black aesthetic.[11] However, despite Jackson's curatorial openness, Acts of Art's exhibiting artists were predominantly men. Though they maintained an alliance with Black men, the founders of WWA were aware that masculine Black exhibition spaces would not reflect their perspective without pressure. As McCannon argued: "some don't give a fuck about Black women. And some will

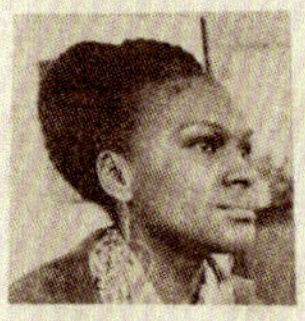

Carol Blank

Don't turn around.

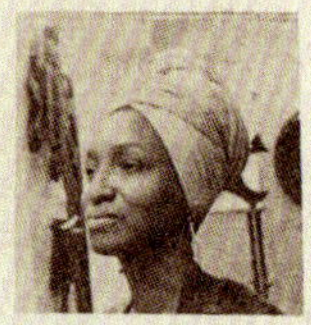

Kay Brown

Black Woman
Yes, the Wisdom of Waiting
For she knew as she strives
That the New Day would finally arrive
And the burden of her life's story
Will worth the eternal glory
No more time for Pain
Past troubles or all that strain
For the Wanton, Wretchedness of life
Has past to emptiness, as her strife
And, yes, the future is no longer
......It is now.

Vivianne Browne

Painting for me
is a kind of visual music:
when all the colors and textures
and forms, etc. work together
it sings!

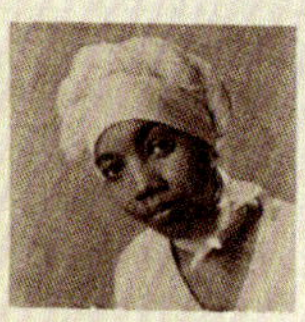

Jerrolyn Crooks

black art?
black outlook.
black fashion art?
yeah.

Exhibition brochure, *Where We At: Black Women Artists 1971*, June 22 to July 30, 1971

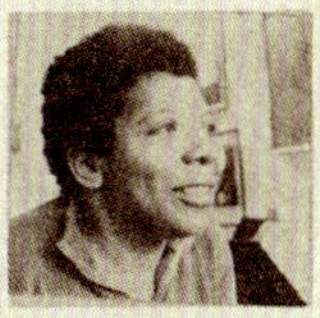

Iris Crump

From tidal waves of black
Emerges a woman.

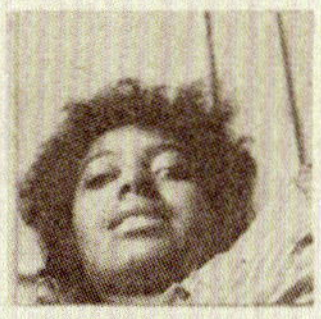

Pat Davis

My photographs are an attempt to
study the aesthetic values of
everyday people and things.

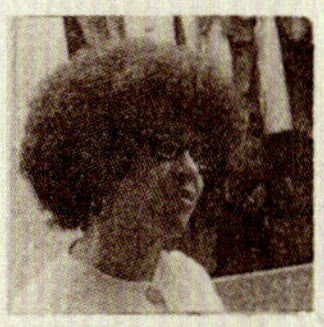

Mai Mai Leabus

My art gives me an opportunity
to not only shout how beautiful
black is but a chance to express
an unforgettable and eye-filling
experience unique to blackness.
Specifically black femaleness.

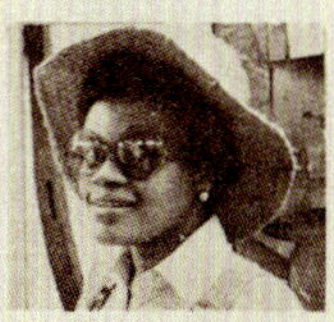

Dinga McCannon

My art is an attempt to remember
Colors, shapes. and form . . .
As I preceived them before
I was old enough to realize
I was in prison.

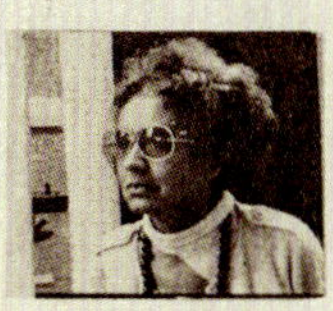

Onnie Millar

Out of the Maze
Out of the Maze
Come now to Wonderous New Days
Crouch no more
Sit in no more
In the World
And Take our minds Now
To the Apex of Wonder.

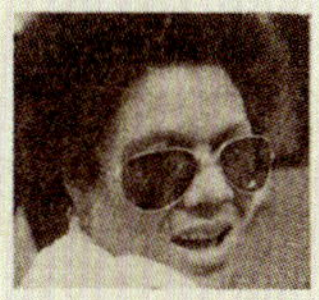

Omolaye

Film, the new drum.

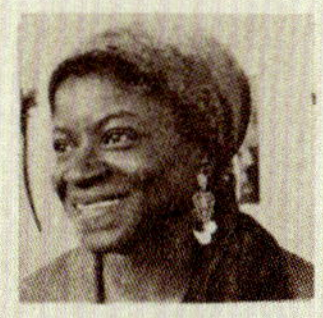

Charlotte Richardson

Black Folks
Beautiful Black Folks
Stimulating Black Folks
Just dig the tempo of Harlems
Capturing the essence of the
People in my art.

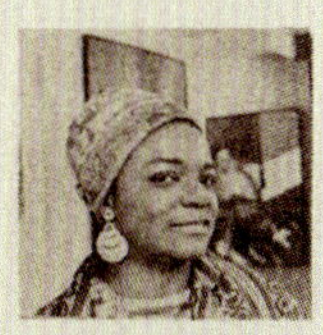

Faith Ringgold

Black Women Artists
"Where we at," is where black
art, life, love, and the bloodless
revolution is at.

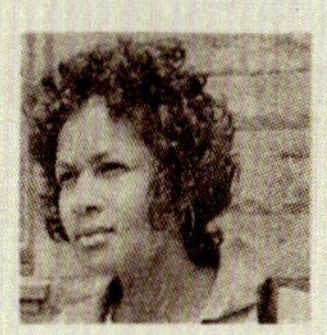

Ann Tanksley

My paintings are my reflections / on prevailing
social attitudes / and contemporary ideas.

accept [our] work but they will not do the same things that they do for men; like heavy advertising."[12] Accordingly, the sisterhood, through its intersectional framework, centralized the importance of Blackness and gender in shaping art production and art opportunities. At the time, McCannon would even extend this need for independence to personal life, advising that Black women artists "try and put off marriage or any permanent relationships" to devote all of their time to their artistic development.[13] Beyond sexism, McCannon believed that the neglect of Black women artists was symptomatic of their restraining familial role as caretakers, a perception not shared by every member of the collective. Despite some internal disagreements, early WWA members all seemed to concur that critical separation from predominantly masculine art spaces was a necessary—if not permanent—political step.

WWA also formed during the height of second-wave feminism. Though a few members identified as feminists—Ringgold, most openly—many artists of the sisterhood did not.[14] From their perspective, which was shared by many Black women in the '70s, the women's liberation movement was organized around white liberalism and fought for the rights of white, middle-to-upper class women.[15] *Essence* magazine editor Ida Lewis explained this dynamic in 1971: "The Women's Liberation Movement is basically a family quarrel between white women and white men. [The] role of Black women is to continue the struggle in concert with Black men for the liberation and self-determination of Blacks."[16] McCannon, who discouraged marriage and promoted independence for women artists, adopted a more radical stance: entrenched sexism complicated the ideal solidarity across gender that Lewis advocated for. For McCannon, there *was* also a quarrel between Black men and Black women but there was nothing feminist about addressing or resolving it, since feminism was intrinsically white. Brown and McCannon approached the collective pragmatically. For them, the compounding power structures of racism and sexism made the Black woman artist into a "double problem;" WWA provided a temporary solution.[17] Hence, they mobilized to carve out a space for Black women within the art world, circumventing its gendered and ethnic blind spots. Conversely, members like Ringgold saw value in WWA as a feminist group and sought to expand who feminism could belong to. It's possible that this differing perspective contributed to Ringgold's eventual distancing from her leadership role within the group. In fact, between 1971 and 1999, group membership shifted as the political priorities of the collective evolved. Nonetheless, WWA's core mission—to fight for the celebration, acknowledgement, and support of Black women artists—always remained intact.

As Kay Brown observed, *Where We At: Black Women Artists 1971* was a "real coming together of creative and talented Black women, unique in its philosophy of mutual support of Black women artists in the creative endeavor [and its dedication] to the cultural education and enrichment of the community."[18] Beyond simply supplying a space for Black women artists, the show also reimagined how art spaces could function, feel, and provide. As Brown recounts: "At the opening, attendees were served deliciously cooked food, a conscious departure from the wine and cheese served at traditional openings."[19] Themes of family and tradition are woven through their works that comment on racial discrimination, disparity of resources, and feminine representation. Phillip Bonosky celebrated the exhibition in a 1971 issue of the communist newspaper the *Daily World*, examining five of the thirteen artists' works, including McCannon's assemblage titled *Revolutionary Sister*. McCannon said of this work, "In the '60s and '70s we didn't have many women warriors (that we were aware of) so I

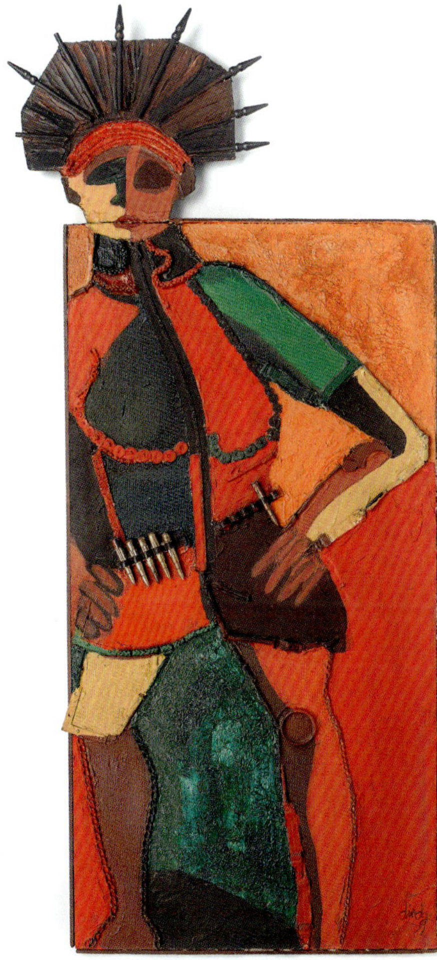

Dindga McCannon, *Revolutionary Sister*, 1971.
Mixed media construction on wood; 62 × 27 inches

created my own."[20] Bonosky notes that this mythological figure appears several times in the exhibition in wood cuts. His critique values the political content of the exhibition, stating that "what qualifies this showing, even with its faults, is the tremendous sense of purpose you sense here."[21] Writing for *New York Amsterdam News*, Mel Tapley praised the group's work in dozens of iterations of his "About the Arts" column, regarding its members as "some of the most talented and creative minds in the arts."[22] Tapley also reported on the festive atmosphere that WWA's events generated, noting jazz performances, poetry readings, and dance performances.[23]

WWA's second major show, *Cookin' and Smokin'*, opened in the winter of 1972 at Weusi's Nyumba Ya Sanaa Gallery and carried on the convivial spirit of the inaugural show as is made explicit by its title.[24] The sisterhood caught the attention of renowned psychologist Kenneth Clark who requested an exhibition at the Manhattan Applied Research Center in downtown Manhattan.[25] Following the success of these shows, they exhibited at numerous colleges, museums, and galleries throughout the '70s.[26] In the 1980s, WWA organized nationally traveling exhibitions like *Adaptation Innovation Black Women Artists* and *She Is*.[27] Though members welcomed these opportunities, some felt the group operated on the periphery of the real art world, "outside of the normal realm," in a world composed of "hundreds of little galleries mostly run by women from their homes," as McCannon recounts.[28] The sisterhood would gradually migrate to Brooklyn, changing their community circle while also following exhibition opportunities.[29] WWA was also politically engaged with members participating in panels like the National Conference of Artists.[30] In a similar vein, members organized community programs such as art classes and workshops for youth, prison inmates, and art students.[31] Their focus on exhibiting at local Black-owned spaces functioned as subversive geopolitical activism.[32] In the report of a 1976 Weusi meeting, Brown closes the minutes with a hopeful sentiment addressing her co-members, "Let us move into the '70s with new heart and spirit, knowing that it is us who have paved the way, and it is also us who must establish the guidelines for this new day."[33]

By the 1980s, the sisterhood had grown to thirty members under the leadership of McCannon, Blank, and Rafala Green.[34] By then, Ringgold and many other original members were no longer part of the collective. In 1981, WWA presented *Directions '81: Creative Expressions* at the Benin Gallery in Harlem. WWA started to exhibit alongside their Black male contemporaries; Weusi member Ademola Olugebefola recounts the relationship between the two groups as that of a brother and sister.[35] Together, WWA and Weusi produced the 1985 show *Close Connections: An Exhibition Featuring the Works of Where We At Black Women Artists and Weusi Artists* at 1199 Gallery in Midtown Manhattan.[36] The 1986 show *Joining Forces: 1 + 1 = 3* at the New Muse Community Museum of Brooklyn was another instance of WWA exhibiting with Black male artists.[37] This follows an ideological shift in the group when Black family unity—as opposed to feminine independence—began to take center stage; *Joining Forces* aimed to address this concern.[38] In 2020, McCannon would retrospectively explain this renewed familial concern, stating: "we wanted to keep our families intact and nobody I knew was able to stay home and paint while the husband went to work."[39]

Where We At's groundbreaking exhibition style remains a historically unparalleled contribution to Black art-activism. Although the group eventually disbanded, the impact of WWA still resonates throughout the twenty-first century. In 2017, the Brooklyn Museum of Art in New York organized the exhibition *We Wanted a Revolution: Black Radical Women, 1965–85* as a survey of Black women's sociopolitical and aesthetic interventions.[40] Several artists in *We Wanted a Revolution* were members of Where We At, including Brown, McCannon, Davis, Browne, and Carole Byard. The exhibition also featured material from *Cookin' and Smokin'*.[41] In 2022, the Irwin House Gallery and the National Conference of Artists of Michigan presented *WHERE WE AT: A Black & Women's History Month Exhibition*.[42] This exhibition honored the women of WWA through the work of a new generation of artists who continue to walk in the footsteps of the sisterhood. These cross-generational conversations between contemporary Black artists and their progenitors weave history into the identity of Black women in twenty-first-century America.

WWA was an urgent collective intervention with the aspiration of ensuring that inherited historical neglect of Black women would not further plague the Black art world. Though they evidently could not change the broader institutional biases of the art world, WWA generated opportunities for Black women artists, and provided them with the support and recognition they had been historically denied on the dual bases their race and gender. In the words of Kay Brown, "the legacy of the WWA's activism, even more than the artists' specific work, has opened doors for younger Black female artists to be recognized by the mainstream art world."[43]

NOTES

1 Kay Brown, "The Emergence of Black Women Artists: The Founding of 'Where We At,'" *Nka: Journal of Contemporary African Art* 29 (Fall 2011): 118–19, <https://doi.org/10.1215/10757163-1496399>.

2 Brown, "The Emergence of Black Women Artists," 120.

3 Dindga McCannon, "An Oral History with Dindga McCannon by Philip Glahn," interview by Philip Glahn, *BOMB Magazine*, August 3, 2020, accessed April 10, 2024 <https://bombmagazine.org/articles/2020/08/03/dindga-mccannon-by-philip-glahn/>.

4 McCannon had collaborated with future Weusi members as far back as 1964 for the Twentieth Century Creators' first annual outdoor show in Harlem. However, she was not an official member of the Weusi collective. Ringgold never became a member of Weusi, though she was collaborating and exhibiting with them as early as the late '60s. See McCannon, "An Oral History."

5 Pat Davis was also part of the Weusi circle at the time, though she was not a core member. See McCannon, "An Oral History."

6 McCannon was one of the three artists who were included in Acts of Art's 1971 *Rebuttal to the Whitney Museum Exhibition*; the others were Ann Tanskley and Vivian Browne. See McCannon, "An Oral History."

7 Dindga McCannon, "Dindga McCannon: An Artist at War with Racism and Sexism," interview by Pat Davis, *Black Creation* 4, no. 2 (1973): 54.

8 Brown, "The Emergence of Black Women Artists," 120.

9 For a comprehensive list of all early members of the sisterhood, see Brown, "The Emergence of Black Women Artists," 120–21; and Where We At, *Where We At: Black Women Artists 1971*, exhibition brochure (Acts of Art Gallery, 1971).

10 Along with Pamoja Gallery, which was affiliated with the Weusi collective, Acts of Art was one of the only Black-owned galleries operating in downtown Manhattan. Howard Singerman and Sarah Watson, eds., *Acts of Art and Rebuttal in 1971*, exhibition catalogue (Hunter College Art Galleries, 2018), 2 and 34.

11 Howard Singerman, "Insisting on Inclusion and Making Space Downtown," in *Reshaping the Field: Arts of the African Diasporas on Display*, ed. Nana Adusei-Poku (London: Afterall Exhibition Histories, 2022), 78.

12 McCannon, "An Artist at War with Racism and Sexism," 54.

13 McCannon, 55.

14 Brown, "The Emergence of Black Women Artists," 123–24.

15 See Brown, 123–24.

16 See Toni Morrison, "What the Black Woman Thinks About Women's Lib," *The New York Times*, August 22, 1971, accessed May 20, 2024 <https://www.nytimes.com/1971/08/22/archives/what-the-black-woman-thinks-about-womens-lib-the-black-woman-and.html>.

17 McCannon, "An Artist at War with Racism and Sexism," 54.

18 Kay Brown, "'Where We At' Black Women Artists," *Feminist Art Journal* 1, no. 1 (April 1972): 25.

19 Brown, "The Emergence of Black Women Artists," 121.

20 Dindga McCannon, "Revolutionary Sister," collection object entry, Brooklyn Museum, accessed August 29, 2024 <https://www.brooklynmuseum.org/opencollection/objects/210707>.

21 Phillip Bonosky, "Powerful Challenge By 13 Black Women Artists," *Daily World*, July 8, 1971, p. 8.

22 Mel Tapley, "About the Arts," *New York Amsterdam News*, August 20, 1977.

23 Tapley, "About the Arts," *New York Amsterdam News*, November 13, 1976.

24 Brown, "The Emergence of Black Women Artists," 122.

25 See Brown, "The Emergence of Black Women Artists," 122.

26 Brown, 122.

27 Brown, 127.

28 McCannon, "An Oral History."

29 The collective built a long relationship with Medgar Evers College where they would often exhibit. WWA also participated in events such as the Second Festival of Black Arts and Culture (FESTAC '77) in Nigeria. See Brown, "The Emergence of Black Women Artists," 122–23.

30 Founded in 1959, the National Conference of Artists (NCA) is the oldest operating African American arts organization in the United States. NCA's mission is "to preserve, promote, develop, and mentor each artist while nurturing their creative forces and expressions as they navigate through the mainstream American art world at large." See "Our History," The National Conference of Artists, New York, Inc., accessed April 11, 2024 <https://www.ncanewyorkart.com/>.

31 Brown, "The Emergence of Black Women Artists," 123.

32 Exhibition spaces included the Restoration Gallery, Benin Gallery, the New York State Office Building, the New York Arts Consortium, and the Downtown Cultural Gallery. See Brown, 123.

33 Weusi Nyumba Ya Sanaa Gallery, meeting minutes, February 12, 1976, New York, reel 7, Ademola Olugebefola Archives, Schomburg Center for Research in Black Culture, New York Public Library, NY.

34 Brown, "The Emergence of Black Women Artists," 125–26.

35 Ademola Olugebefola, "Class Lecture with Ademola Olugebefola" (lecture, Hunter College, New York, NY, April 8, 2024).

36 Brown, "The Emergence of Black Women Artists," 125.

37 Brown, 125.

38 Curator Charles Abramson indeed paired every WWA member with a male artist to show their work alongside one another. See McCannon, "An Oral History."

39 McCannon, "An Oral History."

40 The exhibition's study of Black feminism highlights an overlooked history of activism suppressed by the white American master narrative.

41 Balasz Takac, "Where We At—A Revolution of Black Women Artists," *Widewalls*, February 16, 2021, accessed September 20, 2024 <https://www.widewalls.ch/magazine/where-we-at-black-women-artists>.

42 "WHERE WE AT: A Black Women's History Month Exhibition," exhibition press release, *Irwin House Gallery*, February 12, 2022, accessed April 11, 2024 <https://irwinhousegallery.org/2022/01/27/where-we-at-a-black-womens-history-month-exhibition/>.

43 Brown, "The Emergence of Black Women Artists," 127.

Caribbean and Afro-American Women Artists: Loïs Mailou Jones's Research in Haiti and at Howard

SONDRA McGILL & CHLOE MING

Caribbean and Afro-American Women Artists, curated by Loïs Mailou Jones, ran at Acts of Art gallery between June 25 and July 15, 1974. It featured thirteen artists from Haiti, seven from Jamaica, one from Guyana, and ten from the African diaspora in the United States—including Jones herself. The exhibition was ambitious in scope, aiming to condense the wide-ranging artwork of Black women across several countries into a relatively small exhibition. *Caribbean and Afro-American Women Artists* was a unique exploration of the intersections between gender and the African diaspora, and Jones's work on this exhibition—including her research conducted in the decades prior—set a precedent for women artists of African descent in and outside of New York City. She recognized a cultural absence in the majority of American art scenes and set out to the diaspora to expand her creative and curatorial consciousness.

Jones was an artist, activist, traveler, and scholar with deep ties to Caribbean culture, people, and arts. Her spirited practices allowed her to honor Caribbean and African American women artists that may have been working without Western arts representation or resources; or who were experiencing political and social upheaval in their country of origin and residence. *Caribbean and Afro-American Women Artists* drew upon work Jones had been undertaking for a research project that she had begun on behalf of Howard University in 1973. For this project, entitled "Women Artists of the Caribbean and Afro-American Artists," she researched, documented, and disseminated the work of accredited Black women artists from the United States and the Caribbean. Citing the lack of existing publications on the topic, she felt that this demographic was an important but under-recognized one whose work deserved to be showcased.[1] In the introductory text for the exhibition catalogue, Jones underscored the heterogeneity of the work included. She framed the selection as a "sampling" from a vast and varied field while also emphasizing the inherent solidarity that existed among the participating artists. Jones writes: "No longer need [Caribbean and African American women artists] be excluded

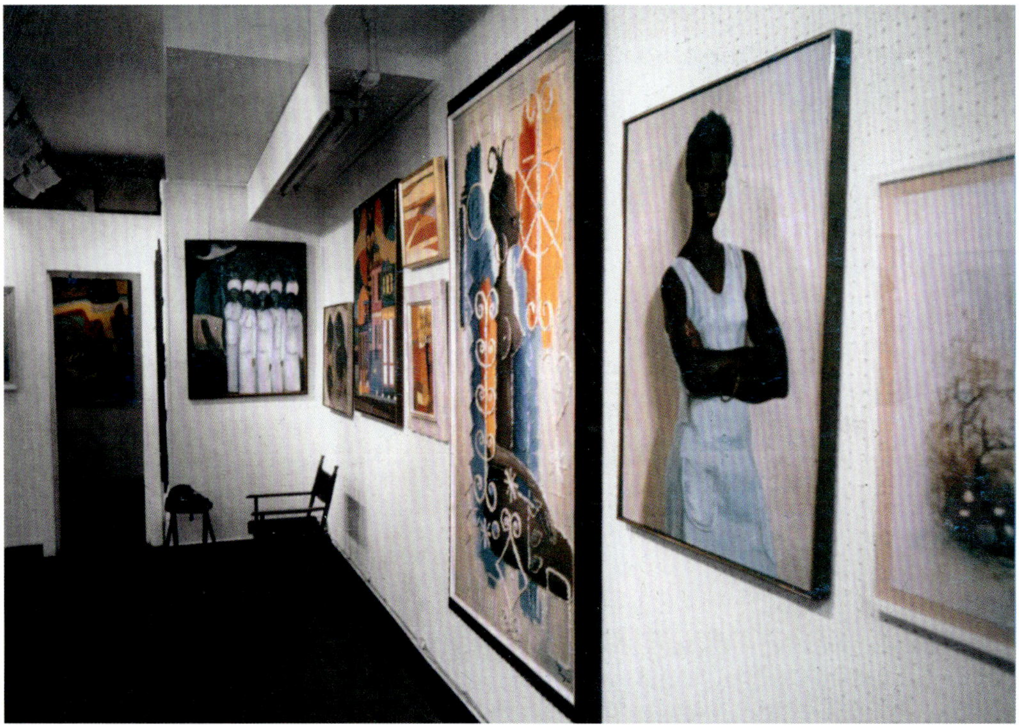

Caribbean and Afro-American Women Artists installed at Acts of Art, June 25 to July 15, 1974

from the art world and isolated from each other…the bringing together of this cross-section of creative work from here and abroad establishes a bind which affirms and supports the importance of the 'WOMAN ARTIST.'"[2]

The significant presence of Haitian artists in the exhibition reflects Jones's longtime artistic, academic, and personal interest in the country. She first traveled to Haiti in 1954. Although the trip was primarily intended to be a honeymoon after her marriage to Haitian artist Louis Vergniaud Pierre-Noël, she had also been invited by the country's president to do a series of paintings depicting the landscape and people of Haiti. She credits this trip with giving her a new visual vocabulary and influencing her perception of the African diaspora; by extension, this visit changed the course of her career. She was struck by how clearly Haitian culture displayed its ties to "mother Africa" and found its Vodou practices especially compelling as source material.[3] She later stated, "I feel that Haiti, Black America, and Africa are one."[4]

The same year Jones made her first trip to Haiti, Hurricane Hazel swept through the country, killing more than 1,000 people and ruining regenerative crops across the island. Shortly after, in 1957, one of Haiti's most notorious leaders—François "Papa Doc" Duvalier—seized power. His tyrannical methods aimed to instill fear among the masses, regain economic control of the land, and boost Haiti's international prowess as a powerful Caribbean nation. Though his status as "president for life" was confirmed in 1964, his tenure was ultimately shortened by his death on April 21, 1971. His son, Jean-Claude "Baby Doc" Duvalier, was immediately sworn into office in his place and assumed the title of the youngest president in the world at age 19—with the same right to rule for life.

In Haiti, Jones developed relationships with various artists and institutions, particularly Le Centre d'Art in Port-au-Prince where she was a guest professor in 1954. Le Centre d'Art was Haiti's first public art center at the heart of Port-au-Prince's burgeoning art scene; founded in 1944 to serve as a gallery, museum, and art school, the Centre functioned as a cosmopolitan meeting ground for artists and intellectuals.[5] In addition to highlighting and instructing Haitian artists, Le Centre d'Art aimed to provide a venue for valuable cross-cultural exchange—something Jones was also trying to foster through her research project.

In the same timeframe, Jones's diasporic mission cast a wide net, engaging with women artists from Haiti, Guyana, Jamaica, and the United States. This research was not new to Jones's practice: she spent decades exploring sites of Blackness. She spent time as a pupil and as a faculty member in Howard University's Department of Art, experienced the New York art scene at the onset of the Harlem Renaissance, traveled to France and neighboring European nations to paint, and studied contemporary arts in eleven African countries. Jones was long searching for the intersections of African diasporic arts and female experiences, and even more so, the places in which those intersections were invited, acknowledged, and protected.

After her initial trip, Jones continued to visit Haiti every summer. In 1968, Jones secured a grant from Howard University titled "The Black Visual Arts: Contemporary Afro-American and Contemporary African Art" to document the work of Black artists in Haiti, Africa, and the United States; the intention of the project was to compile a visual archive for the University. Between ongoing research into American artists, she spent the summer of 1968 in Haiti and visited eleven African countries in 1970, expanding on her intercultural network of Caribbean, American, and African artists, academics, and institutions. "Women Artists of the Caribbean and Afro-American Artists" built on what she had begun in this earlier survey, this time through a lens of female empowerment; Jones hoped to showcase the "creative power of the Black woman artist."[6]

Unfortunately, by 1973 humanitarian crises in Haiti were recurrent—from natural disasters to social uprisings to political corruption. The nation had experienced division and unrest throughout its history, beginning with its indigenous Taíno ancestors. In the ongoing political and social turbulence of Haiti, the Duvaliers' despotic Tonton Macoute (a Haitian police security group and militia) took the nation by force, denying civilian-centered resources and igniting insurgence. The Tonton Macoute operated through fear tactics, utilizing a brand of Black nationalism that wasn't entirely unfamiliar to Jones. *Noirisme*—or Noirism—was a social, cultural, and ultimately political movement that arose in the mid-twentieth century in Haiti. Stemming from values of the Négritude movement and the end of the United States' occupation on the island, Noirism centered poor Haitians in a way that supposedly refined and enhanced their quality of life; in actuality, it functioned to benefit the Duvalier regime. Simply put, Noirism commemorated and favored dark-skinned Haitians, capitalizing on the existing colonial structure that mistreated and marginalized the masses of the rural poor. In enforcing the policies of the Duvaliers' administration, the Tonton Macoute reinforced this ideology, often disguising it as a celebration of dark-skinned Blackness. Jones's interest in the nation was that of an outsider, but also that of a well-resourced American offering a level of access that some Haitian and Caribbean women artists had yet to experience. In turn, Haiti offered Jones something Black people living the United States longed for: unwavering Black nationalism.

By 1974, Jones had established herself as a figure in the art world with a career spanning over forty years. In 1972, her first retrospective, *Loïs Mailou Jones: Forty Years of Painting, 1932–1972*, was exhibited at the Howard University Gallery of Art. This was followed by retrospective exhibits at the Museum of Fine Arts, Boston, and Acts of Art Gallery in 1973. In addition to her prolific career, she trained generations of artists through her long-held faculty position in Howard's art department. However, despite her achievements, Jones felt that being a Black woman presented a double obstacle in terms of receiving recognition: she had to work twice as hard to overcome the dual and intersecting forces of racism and sexism. Jones' mission in taking on the "Women Artists of the Caribbean and Afro-American Artists" project and the ensuing exhibition was to strengthen the self-image of the woman artist; in bringing together Caribbean and African American artists, she could simultaneously provide a similar framework for the Black artist in America.

Jones's 1974 exhibition at Acts of Art was the second out of three projects she would curate based on her research. The first was *An Exhibition of Haitian Art* comprising seventy-nine works from prominent Haitian artists exhibited at the Art Gallery in the College of Fine Arts at Howard University. Running from March through April 1974, this exhibition featured twenty-six watercolors by Marie-José Nadal-Gardère, an internationally recognized artist from Port-au-Prince. The third was a solo exhibition of paintings by Rose-Marie Desruisseau, a Haitian artist and professor of painting and drawing at the Académie des Beaux Arts in Port-au-Prince that was on view at Howard University's James Porter Gallery from November through December of 1974. Nadal-Gardère and Desruisseau, both of whom were also featured in *Caribbean and Afro-American Women Artists*, were closely involved with Le Centre d'Art; in fact, Desruisseau was one of its founding members. The three exhibitions were organized in response to requests from women artists in the Caribbean that Jones present their work in the United States. However, in addition to increasing the visibility of Caribbean artists, these shows also had an educational function for their United States audiences.

Caribbean and Afro-American Women Artists was the second show at Acts of Art featuring all women artists, the first being the 1971 *Where We At* exhibition; however, the two shows were developed with different curatorial frameworks. *Where We At* was highly local in its conception and aimed to emphasize its close ties to the larger Black Arts movement in New York; as such, it placed particular focus on issues specific to Black women, men, and families.[7] *Caribbean and Afro-American Women Artists* took a distinctly international approach, conceptualizing women of the African diaspora as a connected global class. This was the first exhibition at Acts of Art to feature international artists so heavily.

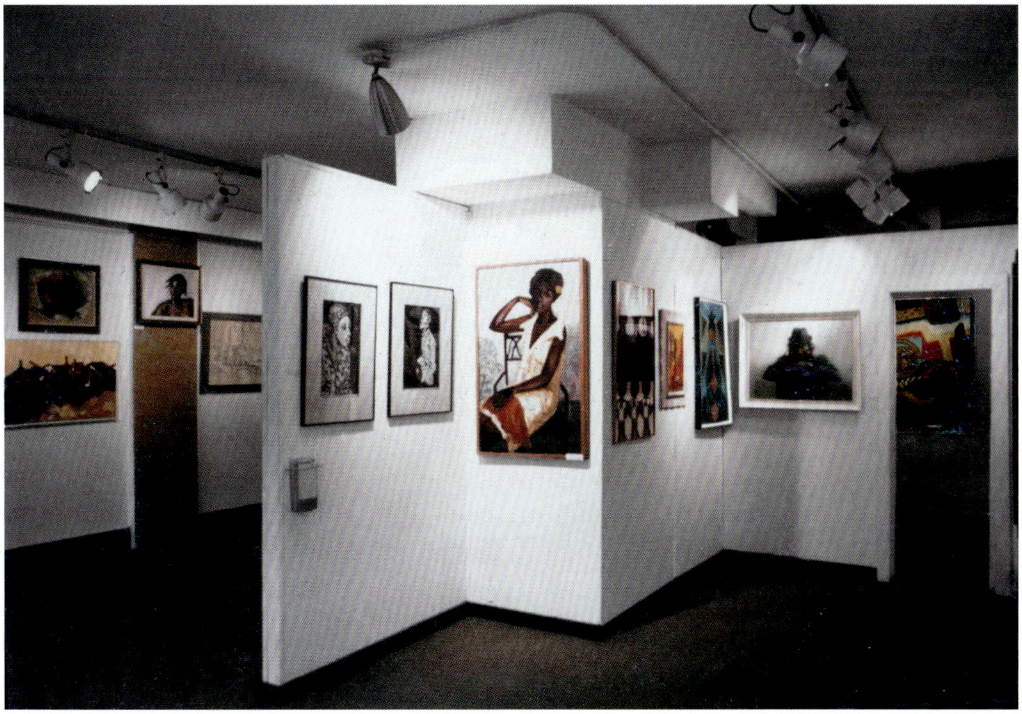

Caribbean and Afro-American Women Artists installed at Acts of Art, June 25 to July 15, 1974

The exhibition's opening was "extremely well-attended."[8] In addition to several of the African American artists present, two Jamaican artists in the exhibit—Hope Parchment and Heather Sutherland—traveled especially for the occasion. None of the Haitian artists came, but over seventy Haitians residing in New York attended. Through this exhibition, Jones was able to expand and strengthen the women's African diasporic artistic network she had helped to forge. While Jones's execution was deemed successful, *Caribbean and Afro-American Women Artists* may appear one-dimensional in its approach. In Jones's personal artistic practice, Caribbean and African American aesthetics were determined through African influence. Although African artistic influence was present on these islands as in the United States, the African diasporic nations of Haiti, Jamaica, and Guyana all sustained pre-existing cultural and creative identities specific to the Caribbean region and their individual countries. Understanding Jones's need to organize this exhibit and her relationship to Haiti during the second half of the twentieth century is crucial in interpreting her curatorial and creative practice and the exhibition's function and impact. Jones realized the importance of artistic exposure and recognition on a global scale—especially in the United States where Black woman artists were departing for "less" racially prejudiced countries for the betterment of their careers and livelihoods. Jones's investment in Haitian, Jamaican, and other Caribbean women artists was based in her belief in their artistry and creative abilities as well as her mission to extend her curatorial and research objectives to Caribbean nations and the African diaspora. Jones's engagement of these thirty-one Caribbean and African American women artists instilled a framework for exhibitions centering Black and Caribbean women artists and offered an environment for those artists to receive the acclaim they deserve.

Loïs Mailou Jones's intentions were unsullied; her love affair with Haiti was intensified by her love for her husband, the African diaspora, and anti-misogynoir beliefs. In its time, *Caribbean and Afro-American Women Artists* was the largest and most comprehensive exhibition to incorporate these themes and this subject matter to highlight a specific group of Black women. The invitation that Acts of Art extended to Jones to utilize their exhibition space was revolutionary for these reasons: it offered her a foundation for the show celebrating and championing international women artists who may have otherwise never had their work leave the Caribbean or Latin America.

NOTES

1 Rebecca VanDiver, *Designing a New Tradition: Loïs Malou Jones and the Aesthetics of Blackness* (University Park: University of Pennsylvania Press, 2020), 171.

2 Loïs Mailou Jones, *Caribbean and Afro-American Women Artists*, exhibition catalogue (New York: Acts of Art, 1974), 1.

3 VanDiver, *Designing a New Tradition*, 112.

4 Tritobia H. Benjamin, *Life and Art of Loïs Malou Jones* (San Francisco: Pomegranate Artbooks, 1994), 8.

5 Veerle Poupeye, "Le Centre d'Art," website of the Haitian Art Society, 2021, accessed July 5, 2024, <https://haitianartsociety.org/le-centre-d-art>.

6 Loïs Mailou Jones, "A Review of Haitian Art," *New Directions* (Spring 1974): 46.

7 Kay Brown, "The Emergence of Black Women Artists: The Founding of 'Where We At,'" *Nka: Journal of Contemporary African Art* Volume 2011, Issue 29 (2011): 120, <https://doi.org/10.1215/10757163-1496399>.

8 Loïs Mailou Jones, personal notes, n.d., box 215-3, folder 5, Lois Mailou Jones Papers, Moorland-Springarn Research Center at Howard University, Washington, D.C.

Black Artists in the New York Scene

JUNE KITAHARA

By the mid-twentieth century, art institutions had already accrued a long history of denying exhibition space, financial support, and recognition for Black artists. Spaces such as Acts of Art Gallery emerged in response. As artist and educator Randy Williams explains in his 1974 essay "The Black Art Institution": "our current art institutions exist because the establishment institutions would not allow us in the first place. It was their fraudulent practices that stimulated the development of our institutions."[1] During this moment, the pressing need for inclusive exhibition venues, proper stewardship of Black artists' work, and opportunities for communal engagement among Black artists in New York City emerged as paramount. Acts of Art Gallery has had a lasting impact on the New York art landscape since its closure in November 1975; this is demonstrated particularly through the gallery's statement exhibition, *Black Artists in the New York Scene.*

Running from September 10 through October 1, 1974, *Black Artists in the New York Scene* featured the works of twenty-six artists deeply entrenched in a number of sociopolitical and artistic milieus of New York City. On the exhibition's invitation, Nigel Jackson offered an impassioned declaration of the indisputable contributions of Black artists to both the New York art scene and art history at large. He wrote:

> The Black artist in the New York scene—he is not a part of the so called grey area. He is not less than complete within himself. Commercially he has a problem—only because of benign neglect. We come to New York like all other artists—for reasons of making a contribution to the spirit and cultural well-being of all the people. The road is long for some of us. Our tools of expression become sharper. Our palettes become brighter with determination. This legacy of the works left behind will serve to change the attitudes of all the people.[2]

Artists in the exhibition included some who had been featured in previous Acts of Art shows: James Denmark, Dindga McCannon, Arthur Coppedge, Manuel Hughes, Nigel Jackson, Enid Richardson Moore, Faith Ringgold, Ernestine Robinson, and Lloyd Toone. Several artists, including Vivian Browne and Greg Ridley, who had only been shown previously in the gallery's fifty-artist *Rebuttal to the Whitney Museum Exhibition: Black Artists in Rebuttal* exhibition in 1971 were invited to participate again. The exhibition also brought in artists whose work had not been shown at Acts of Art before including artists Romare Bearden, Camille Billops, Alvin Hollingsworth, Norman Lewis, Tyronne Mitchell, Otto Neals, Don Robertson, Virginia Smit, Vincent Smith, Grace Williams, Hale Woodruff, and photographers Bunnie Brissett, Fred Floyd, Randolph Floyd, and Pat Davis.

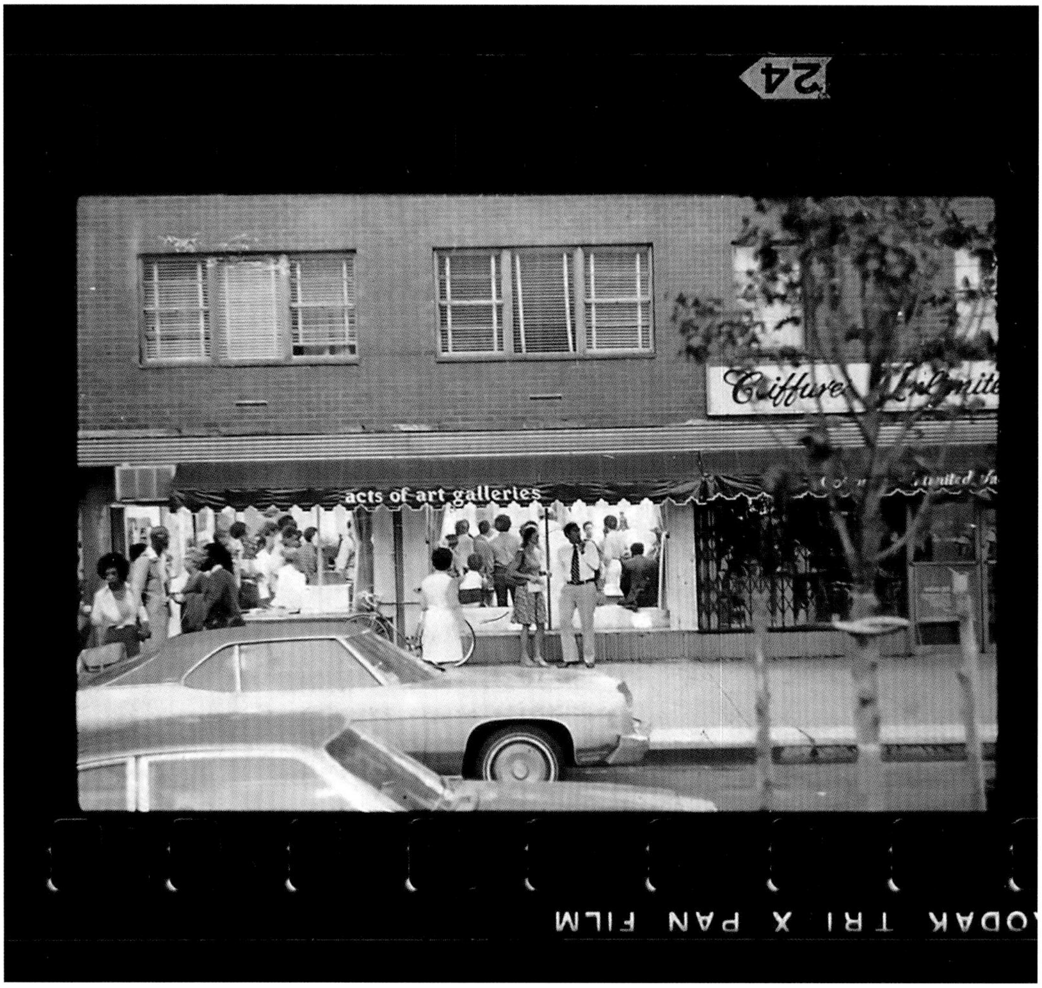

Opening of *Black Artists in the New York Scene*, September 10, 1974

In the exhibition's press release, Jackson charged gallery-goers to "do whatever you can to erase the ugly stigma on the New York art scene."[3] The downtown art scene of the mid-1970s shared a newfound attitude toward the production of art that looked to problematize the function of art and its relationship to institutions. Featuring an array of painters, photographers, sculptors, and collage artists, *Black Artists in the New York Scene* renewed the sense of sociopolitical and artistic urgency of the waning Black Arts Movement and reflected the inclusive push of organizations like the Black Emergency Cultural Coalition, the Art Workers' Coalition, and Where We At. Artist Dindga McCannon's drawing—featured on the front of the invitation—captures the reverberant interplay of dialogue, protest, and creative work that animated New York's cultural landscape of the 1960s and '70s.

Visiting *Black Artists in the New York Scen*e, viewers would have been greeted by the scallop-trimmed awning and open windows of Acts of Art Gallery. The heightened buzz of the show and its very premise is captured in a rare photograph of the night taken by a photographer for the *Daily World*. The invitation of the gallery is pasted onto the window and some of the artists' children sit in the windowsill of the gallery. Entering the space, viewers were met with works including a sculpture by Toone and paintings by McCannon, Richardson Moore, and Coppedge. The show presented a selection of artists who deftly navigated the slippery demands of representation for Black artists within New York's art institutions while also engaging in broader discourse surrounding Black cultural nationalism, integration, and Black aesthetics. Central to this conversation was the inquiry into the formulation of a radical Black aesthetic that echoed throughout larger dialogues on the intersections of aesthetics and politics. Some conversations cited art institutions as physical and ideological embodiments of a continued tradition of Eurocentrism in the United States. Through the intellectual, physical, and political labor of Black artists and scholars, pressure was placed on these institutions which had hitherto practiced an active blindness to the works and voices of Black artists. Black artists in New York City took the initiative to establish spaces and opportunities for the genesis of various coalitions, community gatherings, and collectives.

In the face of inconsistent and often conditional government funding and institutional support for the work of Black artists and art spaces, a sense of urgency pushed artists to forge collectives, artist groups, and communal networks to respond to such shortcomings. Emerging from the grounds of the Harlem Art Center was the Harlem Artists Guild, established in 1935 by a group of US-based Black painters including Lewis, Charles Alston, Bearden, Aaron Douglas, Selma Burke, Robert Blackburn, Jacob Lawrence, and Augusta Savage. Dedicated to attending to the socioeconomic and creative needs of Black artists at the time, the guild served as a space of solidarity during this era of neglect and transformation. Additionally, artists found camaraderie at Blackburn's Printmaking Workshop founded in 1947. The workshop provided a supportive environment for several artists featured in *Black Artists on the New York Scene* including Browne, Neals, Lewis, Billops, Benny Andrews, Emma Amos, and Bearden. The workshop allowed artists to hone their craft and exchange ideas with one another. Later, in 1965, the Weusi Artists collective was founded by Neals and Taiwo DuVall; at the same time, poet Amiri Baraka was establishing the Black Arts Repertory Theatre. By 1967, Weusi Artists had a home base at their gallery—Nyumba Ya Sanaa-House of Art—at 158 West 132nd Street. In this space, the collective provided a variety of tours, lectures, workshops, and exhibitions on Black arts and culture through their inquiry into a radical Black aesthetic that embraced the inextricability of politics from aesthetics. Collectives, galleries, and organizations like these contributed collectively to the formation and proliferation of the Black Arts Movement.

The month after Acts of Art's opening in October 1969, Bearden, Ernest Crichlow, and Lewis opened Cinque Gallery—another space for Black artists downtown. Named after Joseph Cinqué, the leader of the Amistad slave ship revolt of the 1830s, the gallery grew out of the Spiral group associated with Bearden, Hollingsworth, Lewis, and Woodruff. The artists met between the years 1963 and 1965, navigating during this time various definitions of "Black art." Spiral, and subsequently, Cinque Gallery continued initiatives to establish spaces and opportunities for Black artists and to expand community arts education. Similarly recognizing the glaring absence of inclusive spaces within museum institutions and broader artist communities, artists such as Billops and McCannon cultivated vital venues for communal solidarity specifically for Black women artists. When asked about the founding of Where We At, McCannon answered, "I wanted to talk to somebody, but I wasn't quite sure who. I was surrounded by men. All of my friends were men, my fellow artists were men."[4] Stemming from the ethos of the Black Arts Movement, Where We At was founded in 1971 in McCannon's residence on East Second Street. Among its founding members were artists Kay

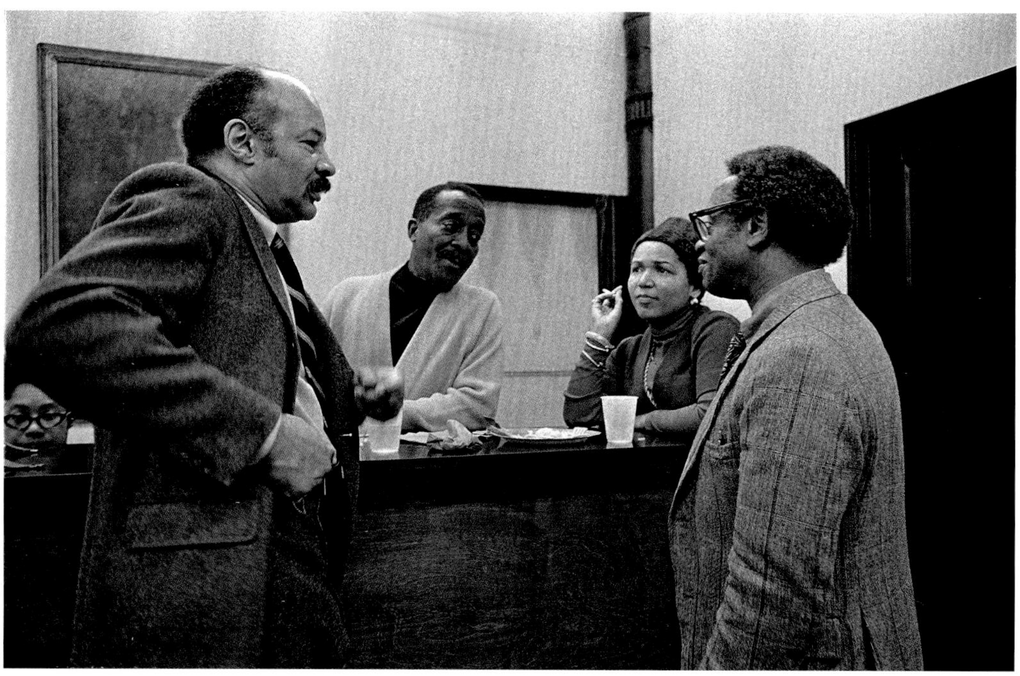

Chester Higgins, *Cinque Gallery, Public Theater*, 1971
Pictured (left to right): Felrath Hines, Norman Lewis, Ouida Bramwell Lewis, and Ernest Crichlow

Brown, Faith Ringgold, Pat Davis, and Carol Blank. Similarly, Billops transformed her SoHo loft into a nexus of dialogue, hosting gatherings that welcomed figures such as Howardena Pindell, Ringgold, Lawrence, and Cliff Joseph. Among the rhizomatic network of noteworthy organizations and artist spaces in New York City that the exhibition title refers to, additional venues included the Art Students League (founded in 1875), where exhibiting artists Bearden, Browne, Coppedge, Jackson, McCannon, Richardson Moore, and Smith were members or took classes. Lewis, Hollingsworth, Richard Mayhew, Alston, and Lawrence also taught at the Art Students League and mentored some of the artists featured in *Black Artists in the New York Scene*. Galleries and museums including—but not limited to—the Studio Museum in Harlem (founded in 1968), Dorsey Gallery (1970), the Storefront Museum (1971), Just Above Midtown Gallery (1974), and Kenkeleba House (1974) further expanded this budding network of Black art spaces. In addition to those listed above, the ubiquitous emergence of collectives also included artist groups such as the African Commune of Bad Relevant Artists (AfriCOBRA), Kamoinge Workshop, and Smokehouse Associates.[5] This period also witnessed a proliferation of publications fueling the national discourse on Black aesthetics and politics. Noteworthy among these was *The Black Photographers Annual* established in 1973 by Beuford Smith, Anthony Barboza, and Shawn Walker. *The Black Photographers Annual* showcased the photography of Brissett whose work was featured alongside photographs by Davis, Fred Floyd, and Randolph in *Black Artists in the New York Scene*.

Acts of Art Gallery emerged as a nexus for dialogue and artistic expression as emphasized by exhibiting artist James Denmark who remarked: "The Acts of Art Gallery was artistic in nature; that was its first priority. It was social to a degree. And, it became political to a degree. It was all those things wrapped up in one; that's what gave Acts of Art its flavor."[6] The exhibition and, more broadly, the Acts of Art Gallery highlighted the contributions of Black artists, Black artistic labor, and artist spaces that were undeniably integral to the fabric of New York's arts landscape. As Norman Lewis, with his honorable frankness, put it, "We are so much part of the mainstream that if Black people would suddenly go on strike for one day in America, it would shake the economy."[7]

NOTES

1 Randy Williams, "The Black Art Institution," *Black Creation: A Quarterly Review of Black Arts and Letters* 6, no. 4 (1974–75): 497.

2 Acts of Art Gallery, *Black Artists in the New York Scene*, invitation to the exhibition, September 10–October 1, 1974.

3 Acts of Art, *Black Artists in the New York Scene* invitation.

4 Dindga McCannon, in "When That Time Came Rolling Down, panel II," *Artist and Influence*, unnumbered (1985): 153.

5 AfriCOBRA was founded in Chicago in 1968 but also had a significant presence in New York during the 1970s.

6 James Denmark, in "When That Time Came Rolling Down, Panel II," 146.

7 Norman Lewis, "Interview of Norman Lewis by Vivian Browne, August 29, 1974," *Artist and Influence* 18 (1999): 86.

artists in the exhibition

BENNY ANDREWS

Benny Andrews (b. 1930, Plainview, GA – d. 2006, Brooklyn, NY) was the first in his family of sharecroppers to graduate high school. He attended Fort Valley State College for two years before dropping out to join the Air Force in 1950. In 1954, he enrolled at the School of Art Institute of Chicago under the GI Bill. He developed a figurative style, even though abstract expressionism was *en vogue* at his and throughout many college art programs. After graduating in 1958, he moved to New York City. His first solo exhibition was in 1960, and by 1962 he was a member of Forum Gallery. His works explored both personal and political narratives of the Black experience, and challenged the formalist emphasis on abstraction and surface flatness by layering expressionist strokes of paint with fabric and found items. In 1968, he began teaching underserved students through the SEEK (Search for Education, Elevation, and Knowledge) program at Queens College, where he remained for three decades. The following year, in 1969, Andrews founded the Black Emergency Cultural Coalition whose activism opened the door for Black artists and professionals in white-led art institutions. He developed the Prison Arts Program in 1971. Andrews received numerous awards and prizes, most notably the John Hay Whitney Fellowship (1965), and a National Endowment for the Arts (NEA) Fellowship (1975). Andrews would also serve as the director of the Visual Arts Program at the NEA from 1982 through 1984. Andrews's commitment to social justice and political engagement through art continued until his passing at the age of 75 in 2006. At the time of the artist's death, he was working on his *Migration* series.

Inmate, 1964
Oil and collage on canvas; 36 × 26 inches

Corner Man, 1970
Mother of the World, 1970
Both pen and ink on paper; 18 × 12 inches

All courtesy of The Andrews-Humphrey Family Foundation and Michael Rosenfeld Gallery, New York

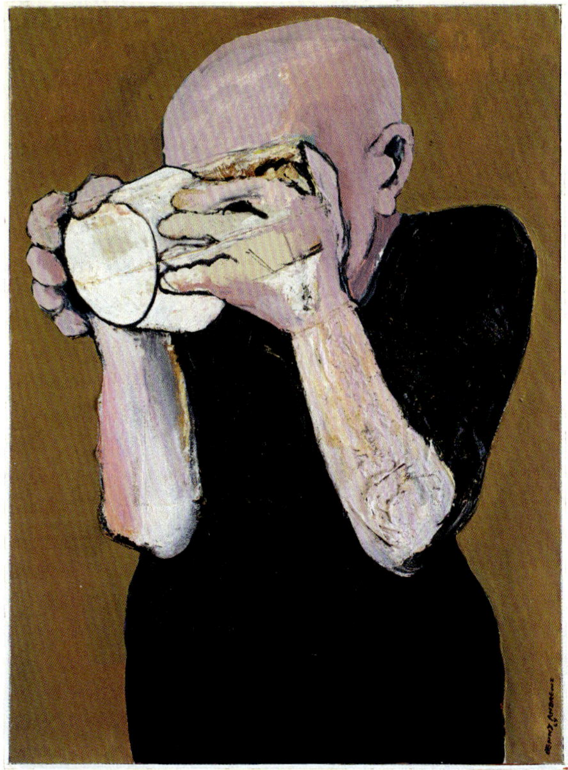

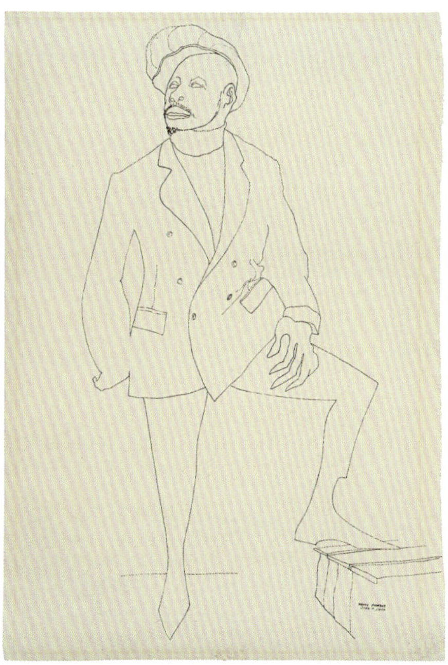

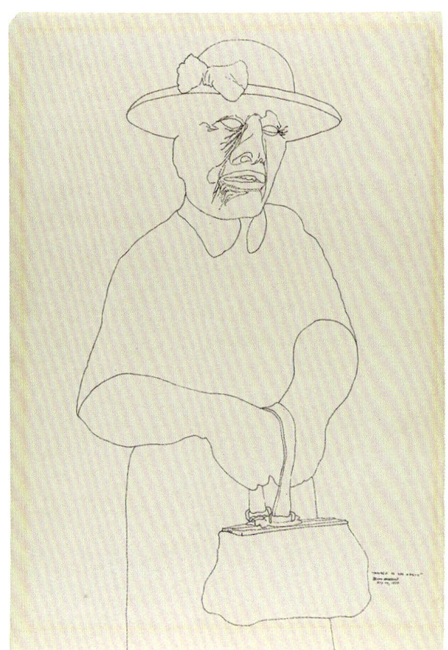

JAMES DENMARK

James Denmark (b. 1936, Winter Haven, FL) is best known for his collages, which incorporate hand-colored paper, objects, and fabric. In addition to these collage works, Denmark has exhibited his watercolors, silkscreen prints, and sculptures widely. Denmark earned his BFA from Florida A&M University in Tallahassee, Florida, where he studied with the leading historian of African American art, Samella Lewis. He later received his MFA from the Pratt Institute in New York. While at Pratt, Denmark was introduced to Jacob Lawrence and Romare Bearden whose artistic practices he was already familiar with from his art historical studies. The influence of Lawrence and Bearden, combined with that of Jackson Pollock and Willem de Kooning, transformed Denmark's work in the 1970s. Since then, Denmark has had over sixty solo exhibitions, and his work has been collected by the Metropolitan Museum of Art; the Museum of Fine Arts, Boston; the Brooklyn Museum; the San Francisco Museum of Modern Art; and the High Museum in Atlanta. In 1980, he was honored with the Living Legends Award from the National Urban League. Denmark lives and works in Yemassee, South Carolina.

Untitled, c. 1980
Cut and pasted fabric and paper on canvas; 30 × 30 inches
Courtesy of Lloyd Toone

Songbird, 1972
Cut and pasted fabric and paper on cardboard; 29 ¾ × 17 ¾ inches
Courtesy of The Metropolitan Museum of Art, Gift of Bertina Carter Hunter, 1978 (1978.313)

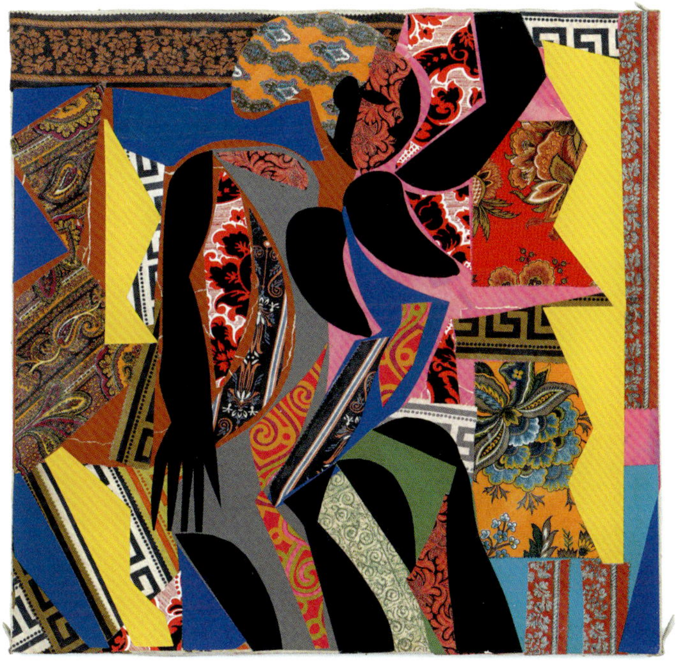

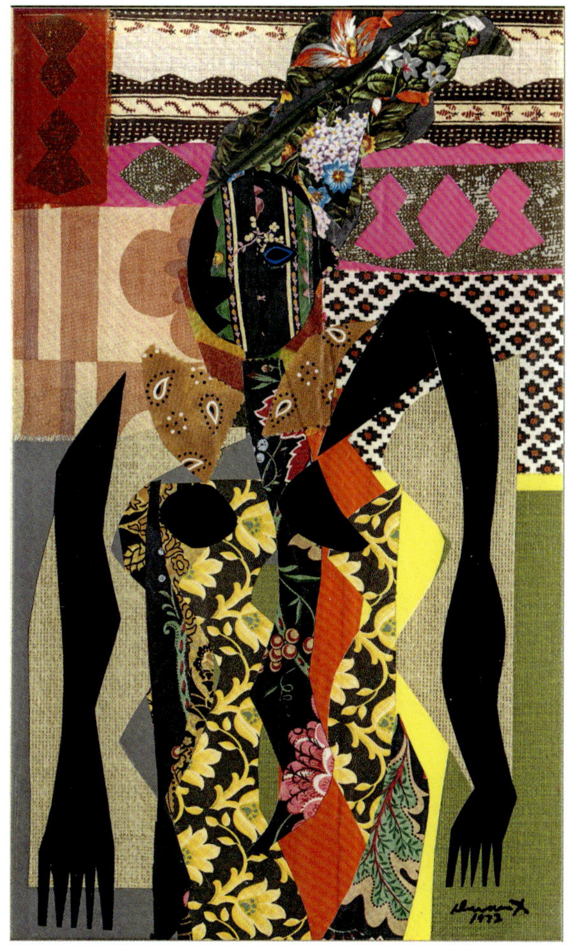

REGINALD GAMMON

Reginald A. Gammon, Jr. (b. 1921, Philadelphia, PA – d. 2005, Albuquerque, NM) was an artist, activist, and teacher whose work focused on the African American experience. His work was primarily figurative with themes of Black America's social, political, and cultural conditions. He drew inspiration from African American history, referencing newspapers and photographs from both family albums and writing by Black leaders such as Henry O. Tanner and James Weldon Johnson. Gammon was educated at the Philadelphia Museum College of Art and the Stella Elkins Tyler School of Fine Art between 1946 and 1949. In 1963, he became a member of Spiral, an artist's group founded in the lead up to the March on Washington by artists Romare Bearden, Norman Lewis, Charles Alston, and Hale Woodruff. In 1965, he showed in the collective's only group exhibition, *First Group Showing: Works in Black and White*. In 1969 he joined the Black Emergency Cultural Coalition (BECC) and participated in protesting the Metropolitan Museum of Art and Whitney Museum's exclusionary racial practices. He exhibited *The Gammon File* at Acts of Art Gallery in 1973 and staged another solo exhibition at the gallery in 1974. Gammon's role as an art educator allowed him to nurture the talent of students through both the Saturday Academy Program for New York City public schools and at Western Michigan University, where he taught beginning in 1970 until he retired as a full professor in 1991. Gammon spent his later years in New Mexico and was a member of the New Mexico Afro-American Artist Guild.

Bon Bon Buddies, 1973
Acrylic on canvas; 48 × 36 inches
Courtesy of the Estate of Reginald A. Gammon

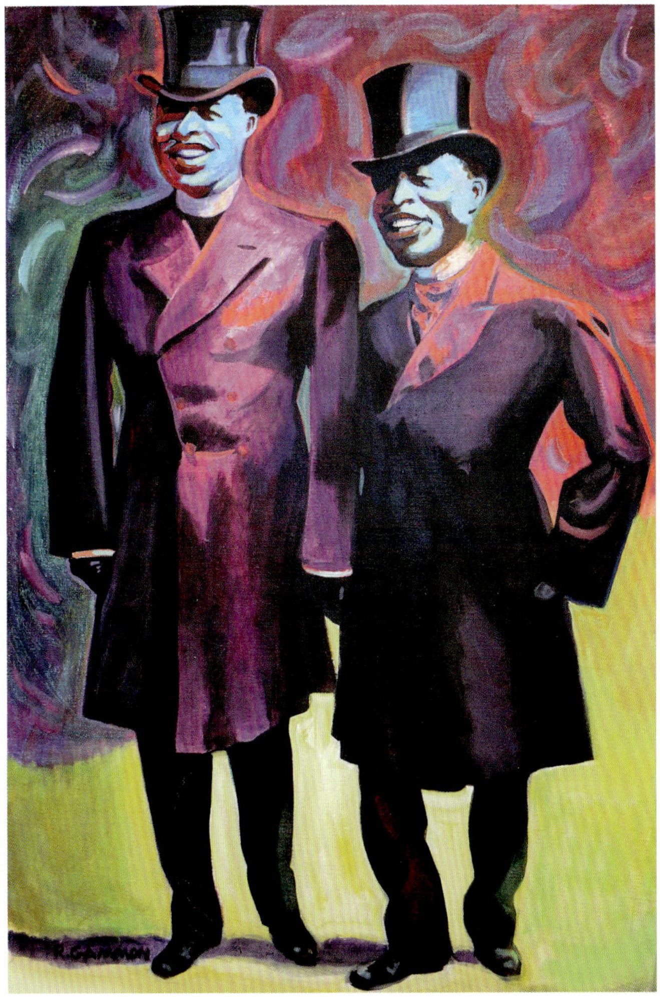

HARLAN JACKSON

Harlan Jackson (b. 1918, Cleburne, TX – d. 1993, Sag Harbor, NY) was raised in Hutchinson, Kansas. He earned his degree in art at Kansas State Teachers College and worked briefly as a cartoonist for the *Houston Reformer* before joining the Navy in 1940. After being discharged, he was a backup player for the Harlem Globetrotters until 1945 when he enrolled at the California School of Fine Arts in San Francisco under the GI Bill. Although he studied with the leading abstract expressionists Clyfford Still and Mark Rothko, his art remained figurative as he explored African themes through a modernist idiom. In 1947, Jackson had his first solo exhibition at the Artists Guild Gallery in San Francisco. Awarded the Abraham Rosenberg Travel Fellowship in 1948, he ventured to Haiti where his study of Vodou deepened his connection to and portrayal of African culture. After graduating from CSFA, Jackson moved to New York City in 1950 to attend the Hans Hofmann School of Fine Art. Under Hofmann's tutelage, Jackson's works became increasingly abstract, though unlike many of his abstract expressionist counterparts he never fully abandoned figuration. Jackson continued to exhibit until the mid 1970s, with one of his final shows at the Acts of Art Gallery in 1975. Despite the emphasis on universalism and non-objectivity within the abstract expressionist movement, Jackson is remembered as a groundbreaking abstract artist whose works explored Black consciousness and ancestry.

Untitled, 1969
Acrylic and paper on canvas; 48 × 42 inches
Courtesy of the Art and Artifacts Division, Schomburg Center for Research in Black Culture, New York Public Library, Astor, Lenox and Tilden Foundations

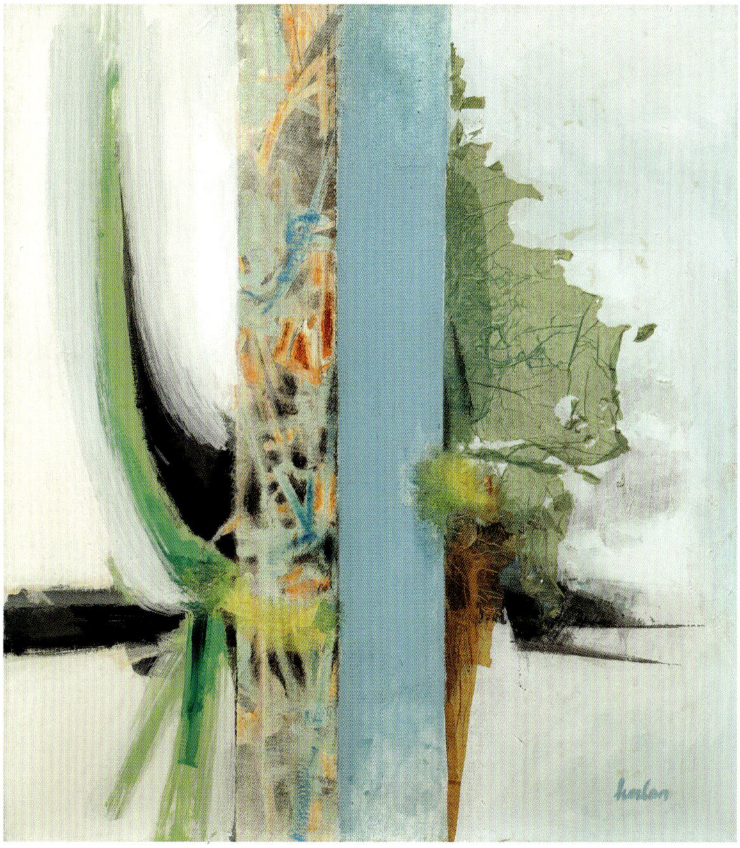

NIGEL JACKSON

Nigel Loring Jackson (b. 1940, Kingston, Jamaica – d. 2005, New York, NY) was the co-founder and director of Acts of Art Gallery. Jackson moved to New York City as a teenager. At the age of eighteen, he enlisted in the United States Marine Corps and served for four years. Originally trained as a machinist, Jackson was introduced to art history at Manhattan Community College where he enrolled in 1964. From 1964 and 1969, Jackson worked as an Assistant Production Manager at *Look*, a biweekly pictorial magazine. During this time, Jackson honed his painting skills and began his formal training at the Art Students League in 1969. He was awarded a three-year scholarship from the League in 1971 and became a member in 1973. In addition to his courses at the Art Students League, Jackson also took art classes at The New School for Social Research in 1970. It is these courses at the New School that he credited with raising his consciousness about Black politics. Jackson opened Acts of Art Gallery in 1969 with Patricia Verdicchio Grey, a fellow student at the Art Students League and his future wife. In addition to two solo shows at Acts of Art, Jackson exhibited in numerous group exhibitions at the gallery over its six-year history. Beyond these shows at Acts of Art, Jackson exhibited work in New York's Black Art Festival at Riverside Church (1970), the Childe Hassam Fund Purchase Exhibition at the American Academy of Arts and Letters (1973), and in exhibitions at the Interracial Council for Business Opportunity, Paula Fuchs Gallery, the Hudson Guild, and Hamline College. His work was shown internationally at Sunnybrook Gallery in Toronto, Canada, and Bolivar Gallery in Kingston, Jamaica. Throughout the 1970s, Jackson supported various Black art exhibitions in New York as a consultant and gave numerous lectures related to African American and Caribbean art and issues in greater New York and beyond. Jackson closed Acts of Art Gallery in November of 1975 before traveling to live and work in Botswana in early 1976. He returned to New York in 1978, but not to the art world. In 1987, Jackson did resume his Art Students League membership, and he remained a member until 1991.

The Seekers, 1970
Acrylic on canvas; 48 × 36 inches

Self-Portrait, c. 1974
Watercolor on paper; 20 × 16 inches

Both courtesy of Fay and Franklin Leeper

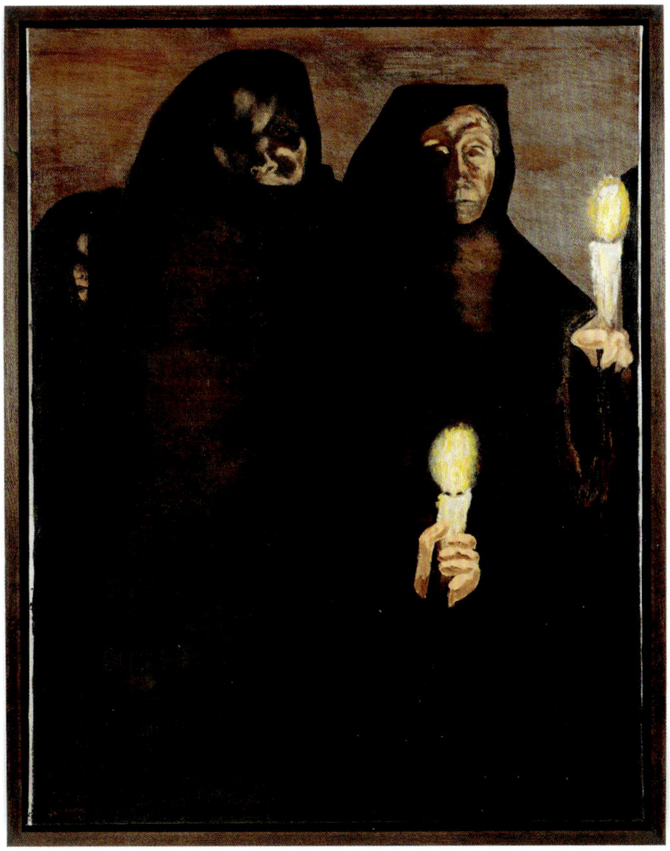

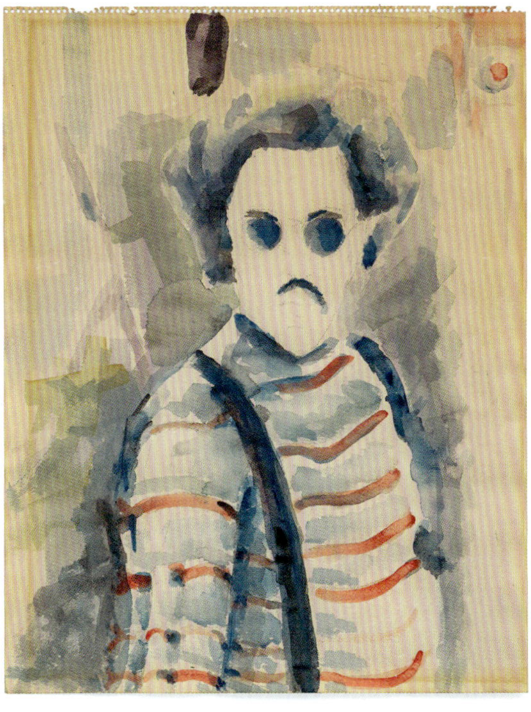

BEN JONES

Ben Jones (b. 1941, Paterson, NJ) is an artist, activist, and educator with mixed media practices in collage, material objects, sculpture, and murals. Jones obtained a BFA from William Paterson University, New Jersey; an MA from New York University; and an MFA from the Pratt Institute, New York. Jones's artwork emphasizes the interconnectedness of human consciousness and political and social ideologies. Ancestry, legacy, and lineage are paramount in Jones's artistic practice and approach to making; his works evoke a connection to Africa and its diaspora through the use of traditional African symbolism, including Shango, the deity thought to be the ancestor of the Yoruba people. His work also regularly references the ongoing civil rights movement, distinguished Black figures, and everyday Black lives. Jones's multicultural capital was earned during his extensive travels to nations of the Afrodiaspora. Jones has made nearly one hundred cultural exchange trips to Cuba since the 1970s. He feels most closely connected to land and individuals who seek an understanding of identity, freedom, and justice while recognizing the power of spiritual and human energy. Actively involved in the Northeast New Jersey arts scene, Jones was one of three original co-founders of the African American Cultural Committee at the Montclair Art Museum. He is a professor emeritus of art at the New Jersey City University, returning his experience and skills to the community he emerged from. In 2022, the Ben Jones Scholarship was created to promote diversity in the arts and support high school students pursuing arts experiences. Jones's work has been exhibited in museums and cultural institutions across the United States and internationally including the Studio Museum in Harlem; High Museum, Atlanta; the Museum of Modern Art, New York; and the Museum of Fine Arts, Boston. Jones has also lectured, taught, and published in a multitude of venues and journals. He works and resides in Jersey City, New Jersey.

Stand/Funk Elegance, 1975
Silkscreen on paper; 38 × 29 ⅞ inches
Courtesy of the artist

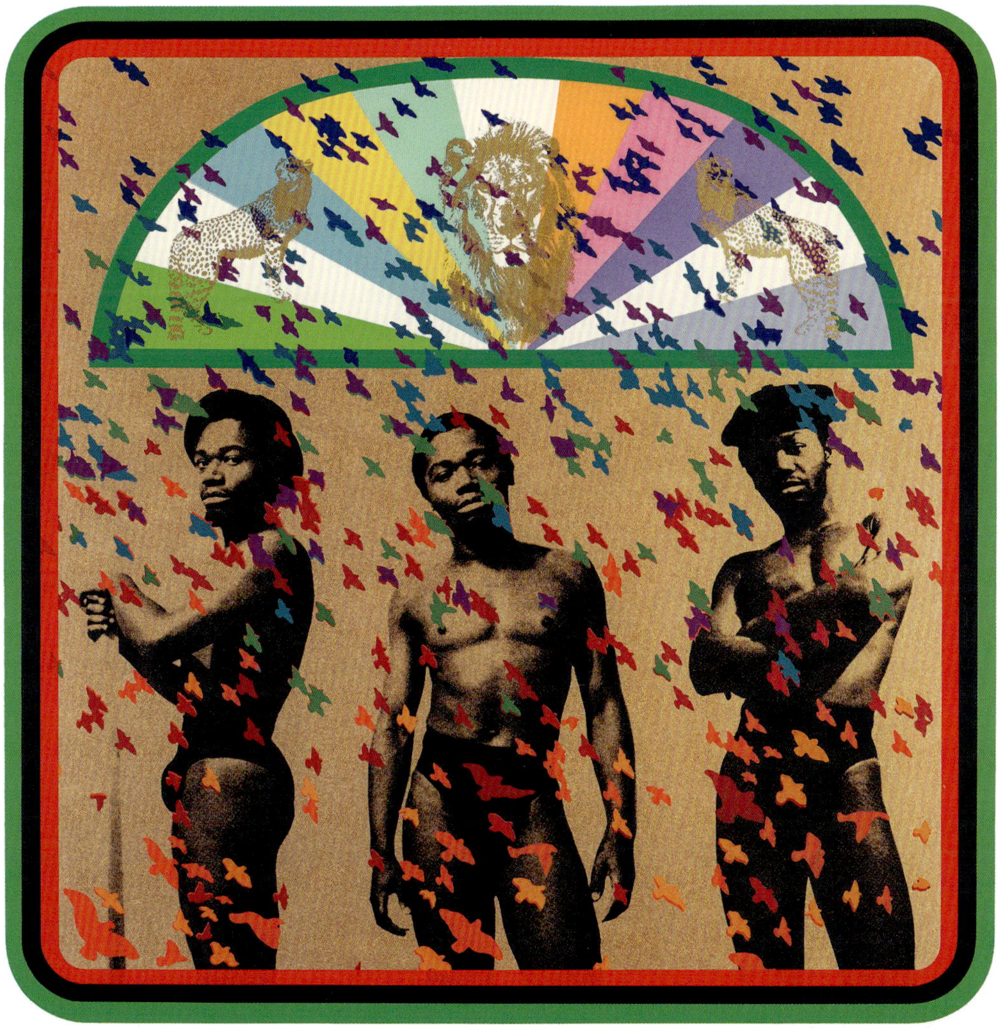

LOÏS MAILOU JONES

Loïs Mailou Jones (b. 1905, Boston, MA – d. 1988, Washington, D.C.) was an artist, educator, and scholar who continuously experimented with visual language throughout her prolific career. She studied at the School of the Museum of Fine Arts, Boston, and went on to earn a graduate degree from the Design Art School (also in Boston), initially pursuing a career in textile design. At only twenty-five, she was recruited as a faculty member in the art department at Howard University, a position she held for most of her career. However, it was her various experiences outside of Washington, D.C., that proved to be the most transformative for her artistic development. In the 1930s, Jones lived briefly in New York; it was there that she witnessed the Harlem Renaissance first-hand and began to gain recognition as a visual artist. While helping design costumes for a dance company in New York, she discovered her interest in African masks, a subject and image she would return to throughout her career. Also noteworthy were her summers spent in France where she studied impressionist painting. The social and artistic climate there further inspired her exploration of African art traditions, and synthesizing European and African aesthetics became a frequent motif in her work. After marrying Haitian artist Louis Vergniaud Pierre-Noël in 1953, Jones began taking frequent trips to the island; Haitian art and cultural practices like Vodou were enormously formative for her practice as an artist and educator. With a research grant from Howard University to study the Black visual arts, Jones traveled to Haiti and eleven African countries to explore contemporary art practices there. She would later present this research in the United States.

Vèvè Vodou III, 1963
Oil and collage on canvas, 37 × 45 ¾ inches
Courtesy of Loïs Mailou Jones Pierre-Noël Trust, Howard University Gallery of Art Collection

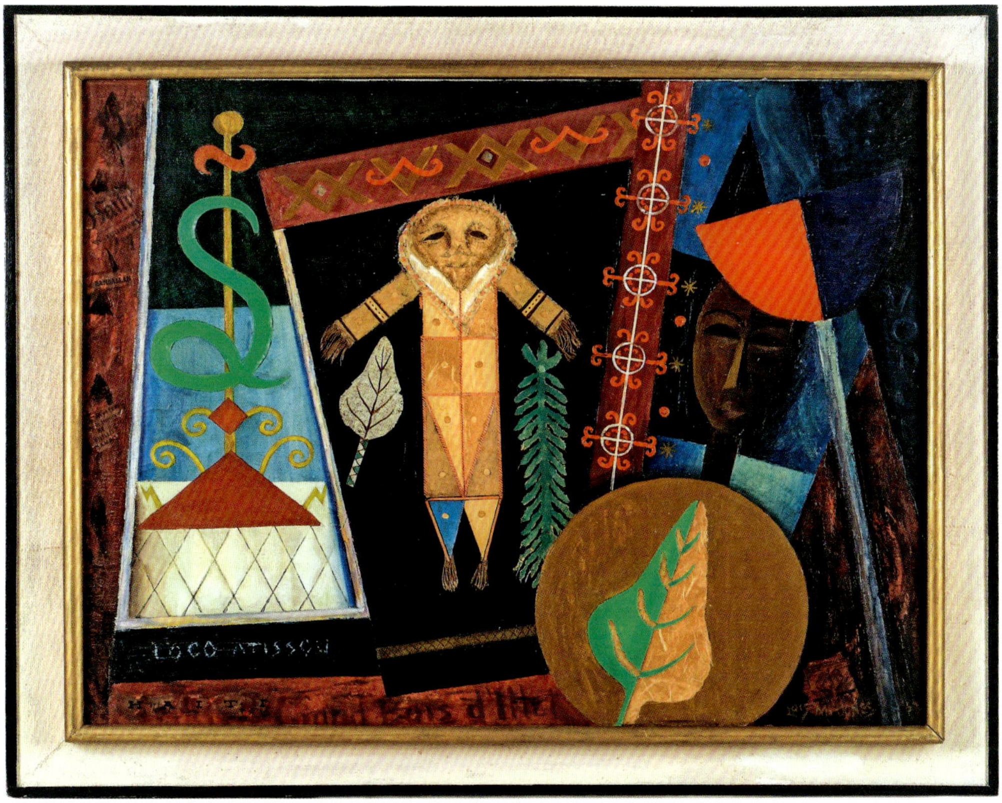
LOCO ATISSOU
HAITI

DINDGA McCANNON

Over the past six decades, Dindga McCannon (b. 1947, New York, NY) has created an oeuvre that focuses on African American history and culture, particularly the experiences of Black women. Her earliest works were linoleum block prints and acrylic paintings on canvas. Her collages include textual and photographic ephemera as well as textiles and objects relating to these subjects. As her career developed, McCannon began to work with textiles, building on a family tradition of sewing and forging connections between identity, African textiles, patterns, and beadwork in her clothing. McCannon began to show with the Twentieth Century Creators in 1964, which led to her participation in the Weusi Artists as one of two original female members. She studied at the Art Students League of New York and at New York City College during this time before co-founding the first Black women's professional artists collective, Where We At, in 1971. The organization's inaugural exhibition at Acts of Art was made possible in part by McCannon's earlier experience exhibiting in the space. In addition to her work as a printmaker, painter, textile artist, muralist, and community leader, McCannon is an author and illustrator for children's books that focus on the lives and aspirations of Black children. Her work as a muralist can be seen on Rikers Island through her installation *Towards a Brighter Tomorrow!* completed in 2024. In the past decade, her work has been acquired by the Brooklyn Museum, the Whitney Museum, and the National Gallery of Art in Washington, D.C., and has been featured in the exhibitions *We Wanted a Revolution: Black Radical Women, 1965–85* (Brooklyn Museum, 2017) and *Afro-Atlantic Histories* (National Gallery of Art, 2022).

clockwise from top left:

Pat is Pregnant, 1977
Acrylic and mixed media on canvas; 30 × 22 inches

Afrodesia at Three, 1979
Acrylic on canvas; 35 × 24 inches

Both courtesy of the artist and Fridman Gallery, New York

Haitian Market Women, 1971
Linoleum block print; 18 × 14 inches
Courtesy of Fay and Franklin Leeper

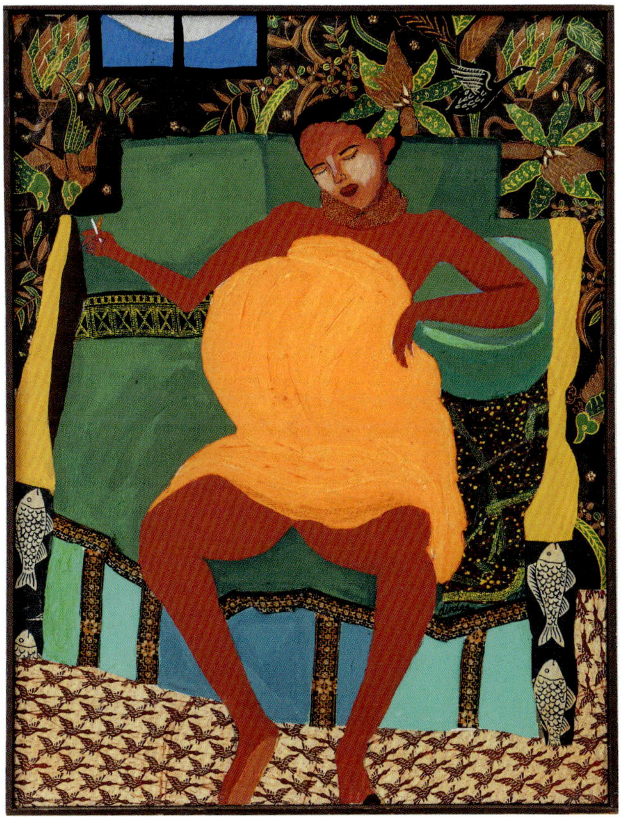

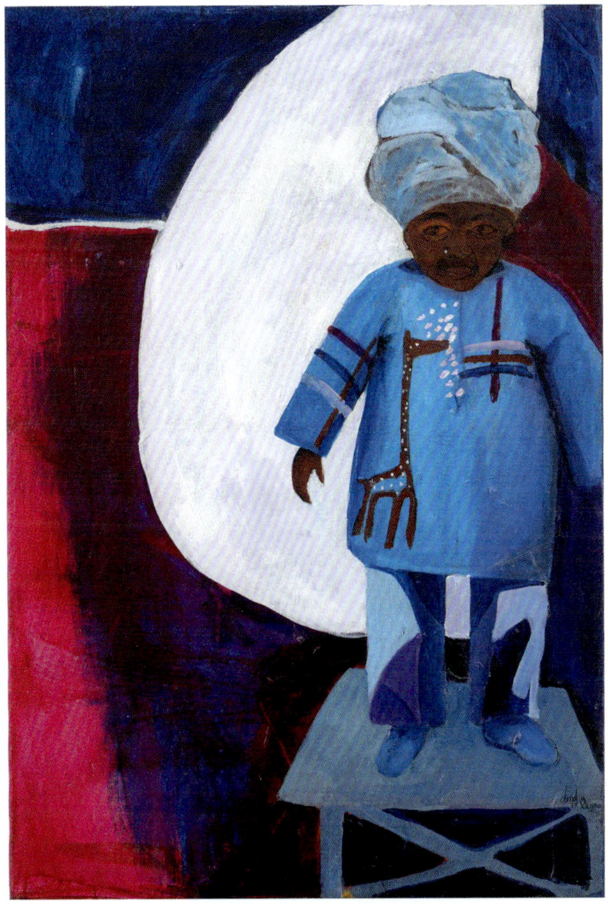

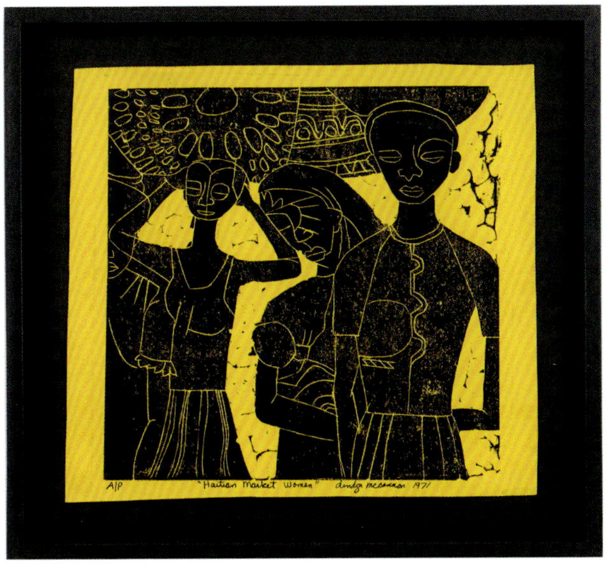
A/P
"Haitian Market Women"
dindga mccannon 1971

ENID RICHARDSON MOORE

Enid Richardson Moore (b. 1937, Jamaica) is a painter and illustrator whose works depict the lives of Black women, their families, and their experiences of everyday life in urban New York and the Caribbean countryside. While Richardson Moore was never afforded a solo exhibition at Acts of Art, her work was included in in numerous group exhibitions from the gallery's first shows in late 1969 and early 1970, to its final exhibition, *The Collection*, in October 1975. Little is known of Richardson Moore outside Acts of Art, either before or after, and the only biography is from a gallery brochure published in February 1970. According to that brief text, Richardson Moore trained at the Art Students League of New York and the School of Visual Arts, and had exhibited at the Afra-Art Gallery in White Plains, New York, as well as in outdoor art shows in Greenwich Village and the Hamilton Grange and the George Bruce Branch of the New York Public Library in Harlem. Also noted was that her work was in the collection of then-Manhattan Borough President Percy Sutton, and she had just illustrated *Naja the Snake and Mangus the Mongoose: A Jamaican Folktale* by Oliver Kirkpatrick, published by Doubleday. Richardson married Cyril Moore in 1970, and her name is listed both with and without her husband's added surname on Acts of Art exhibition announcements. After Acts of Art's closure, Richardson Moore exhibited intermittently at Dorsey's Fine Art Gallery in Brooklyn. A 2012 painting entitled *Water Bucket*, a rural scene of children carrying water, is the most recent work by Richardson Moore we have been able to locate. It was shown at Dorsey's in 2022, in the gallery's *From the Collection* show.

Vickie and Her Brother, c. 1973
Oil on canvas; 19 ¾ × 19 ¾ inches
Courtesy of Gertrude Erwin

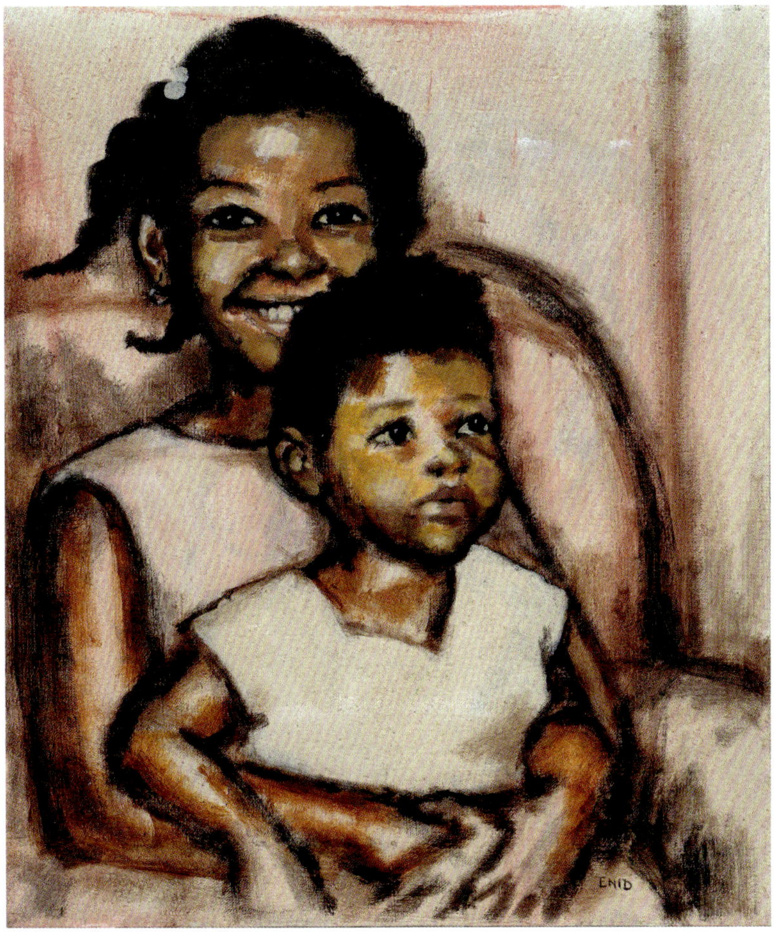
ENID

ADEMOLA OLUGEBEFOLA

Ademola Olugebefola (b. Bedwick Loyola Thomas, 1941, St. Thomas, U.S. Virgin Islands) is a multidisciplinary artist, educator, and activist. He moved to New York City at the age of four and has lived in Harlem since 1966. In that same year, he was given the name Ademola Olugebefola by Baba Oseijeman, founder of the Yoruba Temple in Harlem. Olugebefola joined the Yoruba Temple in 1965 and was later elected to serve as an elder. His creative career began in the 1950s as he found success as a jazz musician. In 1961, he began to work at a printmaking workshop and began painting soon after. He co-founded the Weusi Artists in 1965, which would expand over the next five years into a commercial gallery and academy. Beyond Weusi, Olugebefola forged ties with a variety of creative spaces in the uptown and downtown art communities including Acts of Art Gallery, New Lafayette Theater, National Black Theater, and the Dwyer Arts Center, where he is a founding board member and co-director. He has exhibited in solo and group shows at the Brooklyn Museum (1969); the Studio Museum in Harlem (1970–71); the School of the Art Institute of Chicago (1972); the Second World Festival of Art & Culture, Lagos, Nigeria (1977); Art Students League of New York (2021); and the Hunter College Art Galleries (2022). Throughout his decades-long career, Olugebefola has made a lasting impact in uplifting Black art in and beyond New York City.

clockwise from top left:

Garden of Love: Orionic Etching, 1971
Etching and brushed luma ink; 8 × 7 inches
Edition 14/30
Courtesy of The Studio Museum in Harlem; gift of the artist

Revelations: Orionic Etching, 1971
Etching; 15 × 10 ½ inches
Edition 20/30
Courtesy of The Studio Museum in Harlem; gift of the artist

The Evolution of the Orionic Man is a Phenomena Spoken of in the Sacred Halls of Our Consciousness, 1971
Etching and aquatint; 23 ½ × 28 ½ inches
Artist's Proof
Courtesy of The Studio Museum in Harlem; gift of Golda Matthias Thomas

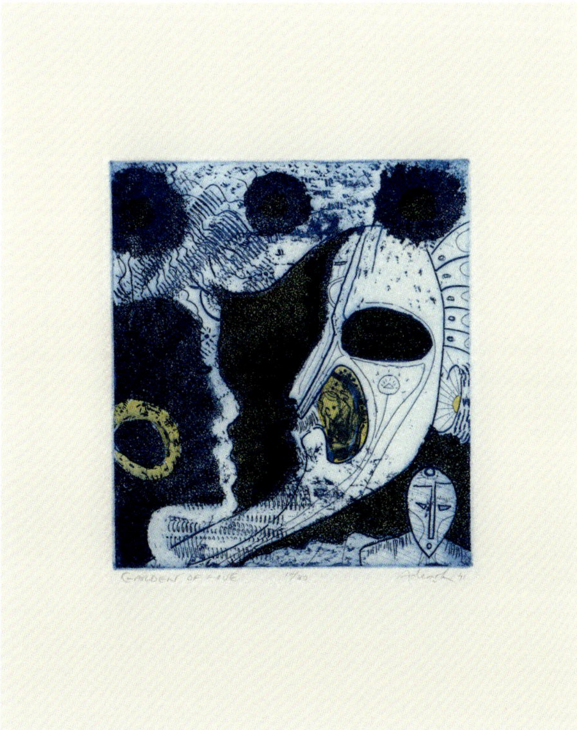
GARDEN OF LOVE

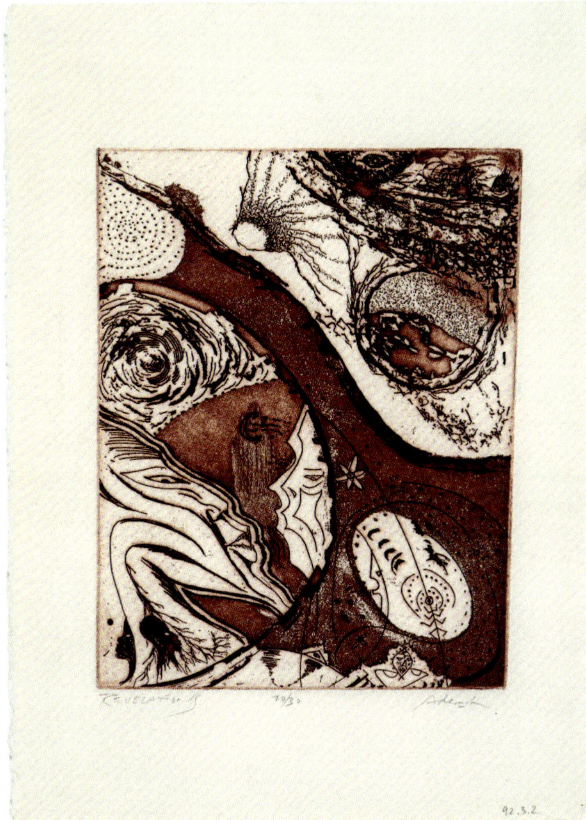
REVELATIONS
92.3.2

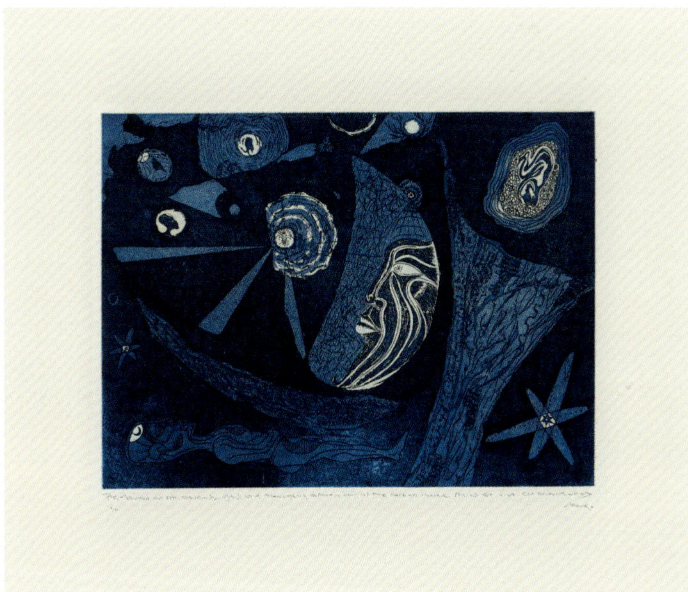

ANN TANKSLEY

Ann Tanksley (b. 1934, Pittsburgh, PA) has always been sensitive to the beauty of ordinary life. She started painting in kindergarten, a talent she would later develop by pursuing a Bachelor of Fine Arts degree at Carnegie Mellon University. After graduating in 1956, she moved with her partner to Brooklyn, New York, where she pursued a career in arts education and teaching. Tanksley has organized art workshops in public schools, community colleges, and youth centers throughout Brooklyn and Queens. Tanksley first exhibited her work professionally at the height of the Black Arts Movement in 1971. Over the decade, Tanksley formed close connections with various networks of Black artists, showcasing her works at Acts of Art Gallery, Dorsey's Fine Art Gallery, Audreon Bratton's apartment gallery, and numerous venues with the Black women art collective Where We At, of which she was a founding member. Her figurative work always centered around Black American life, and included somber paeans of rural labor as well as vibrantly expressionist whimsical tales that blend historical reality and mythology. Among her most striking works is the late-1980s series *Images of Zora*, a portfolio of black-and-white monoprints inspired by the life and writings of Harlem Renaissance author Zora Neale Hurston. Whether she is creating a painting, a woodblock print, a watercolor, or a collage, Tanksley's imagination always radiates. Her work has been exhibited nationwide and internationally in Qatar, Kenya, and elsewhere. It is also included in the permanent collections of the Studio Museum in Harlem and the National Museum of Women in the Arts in Washington, D.C. Today, Tanksley is still painting and exhibiting at the age of ninety.

Retribution, 1974
Oil on canvas; 30 × 40 inches
Courtesy of the artist

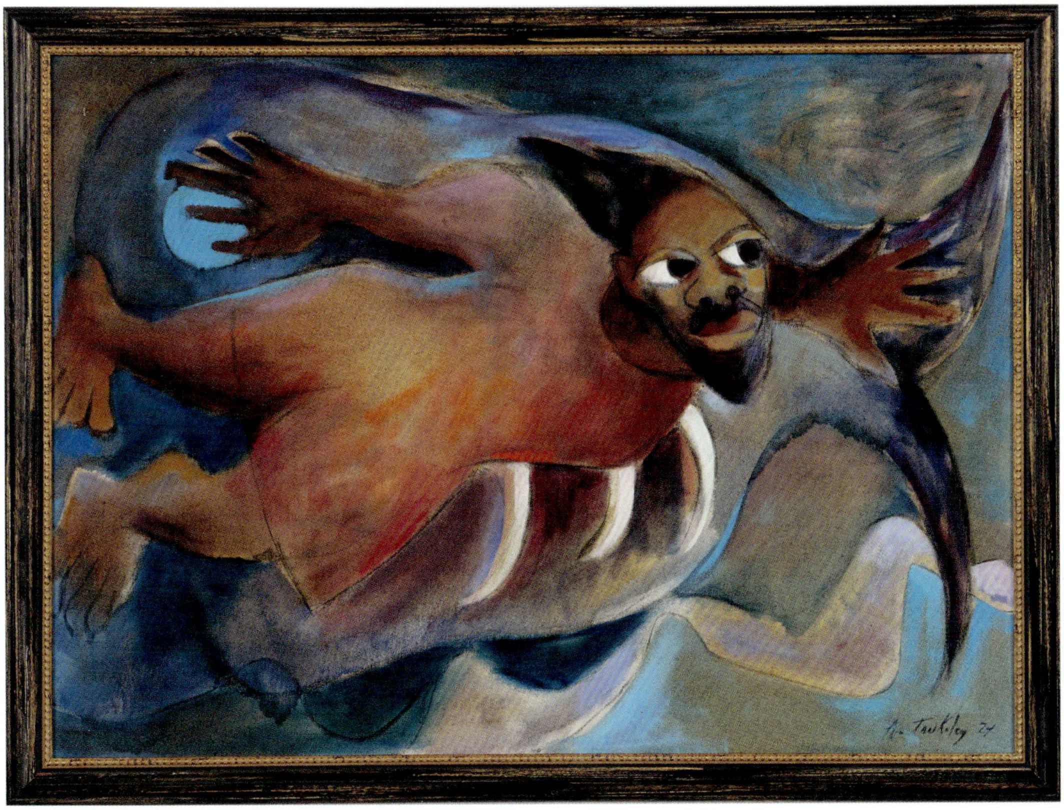

LLOYD TOONE

Lloyd Toone (b. 1940, Chase City, VA) is a master sculptor and painter. He acquired a Bachelor of Science from Hampton University in Virginia. After graduating, he moved to New York where he acquired a Master of Science in Education at Manhattan College. Toone worked as an art teacher for middle schoolers with special needs, an experience that simultaneously bolstered his artistic abilities and his view of art as a critical tool in building community. It was, however, his experience as a world traveler to Southeast Asia, Europe, Africa, and the Caribbean that informed the development of his sculptural practice. During his travels, Toone learned about traditional African sculpting practices that had been referenced—or appropriated—by the work of the great modernists as so-called "tribal" art. Informed by sociopolitical debates sparked by the civil rights movement and the later Black Arts Movement, Toone aimed to adapt traditional practices for the New York landscape of the 1970s using a stylized and inventively eclectic array of cast-off materials found in repair shops and on the streets. In 1969, Toone started to exhibit in local galleries, colleges, and art centers, such as Ruder & Finn Fine Arts, Nassau Community College, LIU Post, and River View Galleries, among others. In 1971, he started a fruitful relationship with Acts of Art Gallery, becoming one of the few artists to have two solo exhibitions with the gallery in 1972 and 1974. He also participated in major exhibitions including the Museum of Fine Arts, Boston's *Afro-American Artists: Boston and New York* (1970). In 1980, Toone and his wife acquired a Victorian brownstone in Harlem which went on to double as a gallery for emerging and experienced Southern artists and helped to revitalize the art scene in the area. Now represented by Blue Leaf International Arts Gallery, Toone still creates sculptures and paintings today.

Natural Look, 1969
Wood and nails; 24 × 12 × 12 inches

Heavyweight Champ, 1975
Leather and wood; 20 × 16 × 9 ½ inches

Both courtesy of the artist

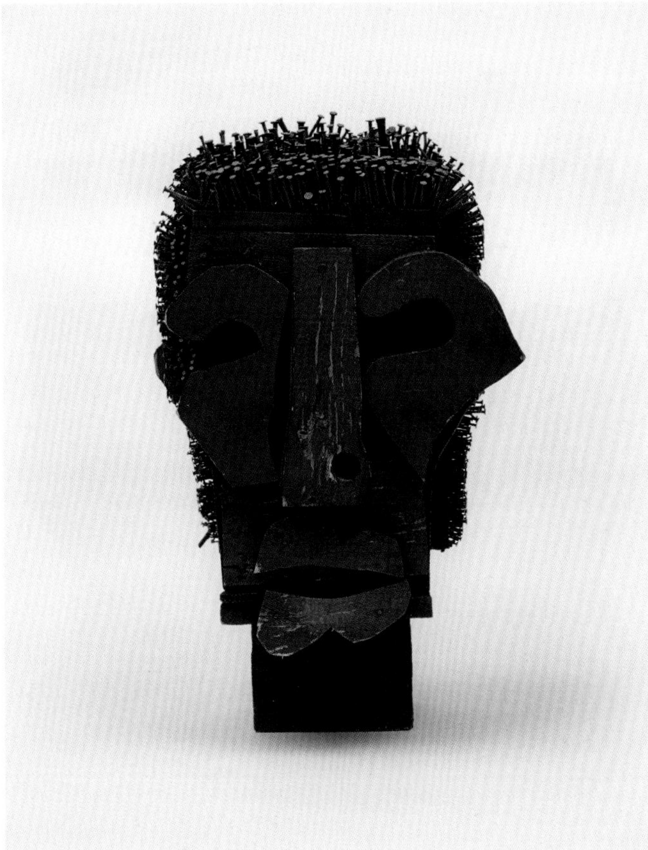

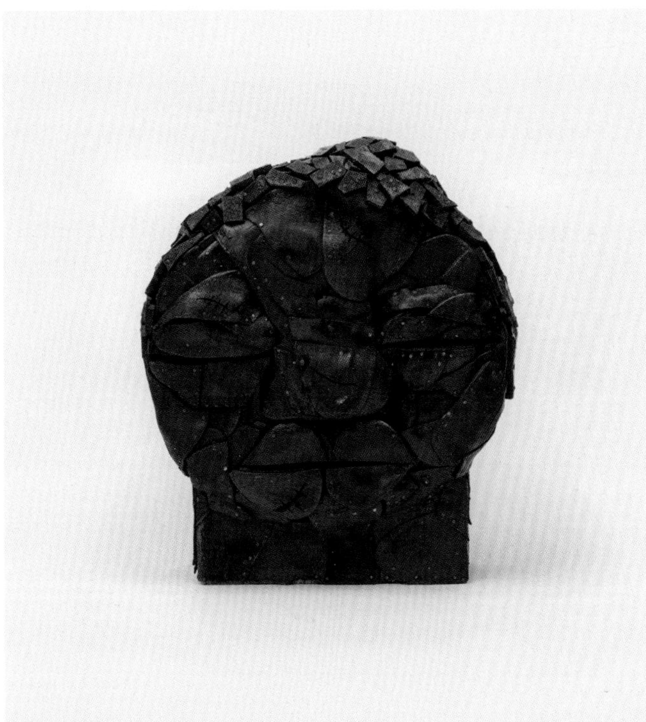

FRANK WIMBERLEY

Frank Wimberley (b. 1926, Pleasantville, NJ) is an abstract expressionist painter, printmaker, and collagist known for his use of color, texture, and movement largely rooted in his love of jazz music. He played jazz himself and had friendships with many jazz greats, including Miles Davis who was an early supporter of his work. As a child, his parents had encouraged his pursuit of art and music; after serving in the United States Army, Wimberley studied painting at Howard University under the guidance of James A. Porter, James Lesesne Wells, and Loïs Mailou Jones. In the 1950s he moved to Queens, New York, with his wife Juanita, working the night shift at their local post office to accommodate his studio practice and caring for their son during the day. He began showing his work publicly in the late 1960s, and in 1973 he had his first solo exhibitions, one of which was at Acts of Art Gallery. A regular on the Acts of Art roster, Wimberley was included in nine exhibitions throughout the gallery's six-year run. He had another solo exhibition at the Gallery in 1974 and was featured in *Rebuttal to the Whitney Museum Exhibition: Black Artists in Rebuttal* (1971); a three-person show with James Denmark and Ann Tanksley (1972); and *Black Artists in the New York Scene* (1974). Wimberley's work is featured in many institutional collections including the Metropolitan Museum of Art, the Smithsonian American Art Museum, and the Parrish Art Museum. Today he maintains his art practice, living and working between New York City and Sag Harbor, New York.

Untitled (Collage), 1977
Newsprint, handmade paper, Color-aid, and painted paper on Arches paper; 21 ½ × 30 inches
Courtesy of Berry Campbell Gallery, New York

Untitled, 1971
Collage with paint on paper; 21 ⅛ × 28 inches
Courtesy of Renee V.H. Simons Family Collection and Berry Campbell Gallery, New York

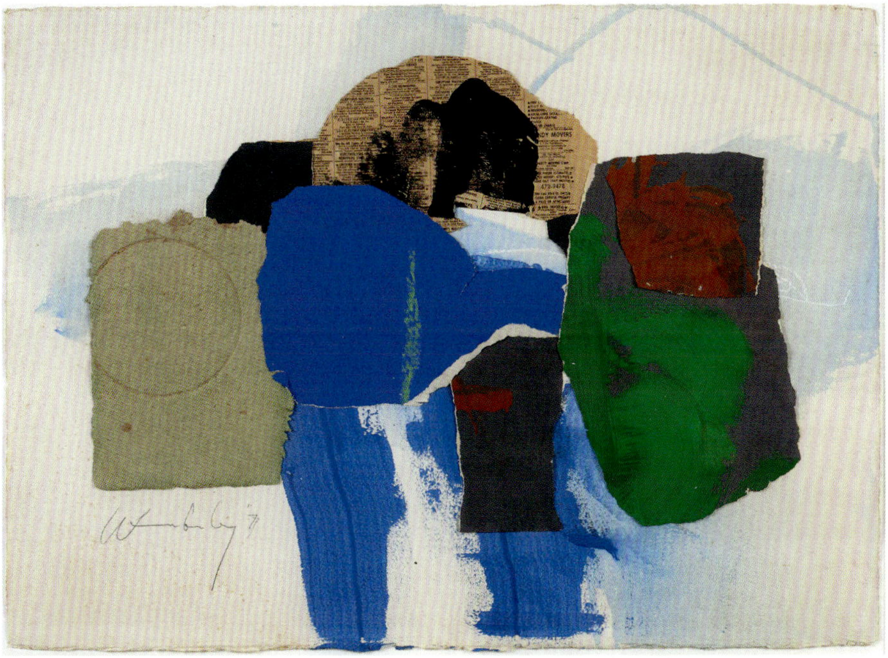

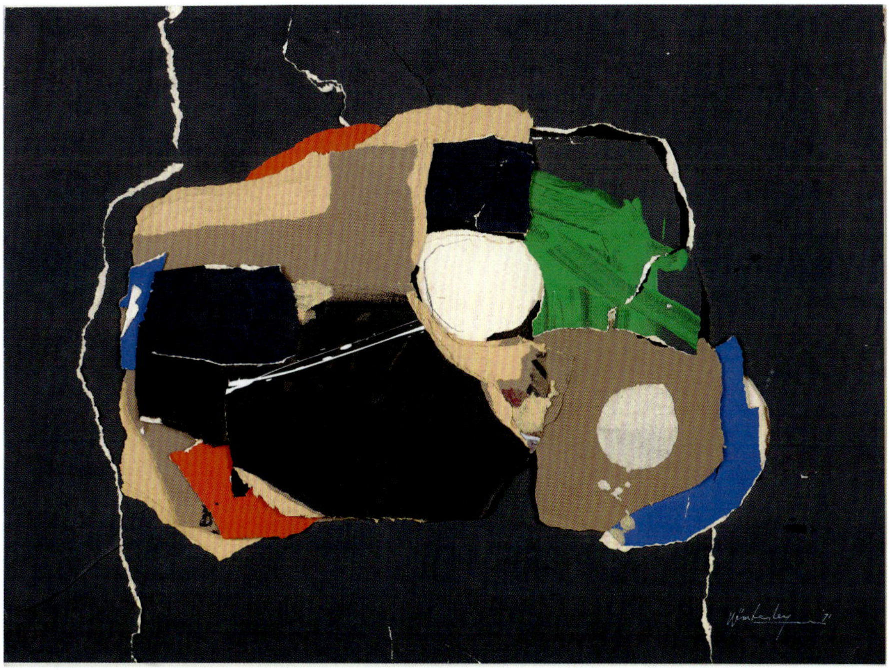

HALE WOODRUFF

Hale Woodruff (b. 1900, Cairo, IL – d. 1980, New York, NY) was a painter, printmaker, muralist, and arts educator. After finishing high school in 1918, Woodruff enrolled at the John Herron Art Institute in Indianapolis where he received his first formal art training. In 1926, Woodruff was granted the Harmon Foundation Award for Distinguished Achievement, the first notable recognition of his talent. The prize enabled Woodruff to travel to Paris, where he studied at the Scandinavian Academy. He returned to the United States in 1931 to take a position as an art instructor at the Atlanta University Center. In 1936, Woodruff traveled to Mexico to study fresco painting with Diego Rivera, which led to the creation of three significant mural cycles. The best known are the *Amistad Murals* (1938–42) at Talladega College; these murals tell the story of the revolt of enslaved Africans on the slave ship Amistad and the victory of its mutineer leader, Cinqué. In 1946, Woodruff became a professor at New York University, where he worked for over twenty years. Over time, Woodruff's work became increasingly abstract by integrating imagery from African motifs such as Ashanti gold weights. Major exhibitions honoring Woodruff's work have included *Hale Woodruff: 50 Years of His Art* at the Studio Museum in Harlem (1979); *Homage to Hale Woodruff*, Waddell Gallery, Atlanta University (1981); and *Hale Woodruff in Atlanta* at the High Museum of Art (2004).

Celestial Gate, c. 1965
Oil on linen canvas; 36 × 24 inches

Cow Woman, c. 1970
Charcoal on paper; 36 ⅝ × 26 ¼ inches

Both courtesy of the Petrucci Family Foundation Collection of African American Art

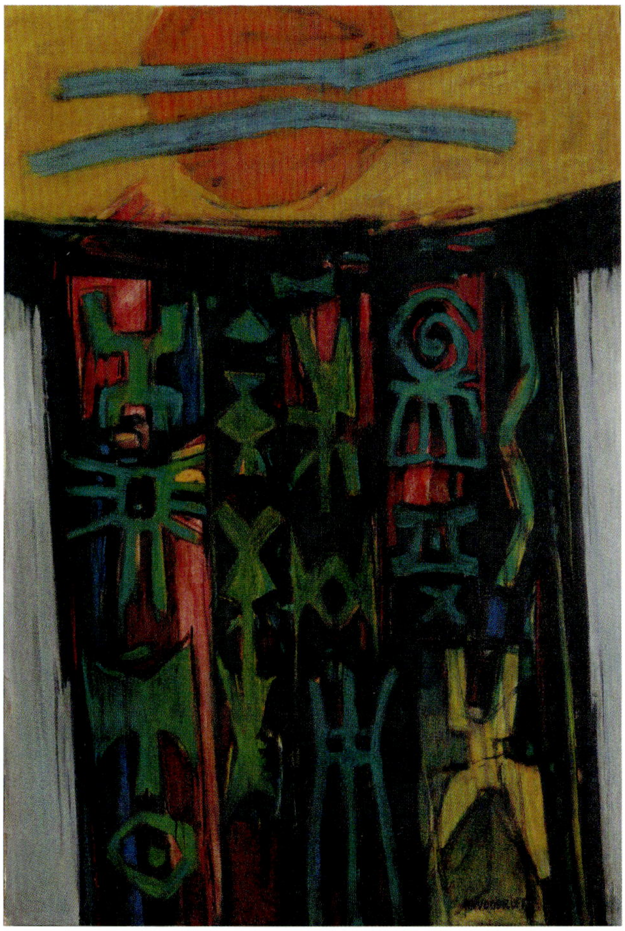

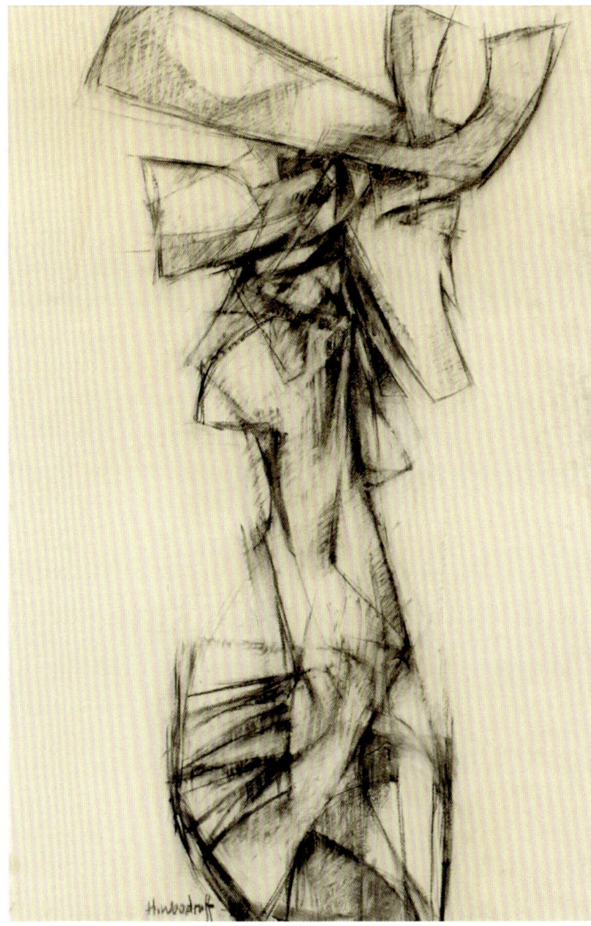

ACKNOWLEDGMENTS

Acts of Art in Greenwich Village has its origins in another Hunter College Art Galleries project, 2018's *Acts of Art and Rebuttal in 1971*. That earlier exhibition and its accompanying catalogue were the product of a graduate curatorial seminar, the culmination of more than a year's worth of interviews, conversations, and archival research. Rather than ending our research, however, the exhibition revealed sources and connections previously unknown to us and opened up new avenues for exploration. Most importantly, it connected Hunter to the family of Acts of Art's co-founder, Nigel Jackson. We are grateful that Fay and Franklin Leeper, Nigel Jackson's sister and brother-in-law, came into the gallery to see the exhibition in late November 2018, and invited us to call. Their visit began the conversation—now in its sixth year—that made *Acts of Art in Greenwich Village* possible. We are also indebted to Thelma Golden, Director and Chief Curator of the Studio Museum in Harlem, who thought to steer Fay to the exhibition that Hunter College had on view about her brother's gallery.

Since we began to envision a new exhibition and catalogue and to work in earnest after the pandemic, we have relied on so many people who have worked together to bring this project to fruition. We thank all the artists, their families, and the lenders to the exhibition who have shared not only works of art but also their time, their stories, and their support. A special thanks to artists Ben Jones, Dindga McCannon, Ademola Olugebefola, Ann Tanksley, and Lloyd Toone, who have taken the time to meet with students enrolled in the Advanced Curatorial Certificate Seminar. We would also like to thank the students who have been so dedicated to this project and to Acts of Art and its history. Their names are reflected in the table of contents and their writing is present throughout this book.

We extend our gratitude to Gertrude Erwin; Renee V. H. Simons; Christine Berry of Berry Campbell Gallery; Iliya Fridman of Fridman Gallery; hallie k harrisburg of Michael Rosenfeld Gallery; Kyle Williams, Director of the Andrews-Humphrey Family Foundation; and Russell Jackson of the Reginald Gammon Estate. We thank our colleagues at the Petrucci Family Foundation Collection of African American Art, the Schomburg Center for Research in Black Culture at the New York Public Library, and the Studio Museum in Harlem, all of whom worked patiently with us to ensure the loans and provide the permissions necessary to build the exhibition and catalogue. We thank everyone at the Metropolitan Museum of Art who made it possible for us to show James Denmark's *Songbird* for the first time in a long time. And we are grateful to Kathryn Coney-Ali, Co-Director of Howard University Gallery of Art—not only for the loan of a beautiful work by Loïs Mailou Jones, but also for sending Howard University undergraduate Kelis George to us as curatorial fellow.

We thank the librarians and archivists who have helped us retrieve the images and ephemera we have used to reconstruct Acts of Art's history. Special thanks to Rachel Detzler in the Stuart A. Rose Manuscript, Archives, & Rare Book Library at Emory University, as well as archivists at the Moorland-Spingarn Research Center at Howard University, the Amistad Center at Tulane University, and the Tamiment Library and Robert F. Wagner Labor Archives at New York University. We are indebted to Chester Higgins for his striking photographic portrait of Nigel Jackson, and for all of the images of the gallery he shared with us.

My personal thanks go to Katie Hood Morgan, Chief Curator and Deputy Director of the Hunter College Art Galleries, and to the gallery staff—Phi Nguyen, Tara Ohanian, Aleeq Kroshian, and Amy Tidwell—for their commitment to this project and their unflappability. Thanks are due, as well, to the book's designer Natalie Wedeking, editor Re'al Christian, and copyeditor Liz Rae Heise-Glass, each of whom were instrumental in bringing this book to fruition. And I am truly grateful to those who have understood and supported my research into Acts of Art from the outset including: Anastasia Davis, Ruth Wilson Gilmore, Craig Gilmore, Mary Ryan, Susan Steadman, Vickiy Strutt-Hackman, John David Treadwell, and Sarah Watson.

Finally, I want to thank my colleagues in the Department of Art and Art History and the Hunter College administration for championing the gallery's programming, and Leonard A. Lauder and the Wolf Kahn and Emily Mason and Alice Trumbull Mason Foundations for their sustaining support and ongoing commitment to our mission.

Howard Singerman
Phyllis and Joseph Caroff Professor of Art History

Notes on Style

The contributors to *Acts of Art in Greenwich Village* have drawn on a variety of primary sources to build the gallery's story: letters and journal entries, invitation cards and mailers, calendar listings and reviews in monthly art magazines and daily and weekly newspapers, both national and neighborhood. Bringing together these disparate resources, each with their own editorial habits, has posed questions that are at once stylistic, historical, and political. Here is a short list of decisions we have made, understanding that other authors or editors might have chosen otherwise.

By the 1970s, Black as the name of a people was capitalized in the pages of the *New York Amsterdam News* and *The Black American,* but not in *The New York Times* or the *The Village Voice.* Most of Acts of Art's own publications, whether press releases or its short-lived newspaper *Raven Art Rap,* also used a lowercase "b." It is important to note here that the gallery's founders consistently rendered its own name uncapitalized in all of its published materials and as its logo: acts of art. For reasons both pragmatic and political, we have chosen to capitalize both Black and Acts of Art throughout, even in direct quotes.

Two further comments: Acts of Art's own publications were most often handmade—typewritten and press-typed rather than commercially typeset—and spelling and titling could be inconsistent. The poster and mailers for the Gallery's 1971 *Rebuttal* list its title as *Rebuttal to Whitney Museum Exhibition,* but it appears in prose as *Rebuttal to the Whitney Museum Exhibition.* We have chosen to use the latter, and we have avoided the use of [sic] in this case and throughout. Finally, Acts of Art was sometimes Acts of Art Gallery and at other times Acts of Art Galleries; we have chosen to use the singular for clarity.

Published in association with the exhibition
Acts of Art in Greenwich Village
Hunter College Art Galleries
Bertha and Karl Leubsdorf Gallery
November 7, 2024–March 22, 2025

Curated by
Howard Singerman, Phyllis and Joseph Caroff Professor of Art History, with Katie Hood Morgan, Chief Curator and Deputy Director, and with MA and MFA students enrolled in the Advanced Curatorial Certificate Seminar: Ansley Browning, Karewith Casas, Erin Chase, Yayun Deng, Brianna Golub, June Kitahara, Laura Luo, Sondra McGill, Chloe Ming, Mary Lisette Morris, and Grace Sanabria. Curatorial fellows: Eve Arballo, Kelis George, and Nicolas Poblete.

Acts of Art in Greenwich Village is made possible by The Leonard A. Lauder Exhibition and Catalogue Fund Endowment. The exhibition's catalogue has been supported by a grant from the Wolf Kahn Foundation and the Emily Mason and Alice Trumbull Mason Foundation on behalf of artists Emily Mason and Wolf Kahn.

EMILY MASON ALICE TRUMBULL MASON
WOLF KAHN FOUNDATION

Published by

Hunter College Art Galleries	Hirmer Publishers
695 Park Avenue	Bayerstrasse 57-59
New York, NY 10065	80335 Munich, Germany
www.huntercollegeartgalleries.org	www.hirmerpublishers.com

Edited by Howard Singerman with Re'al Christian and Katie Hood Morgan

Senior Editor Hirmer Publishers: Elisabeth Rochau-Shalem
Project Manager Hirmer Publishers: Rainer Arnold
Design: Natalie Wedeking
Copyediting and proofreading: Liz Rae Heise-Glass
Pre-press: Reproline Mediateam, Munich
Paper: GardaMatt Art 170 g/m²
Typefaces: Minion Pro and Basic Sans
Printing & binding: Optimal Media, Röbel/Müritz
Printed in Germany

FSC www.fsc.org MIX Paper | Supporting responsible forestry FSC® C108521

Library of Congress Control Number: 2024949380
ISBN 978-3-7774-4399-7

Bertha and Karl Leubsdorf Gallery
Hunter West Building
132 E. 68th St.
New York, NY 10065
www.leubsdorfgallery.org

Additional Image Captions:
Cover: Nandi Guillaume, "Opening of *Black Artists in the New York Scene*," *Daily World*, September 10, 1974. © *Daily World.* Courtesy Tamiment Library & Wagner Labor Archives, NYU Special Collections.

Image Credits:
All artworks are copyright the artist(s) or their estates. Every effort has been made to trace right-holders and obtain permissions for the use of copyrighted materials. If there are errors or omissions, please contact Hunter College Art Galleries. **Page 4:** © Chester Higgins. All rights reserved. Courtesy Bruce Silverstein Gallery. **Page 12:** Group Exhibits: Printed, 1971–1977, undated, 2, Box: 56, Folder: 2. Benny Andrews papers, Manuscript Collection No. 845. Stuart A. Rose Manuscript, Archives, and Rare Book Library, Emory University. **Page 18:** Acts of Art, Inc., Art and Artist Files, Smithsonian American Art and Portrait Gallery Library, Smithsonian Libraries, Washington, D.C. **Exhibition History, pages 26–49:** All photos courtesy the Stuart A. Rose Manuscript Archives and Rare Book Library, Emory University, Acts of Art, Inc. Collection unless otherwise noted. **Exhibition History, pages 26–28:** Benny Andrews papers, Stuart A. Rose Manuscript Archives and Rare Book Library, Emory University. **Exhibition History, page 45:** (top) Adobe Krow Archive Collection; (bottom) Nandi Guillaume, *Daily World.* Courtesy Tamiment Library & Wagner Labor Archives, NYU Special Collections. **Exhibition History, page 48:** (right) Hale Woodruff papers, Amistad Research Center, New Orleans, LA. **Page 51:** Jack Manning/*The New York Times*/Redux. **Page 53:** © Jan van Raay. All rights reserved. **Page 57:** Tyrone Dukes/*The New York Times*/Redux. **Page 58:** Courtesy Fay and Franklin Leeper. **Page 62:** Courtesy Adobe Krow Archive Collection. **Page 65:** © 2024 Frank Wimberley. Courtesy Fay and Franklin Leeper. **Page 67:** Bill Andrews, *Daily World.* Courtesy Tamiment Library & Wagner Labor Archives, NYU Special Collections. **Page 69:** Photographer unidentified, *Daily World.* Courtesy Tamiment Library & Wagner Labor Archives, NYU Special Collections. **Pages 72, 75:** Jeff Donaldson papers, 1918–2005, bulk 1960s–2005, series 5: Artist Files, Box 4, Folder 44, Weusi Artists, circa 1971. Archives of American Art, Smithsonian Institution. **Pages 78–79:** Acts of Art, Inc. collection, Stuart A. Rose Manuscript, Archives, and Rare Book Library, Emory University. **Page 81:** © Dindga McCannon. Courtesy of the artist and Brooklyn Museum. Gift of R.M. Atwater, Anna Wolfrom Dove, Alice Fiebiger, Joseph Fiebiger, Belle Campbell Harris, and Emma L. Hyde, by exchange, Designated Purchase Fund, Mary Smith Dorward Fund, Dick S. Ramsay Fund, and Carll H. de Silver Fund. **Pages 86, 89:** Loïs Mailou Jones Collection 215-1 to 215-80, Series A: Personal Papers, box 215-3, folder 5, Manuscript Division, Moorland-Springarn Research Center, Howard University, Washington, D.C. **Page 92:** Nandi Guillaume, *Daily World.* Courtesy Tamiment Library & Wagner Labor Archives, NYU Special Collections. **Page 94:** © Chester Higgins. Courtesy of the artist and Bruce Silverstein Gallery. **Page 99:** © Benny Andrews Estate/Licensed by VAGA at Artists Rights Society (ARS), NY. Courtesy The Andrews-Humphrey Family Foundation and Michael Rosenfeld Gallery, New York. **Page 101:** © James Denmark (left) Courtesy Lloyd Toone. Photo: Stan Narten (right) Courtesy The Metropolitan Museum of Art, Gift of Bertina Carter Hunter, 1978.313. Image: Art Resource, NY. **Page 103:** © Estate of Reginald A. Gammon. Courtesy the Estate of Reginald A. Gammon / Licensed by VAGA at Artists Rights Society (ARS), NY. **Page 105:** © Harlan Jackson. Courtesy the Art & Artifacts Division, Schomburg Center for Research in Black Culture, The New York Public Library, Astor, Lenox and Tilden Foundations. **Page 107:** © Estate of Nigel Jackson. Courtesy Fay and Franklin Leeper. (top) Photo: Jorge Morocho. (bottom) Photo: Stan Narten. **Page 109:** © Ben Jones. Courtesy of the artist. **Page 111:** © Loïs Mailou Jones Pierre-Noël Trust. Courtesy Loïs Mailou Jones Pierre-Noël Trust, Howard University Gallery of Art, Washington, D.C. **Page 113:** © Dindga McCannon. (top left and right) Courtesy of the artist and Fridman Gallery, New York. (bottom) Courtesy Fay and Franklin Leeper. Photo: Stan Narten. **Page 115:** © Enid Richardson Moore. Courtesy Gertrude Erwin. Photo: Stan Narten. **Page 117:** © Ademola Olugebefola. Courtesy of The Studio Museum in Harlem. **Page 119:** © Ann Tanksley. Courtesy of the artist. Photo: Stan Narten. **Page 121:** © 2024 Lloyd Toone. Courtesy of the artist. Photos: Stan Narten. **Page 123:** © Frank Wimberley. (top) Courtesy Berry Campbell, New York. (bottom) Courtesy the Renee V. H. Simons Family Collection and Berry Campbell, New York. **Page 125:** © Estate of Hale Woodruff / Licensed by VAGA at Artists Rights Society (ARS), NY. Courtesy the Petrucci Family Foundation Collection of African American Art. Photo: Phil Stein.